JEFFERSON'S EMPIRE

The Language of American Nationhood

JEFFERSONIAN AMERICA

Jan Ellen Lewis and Peter S. Onuf, Editors

JEFFERSON'S EMPIRE

The Language of American Nationhood

❧

PETER S. ONUF

UNIVERSITY PRESS OF VIRGINIA

CHARLOTTESVILLE AND LONDON

THE UNIVERSITY PRESS OF VIRGINIA
©2000 by the Rector and Visitors of the University of Virginia
All rights reserved
Printed in the United States of America

First published in 2000
First paperback edition published 2001
ISBN 0-8139-2090-6

⊛The paper used in this publication meets the minimum require-
ments of the American National Standard for Information Sciences—
Permanence of Paper for Printed Library Materials, ANSI Z39.48-1984.

The Library of Congress has cataloged the hardcover edition as follows
LIBRARY OF CONGRESS CATALOGING-IN-PUBLICATION DATA
Onuf, Peter S.
    Jefferson's empire : the language of American nationhood / Peter
S. Onuf.
        p.   cm.   —   (Jeffersonian America)
    Includes bibliographical references and index.
    ISBN 0-8139-1930-4 (alk. paper)
    1. Jefferson, Thomas, 1743–1826—Political and social views.
2. United States—Politics and government—1783–1865.   3. United
States—Politics and government—1775–1783.   4. Republicanism—
United States—History.   5. Liberalism—United States—History.
6. United States—Territorial expansion.   7. Jefferson, Thomas,
1743–1826—Views on slavery.   I. Title .   II. Series.
    E332.2.O58   2000
    973.4′6—dc21   99-39129
                                                                    CIP

To *el jefe*, David T. Konig,
and the *amigos*

Contents

Acknowledgments

Many friends, colleagues, students, and family members offered critical support while I was writing this book. My roster of friendly critics includes: Joyce Appleby, Ed Ayers, Brian Balogh, Lance Banning, Andy Burstein, Joe Ellis, Joanne Freeman, Annette Gordon-Reed, Constantine Gutzman, Ari Helo, David Hendrickson, Mike Holt, Dick Holway, Steve Innes, David Konig, Mel Leffler, Ralph Lerner, James Lewis, Jan Lewis, Rob McDonald, Kristin Onuf, Nicholas Onuf, Lindsay Robertson, Herb Sloan, and Jean Yarbrough.

I am particularly indebted to my brother Nick for his enthusiastic engagement in this project. Writing *Jefferson's Empire* postponed work on our collaboration (now with James Lewis) on the second volume of *Federal Union, Modern World*. Nick's most recent book, *The Republican Legacy in International Thought* (1998), has helped shape my understanding of federalism. Along with my mentor Jack P. Greene, Nick has been the crucial figure in my intellectual development; he is also a wonderful brother.

Chapter 1 of this book was first presented at a Seminar on Indigenous People's Rights in the Americas in Buenos Aires in July 1998 and was subsequently published as "'We Shall All Be Americans': Thomas Jefferson and the Indians," in the *Indiana Magazine of History* 95:2 (June 1999): 103–41. Many thanks to Edgar Krebs for the invitation to Buenos Aires. I am grateful to editor Bernard Sheehan for his generous criticism and to the *Indiana Magazine* for permission to republish.

Chapter 2 was originally prepared for a conference on "Centers and Peripheries" at Michigan State University in November 1997 organized by Chris Daniels and inspired by Jack Greene. Jack provided another opportunity to develop some of the ideas in chapter 2 by inviting me to give a paper on the "American Revolution and National Identity" at the Mellon Sawyer Seminar at Johns Hopkins University in April 1998.

A very early version of part of chapter 3 was first drafted as a paper for a conference on Immanuel Kant at the University of Jena, Germany, in May 1996 and was published in German as "Redefreiheit, öffentliche Meinung und die repräsentitive Regierungsform: Jefferson under die Krise der Vereinigten Staaten, 1797–1801," in Klaus Dicke and Klaus-Michael Kodalle, eds., *Republik und Weltbürgerrecht: Kantische Anregungen zur Theorie politischer Ordnung nach dem Ende des Ost-West-Konflikts* (Weimar, Koln, Wien: Bohlau Verlag, 1998), 277–307, translation by Michael Dreyer. I later presented this paper at the annual meeting of the Organization of American Historians in San Francisco in April 1997.

Thanks to Merrill D. Peterson for getting me started on this study by inviting me to a conference he organized in St. Louis, Missouri, in November 1994 to commemorate Jefferson's 250th birthday. The paper I wrote for the conference was published as "Thomas Jefferson, Missouri, and the 'Empire for Liberty,'" in James P. Ronda, ed., *Thomas Jefferson and the Changing West* (Albuquerque: University of New Mexico Press, 1997), 111–53, and appears in revised form in this volume as chapter 4. The Press's permission to republish it is gratefully acknowledged.

Chapter 5 was delivered as my presidential address at the annual meeting of the Society for the Historians of the Early American Republic at Penn State University on July 1997 and was subsequently published as "'To Declare Them a Free and Independant People': Race, Slavery, and National Identity in Jefferson's Thought," and is reprinted by permission from the *Journal of the Early Republic* 18 (Spring 1998): 1–46. Copyright © 1998 Society for Historians of the Early American Republic. Thanks to John Larson for his able editing of it.

Thanks finally to my friends in the history department at the University of Tennessee for the opportunity to deliver a preliminary version of my introduction as the Milton Klein lecture in November 1998.

David T. Konig of Washington University, known to his devoted *amigos* as *el jefe,* is an exemplary scholar, friend, and leader. The original *amigos,* Paul Gilje, Jan Lewis, Alan Taylor, and I, were fellows at the

Center for the History of Freedom at Washington University in St. Louis in spring 1991, recruited by David to contribute essays to his *Devising Liberty: Preserving and Creating Freedom in the New American Republic* (1995). This small band of true and loyal friends has recently been enlarged by the addition of the newest *amigo,* Ed Ayers. Many, many thanks to *el jefe* for making it all possible.

JEFFERSON'S EMPIRE

The Language of American Nationhood

INTRODUCTION

Jefferson's Empire

✥

THOMAS JEFFERSON cherished an imperial vision for the new American nation. Future generations of Americans would establish republican governments in the expanding hinterland of settlement. This rising empire would be sustained by affectionate union, a community of interests, and dedication to the principles of self-government Jefferson set forth in the Declaration of Independence. It would not be, as the British empire in America had become over the previous decade, an empire built on force and fear, remote provinces subject to the despotic rule of a distant metropolitan government. Instead, the new regime, deriving its "just powers from the consent of the governed," would show that the empire of liberty was illimitable.[1]

"Who can limit the extent to which the federative principle may operate effectively?" an exultant Jefferson asked in his Second Inaugural Address (4 March 1805).[2] The British empire had overreached and collapsed because it was insufficiently republican, not because popular forces exercised disproportionate power in radically imbalanced colonial constitutions. Too much democracy was not the problem; it was instead the sovereign solution to the problem of size, for only a free people could sustain its own union over the vast spaces of the American continent. "We can no longer say there is nothing new under the sun," Jefferson told his English friend Joseph Priestley in 1801, "for this whole chapter in the history of man is new." The greatest novelty was "the great extent of our Republic," its imperial domain.[3]

Jefferson's vision of the American future has seemed prophetic to subsequent generations as they pursued their own happiness and fulfilled the nation's destiny. If in March 1801, in the aftermath of a crisis that had threatened disunion and civil war, and at a time when the federal government had virtually no military capability, Jefferson could say that this was "the strongest Government on earth," he must have sensed something of the new nation's future power, its awesome potential for continental, hemispheric, and, ultimately, global preeminence.[4] Yet by invoking Jefferson's vision Americans could assure themselves that their great power would only be exercised for good purposes, to serve the interests of mankind. Jefferson's optimistic account of the new nation's and the world's glorious future has been contagious and inspirational. Articulating the fundamental premises of democratic self-government in the Declaration and projecting them across space and time—for subsequent generations of Americans, for peoples everywhere—he has been for grateful followers of many political persuasions nothing less than the "man of the millennium."[5]

In celebrating Jefferson's progressive vision, Americans congratulate themselves on their own good fortune. But did the author of the Declaration of Independence have any idea of what the new nation would become? Was its destiny manifest to him? This book is my answer to these deceptively simple questions. It revolves around two major themes, "empire" and "nation," and their relationship to one another. For American Revolutionaries "empire" did not necessarily suggest, as it does now, dangerous concentrations of power and schemes of world domination. Jefferson envisioned "an empire for liberty," an expanding union of republics held together by ties of interest and affection. For this bold experiment in republicanism to succeed, Americans would have to be a united people, conscious of themselves as a nation with a crucial role to play in world history. Their destiny was not to be a great power in the conventional sense but rather an inspiration to other peoples to "burst the chains" of despotism "and to assume the blessings and security of self-government."[6]

It is all too easy for us to see through such rhetoric to the interests it so obviously served.[7] From Jefferson's day to our own, critics have emphasized discrepancies between his idealistic professions and less exalted practices, often concluding that the Virginia planter was a great hypocrite. For many present-day commentators Jefferson's failure to address the problem of slavery generally and the situation of his own human chattel in particular is in itself the most damning possible commentary on his iconic standing as "apostle of freedom." If further evidence was needed to banish Jefferson from the national pantheon, the recent confirmation of his relationship with his slave Sally Hemings provides it: the master of Monticello could not even live up to his own infamous strictures against race mixing in his *Notes on the State of Virginia*.[8]

No historian can avoid the controversies swirling around Jefferson. I may disclaim any intention to inflate, deflate, or reposition the mythic Jefferson. But readers will want to know how I really feel: what undisclosed biases are at work in this book? Let me say, as I always do when pressed, that I am "deeply conflicted." And let me ask my readers, how can you not be conflicted about this enlightened man of reason who preached the gospel of liberation while implicated in what he called the "unremitting despotism" of slavery, perpetually exercising "the most boisterous passions"?[9] We might wonder why Jefferson, so conscious of posterity, did not leave us the kind of evidence—of inner conflict, agonizing self-doubt, guilt, and despair—that would enable us to identify with him. I can understand why my distinguished predecessor at the University of Virginia, Merrill D. Peterson, called Jefferson "impenetrable," for by insisting that the "real" man can never be known, we can sustain our belief in an inner space where his contradictions were engaged, if not resolved, and his ideals were securely grounded, a space within which Jefferson silently suffered.[10]

I do not pretend to know Jefferson better than his biographers, though I would suggest that we already knew a great deal about the inner Jefferson when Peterson published his *Jefferson and the New Nation* in 1970, and that much excellent scholarship since then has illuminated formerly obscure aspects of his personality.[11] Our problem here is not lack of knowledge or insight. It is instead that we have failed to grasp the large contours of Jefferson's political philosophy, his vision of the future, his understanding of the meaning of the American Revolution. Jeffersonian ideals are so woven into the fabric of our national self-understanding that we have trouble distinguishing one from the other, Jefferson from America. To understand Jefferson—and ourselves as well—we need to explore his nation-making project, extricating his intentions, as much as we can, from the outcomes that constitute our history. The point is not to explain, extenuate, or forgive him for his sins, by surrounding him with a generation of equally great sinners or by invoking the material conditions—namely, his dependency on slave labor—that prevented him from living up to his own ideals. Rather, my goal is to reconstruct the moral and ideological framework within which Jefferson made his "bold and doubtful" choice for independence, the moment that defined his conception of himself even as it launched the American experiment in republican government.[12] Even though Americans—like all other peoples—have redefined themselves continuously throughout their history, Jefferson's conception of American nationhood has been the touchstone for all these definitions, their deepest source.

The American Revolution was the central event of Jefferson's life. The protracted political and constitutional crisis preceding the break with Britain prepared the way for his republican revelation. As the fundamental opposition between British despotism and American freedom became suddenly clear, Jefferson embraced the new gospel with a convert's zeal. Until his dying day, his experience of the political world was shaped by this republican faith. Every great crisis was a test of patriotism and loyalty, requiring a return to Revolutionary first principles. Jefferson's strength as a party leader was his obliviousness to the changing character of American political life: his opponents were always the new nation's enemies, counter-Revolutionary conspirators against independence and union or their uncomprehending dupes. Yet if, as historians generally agree, Jefferson was a poor judge of his opponents' motives, his ideological convictions helped keep memories of the Revolution fresh, thus fostering popular patriotism and national identity in the post-Revolutionary age. Jefferson's fixation on the recent but ever receding Revolutionary past has also, paradoxically, kept his memory fresh for subsequent generations of Americans. As Jefferson looked backward to the timeless truths he believed had animated the Revolutionaries, his followers have taken him to be a visionary, looking forward to the progressive vindication of republican principles in the unfolding narrative of American history.

The past, we are told, is a "foreign country" or, as Daniel Boorstin put it in the title of his influential study of Jefferson's thought, a "lost world."[13] There is a rich literature on Jefferson as a Renaissance man or as a man of the Enlightenment, suggesting his extraordinary range of achievements and situating him in a European frame of reference. But when it comes to his great life's work, the creation of a new nation, we see him in a much more narrowly American frame: as his past is telescoped into our present, the "foreign country" dissolves into "America." These two images of Jefferson, European and American, accurately reflect the ambivalent position of his youth when, as an ambitious Anglo-American provincial on the edge of the civilized world, he looked across the Atlantic to the British metropolis for markets, credit, consumer goods, cultural standards, political ideas, and self-definition. Independence may have made a self-conscious "American" out of Jefferson, but the gravitational pull of the metropolis remained powerful for the former provincial. The Anglophile now became Anglophobe, redirecting his gaze toward France and a more diffuse and expansive conception of (European) civilization and a "republic of letters" in which provincial Americans could aspire to an equal standing.[14]

Jefferson could never escape Europe.[15] Indeed, it was the strength of Europe's attraction that animated his nation-making project. Jefferson's *Notes on Virginia,* an encyclopedic effort to comprehend his own state, was drafted with an elite European readership in mind. Challenging the comte de Buffon's degeneracy thesis, Jefferson vindicated American nature in the *Notes,* showing that American animals, including Indian peoples, were as large or larger and as well endowed as their European counterparts. Cultural nationalists were obsessed with such comparisons: their "new world" was always, necessarily, defined against—and therefore in terms of—the Old World. This seems obvious enough from our modern perspective: after all, it would take many generations before the new national culture could transcend its provincial sources, before there would be sufficient wealth, leisure, and historical experience for an enterprising people to fashion a culture for itself befitting the founders' bold experiment in nation making. But the distinction we make between politics and culture would have been meaningless to Jefferson, for claims to independent nationhood themselves expressed powerful provincial impulses. The idea of "nation," a characteristically modern idea that Americans themselves helped invent, constituted an imaginative bridge across the great chasm between center and periphery, metropolis and provinces.[16]

Revolutionary Americans did not aspire to isolation but rather to closer integration in the European world.[17] In Jefferson's memorable words, the United States would "assume among the powers of the earth, the separate and equal station to which the Laws of Nature and of Nature's God entitle them"; as a nation among nations, Americans would be "separate" from Britain, no longer subject to the despotic rule of the foreigners Britons had revealed themselves to be in the imperial crisis, yet fully the "equal" of all other recognized nations and sharing in their common civilization.[18] The Revolutionaries' boldest claim, that there was a distinct American people, capable of asserting its rights before the world, was bold because it had so little basis in historical experience or collective self-consciousness before the Revolutionaries began to make their claims, rewriting British and colonial history to support them and vindicating them on the battlefield. Few patriots were fully conscious that they were inventing themselves as a people before the brute facts of the case, war itself, stared them in the face; even then, reluctant Revolutionaries talked of reconciliation, seeking to avert or at least delay the final rupture. The differences between American whigs and tories, the central pivot of Jefferson's political worldview, were not so great after all: patriots of all stripes were first of all provincial Britons, anxious about their identities as well as their rights. As the imperial crisis deepened, Jefferson and his radical colleagues recognized that nothing less than independent nationhood would secure full and equal participation in the civilized, European world, the pinnacle of provincial ambition.

My depiction of Jefferson as the quintessential provincial, proud of his own "country" of Virginia yet inexorably drawn toward the imperial metropolis, constitutes the crucial link between the two major themes of this book, "empire" and "nation." For provincial Britons "empire" did not evoke, as it now does, centralized, despotic, and arbitrary rule; to the contrary, it was only by imagining a transcendent, inclusive, imperial community, a greater Britain that reached across the Atlantic, that colonists could plausibly claim—to their own satisfaction, at least—the "rights of Englishmen." Thinking of themselves as Britons, provincial patriots could also take pride in being part of an empire that, as Anthony Pagden writes, was widely admired by contemporary European commentators for securing law and liberty and fostering extraordinary prosperity in a widening sphere of common "interests and benefits."[19]

Of course, the patriots' idealized image of empire was not widely shared in British policy-making circles, nor was it embraced by all segments of the provincial ruling classes. Even the most sympathetic "friends of America" in Britain could not overcome the condescending attitude characteristic of metropolitans or understand, finally, how the increasingly exaggerated claims of the colonial radicals could be reconciled with any sort of political connection at all. But it was nonetheless true that the provincial apotheosis of empire drew inspiration and strength from powerful tendencies in metropolitan political culture: this is, after all, precisely what makes provincials provincial. The language of British nationalism, the celebration of Britain's vaunted constitution, its Protestant heritage, its imperial domain, enabled provincials to articulate their own identities in their own increasingly idiosyncratic idioms. This was the language that Jefferson and his fellow nation makers invoked when they declared that George III's tyrannical abuses had made one people, the people of a united empire, into two, British and American. "We might have been a free & a great people together," Jefferson lamented in the original draft of the Declaration, "but a communication of grandeur & of freedom" was now all too clearly beneath the "dignity" of proud Britons who no longer acknowledged the ties that sustained imperial union. "We must endeavor to forget our former love for them."[20]

Jefferson's rage was directed at George III and, through him, at a British people who were suddenly revealed to him as distinct and alien. His sense of betrayal was a measure of his devotion to the imperial ideal that the British king had so egregiously violated. Jefferson's empire was thus republican in several senses, most conspicuously in its rejection of the aristocratic and monarchical old regime and its corrupt state apparatus. For Jefferson, the new American "empire for liberty" would be defined against monarchy. He was always on the lookout for monarchical tendencies that might subvert the new regime—tendencies that his nemesis Alexander Hamilton seemed perversely delighted to display. As Jefferson fought the good fight against "aristocrats" and "monocrats," his republicanism focused increasingly on the need for a virtuous and vigilant citizenry, capable of defending its liberties against internal as well as external threats. This is the republicanism that seems so "classical" to modern writers, though the emphasis on the equal rights of consenting citizens is also, indistinguishably, "liberal."[21]

Jefferson's empire was republican in yet another, less familiar, and less equivocally classical way: American experience with the British empire notwithstanding, Jefferson cherished the belief that the new nation would be able to sustain a hierarchy of legitimate authorities, grounded in the sovereignty of the people, ascending from village or "ward" to an all-inclusive union of state-republics.[22] Each successive layer or "sphere" of authority secured the rights of its constituent elements—whether individual citizens or corporate entities—while its own rights were in turn secured at still higher levels of association. The desideratum at each level was equality: within the citizen body, "all men are created equal"; in the union, all states were equal. The tattered remnants of this republican legacy are barely recognizable to us in what we now call "federalism." Jefferson's republican empire, an expanding federal union of free republican states, was demolished in the Civil War.

Jefferson's hopes for the federal union, this "new thing under the sun," reflected the continuing power of the imperial ideal in his thinking. Yet this ideal was always yoked to, and defined by, Americans' actual experience in the far-from-ideal British empire. Thousands of patriots had to lose their lives in a bloody war for independence, the new nation's self-defining moment, so that liberty might be secured. Americans learned that they must be vigilant, ever ready to make the last sacrifice, in order to check the designs of illegitimate, overreaching power. To defend their rights, a free people must first know what those rights are. The British empire failed because it did not have a constitution, defining spheres of authority and so securing the rights of colonies and colonists. With the ratification of the federal Constitution, the Americans rectified this fundamental defect. As long as the Constitution was properly construed, their union would be perfect.[23] This was Jefferson's message in his First Inaugural: "Let us, then, with courage and confidence pursue our own federal and republican principles, our attachment to union and representative government." The fulfillment of the imperial ideal, true and enduring union, was attainable: "Let us, then, fellow-citizens, unite with one heart and one mind."[24]

Jefferson's paean to union beautifully encapsulates the historical problem I address in this book. In our minds Jefferson's federalism is closely associated with a union-destroying devotion to states' rights, local privilege, and the defense of slavery. Such associations are not mere anachronisms but rather plausible characterizations—repeatedly made by contemporary political opponents—of the reactionary and regressive tendencies of Jeffersonian Republicanism. In his darker moments Jefferson himself despaired of the union as it actually was, wondering if there had been any point, after all, in the break with Britain. How can we, in turn, not despair of Jefferson himself when he tells us in the midst of the Missouri crisis that the effort of the "restrictionists" to keep the new slave state out of the union would constitute "treason against the hopes of the world" and thus make the sacrifices of the "generation of 1776" utterly "useless"?[25]

Jefferson was convinced that congressional interference in Missouri's self-constitution as a republic would lead to the "scission" of the union, thus demonstrating the futility of American aspirations to transcend the never-ending cycle of wars among the disunited states of Europe. Convinced as we now are that racial slavery was the early republic's radical flaw, Jefferson's concerns can only seem pathetically, even tragically misplaced. But we should listen carefully to what Jefferson was saying. Jefferson did not think the world's hopes were pinned to the spread of slavery, or that the particular provisions of the federal compact securing the peculiar institution were deserving of veneration. Jefferson, the republican Revolutionary, did not think he was defending the status quo. For him, the crucial connection was between union and hope. Harking back to an idealized vision of the British empire, looking forward to the republican millennium of a world of free peoples in ever more harmonious union, Jefferson despaired for his country because of his vaulting idealism, not because he was determined to secure his class position or the dominion of his class over a captive nation held in unjust subjection. Jefferson heard the "fire-bell in the night" because the union was at risk; the union, the new republican empire of liberty that Jefferson saw spreading across the continent, was to him the whole point of the American Revolution.[26]

When we look at Jefferson in moments of crisis—in the Missouri controversy, during the "reign of witches" of the late 1790s,[27] in the years when the British empire was torn apart—his hopes for the future are thrown into stark relief. The dialectic of hope and fear characterized the whole Revolutionary generation, of course, though in Jefferson it took an extreme, schematic form, deriving from and sustaining a series of powerful binary oppositions: New World against Old, republicanism against monarchy, consent against coercion, independence against submission, freedom against slavery. The positive terms in these pairs described Jefferson's great political project: liberation from tyranny in order to achieve union. Jefferson did not make a fetish of a strictly construed constitution as an end in itself but rather as the guarantee of equality, the fundamental precondition of uncoerced consent, the threshold of genuine union. This was, finally, a union that transcended mere interest. It was also a union of "heart" and "mind," of a people bound by the love that dedication to republican principles made possible.

This account of Jefferson's political thought is not offered in anything resembling a conventional biographical narrative. Each chapter ranges widely through Jefferson's career, seeking to get at the illuminating moments when his thinking on a crucial theme took on its characteristic and influential form. As I wrote, Jefferson's personal presence became increasingly palpable to me, even though I had not intended to look for him. The Jefferson I have come to know is not the proverbial flawed founder, the great visionary with the feet of clay. My Jefferson may be those things but is more interesting to me because he responded with so much feeling to the ideological currents of his day, currents that he hoped to direct, but that sometimes, as he stood by hopelessly, flowed on in unexpected directions. I am no less deeply conflicted than I was when I started this project, perhaps more so, but it is not because I am disappointed in Jefferson or feel that he has let me or us down by not being a better man than he was. My conflicted feelings are instead about Jefferson's larger project itself, the project that inspired in him such hope and such despair. Perhaps, antibiographer though I am, I have begun to identify with my subject.

Jefferson's Empire is not organized according to a straightforward chronological scheme. Indeed, in chapter 4, on "Federal Union," where I come closest to biography, I follow a reverse chronology, beginning with Jefferson's response to the Missouri crisis and the autobiographical reflections it prompted and moving back to the drafting of the Declaration of Independence when he gave voice to the new nation's aspirations for a more perfect union. My intention is to take a fresh look at what we think we already know so well. According to the conventional reading of his political life, the aging Sage of Monticello departed from his true principles when he advocated admitting Missouri as a slave state, betraying the American Revolutionary creed he had so memorably expressed in younger, better years. But what if Jefferson's position on Missouri, repellent as we now find it, was in fact consistent with his Revolutionary principles? This possibility may not make us any more sympathetic to his antirestrictionist, proslavery posture, but it will force us to take another look at the Revolution itself. As we do so, Jefferson's hopes for the new republican empire will come into clearer focus. With the overthrow of King George III's corrupt and despotic regime, Jefferson fervently believed, republican America would enjoy the peace, prosperity, and progress that the British imperial connection had once promised.

Americans sought to secure their new republican empire in a federal union that preempted the concentration of despotic power in a domineering metropolis. Secured in their respective rights, the new state-republics would be drawn into ever closer union by their harmonious interests, common principles, and reciprocal affection. Yet, as Jefferson discovered, these exalted expectations were repeatedly frustrated, and never more ominously than when Americans were divided along sectional lines, whether over the expansion of slavery, the conduct of the War of 1812, commercial diplomacy, or financial policy. In these perilous moments Jefferson and his fellow Americans were prone to forget that they constituted a single great people, poised to spread republican institutions across the continent. The expansive notion of American nationhood, predicated on a spontaneous harmony of interests in a decentralized federal regime, then threatened to give way to parochial loyalties and mutually destructive impulses. The inclusive boundaries of nationhood thus could suddenly contract, making righteous Americans foreigners to one another, and so obliterating the supposed difference between New World and Old.

If it were merely a matter of writing another obituary for antebellum America, my own feelings might not be so engaged in this project. Jefferson's blasted hopes for the union as a peaceful and progressive alternative to the European balance of power could be treated with the historian's customary detachment, perhaps as a sobering reminder of the intractability of international politics. Jefferson's union is fading from memory, remembered only for its bloody demise in the Civil War or its brutal exploitation of enslaved African Americans. But if the old federal system collapsed, the new nation that Jefferson helped to create is very much with us. The historical irony is that Jefferson's nationalism grew out of his devotion to the union: Americans could only sustain a decentralized regime, an empire without a metropolis, a consensual union of free republics, if they were a truly united people. The ambitious young provincial became a precocious nationalist because of his abiding fealty to the imperial ideal; he invoked the language of nationhood against the state-building designs of centralizers and consolidationists, the "nationalists" of our conventional founding narrative. These nationalists may have triumphed with the destruction of Jefferson's union in the Civil War. But the echoes of Jefferson's imperial vision can still be heard in the language of American nationhood.

What did "nation" mean to Jefferson? What does it mean to us now? These are not questions historians have often asked themselves, at least until recently.[28] We know who "we" are; our collective identity as a people is the premise and point of departure of modern American historiography. Even, perhaps especially, when we focus on the conflicts, divisions, and exclusions that now give our history its narrative structure, we take the national framework for granted. It is hard to resist the judgment, for instance, that by failing to deal effectively with slavery, the founders failed to live up to their own nation-defining ideals; yet we also know that we are somehow implicated in, somehow obliged to acknowledge and rectify, this tarnished legacy. The myth of nationhood authorizes these complex and ambiguous transactions with previous generations. But how did the Revolutionaries come to see themselves as a generation, as a nation that could legitimately determine its own destiny? In his most famous meditation on the problem of generations, in a letter to James Madison in 1789, Jefferson wrote, "We seem not to have perceived that, by the law of nature, one generation is to another as one independant nation to another."[29] The existence and integrity of every people, or nation, or generation should be self-evident, if only we would look. Yet the reasoning here was obviously circular: in some sense we already have to know ourselves as a people before there can be anything to see. Where did this knowledge come from?

Historians have identified "popular sovereignty" as the great invention of the Revolutionary age, the liberating "fiction" that enabled Americans to justify their self-constituted political societies.[30] The concept was indeed a protean one, capable of covering much confusion and avoiding many hard questions about who would govern whom. The crucial issue could not be finessed, however: real people had to see themselves as part of the "people"—or "peoples"—who were supposed to be the ultimate source of legitimate authority, if the new republican regime was to survive and prosper. This self-understanding, the intuitive knowledge Jefferson prescribed, had concrete implications for political life, as the people's duly elected (or self-appointed) leaders waged war against their presumed enemies, foreign and domestic. The political and constitutional conflicts that marked the progress of state building, like the mobilization of patriot forces against British tyranny during the Revolution, sustained a continuing, creative tension between the lofty idea of a sovereign people and more mundane struggles for advantage.

Jefferson never doubted who the "people" really were. But he also knew that his countrymen were all too frequently ignorant and complacent, and thus vulnerable to the seductive wiles of their real enemies. Chronic concern that Americans would sink into a state of collective unconsciousness, forgetting that they were a people, made Jefferson into a self-conscious nationalist, ever vigilant in the face of pervasive threats to the new nation's integrity and security. This was a nation defined by its enemies, at home and abroad. But it was also the ultimate culmination of Jefferson's imperial ideal: a republican people, fully conscious of itself, would be enlightened enough to sustain consensual union and strong enough to resist coercion by any enemy. Union was predicated on shared commitment to "federal and republican principles" that in turn depended on reciprocal recognition and identification among citizens in an inclusive national community.

During the great party struggles of the 1790s, the lineaments of national community came into sharpening focus for Jefferson. When Republicans identified themselves with the patriots of 1776 and called on their fellow citizens to return to Revolutionary first principles, they also offered an imaginative genealogy that linked two generations to a common purpose. For Jeffersonians, the "revolution of 1800" constituted a reenactment of the War for Independence, thus sustaining the founders'

living presence, the myth of identity across generations, that makes nations seem immortal.[31] At the same time, the consciousness of one generation giving way to the next suggested an organic, quasi-familial conception of the nation. Over time the thickening weave of family
connection, interdependent interest, and affectionate fellow feeling
would provide rich soil for raising young patriots.

Imagining America's future in the passage of one generation to the
next, Jefferson showed himself to be a sentimental nationalist.[32] The
sentimental assumptions of his nationalism are most clearly apparent in
his thinking about the three great races, European, African, and Indian,
who called the American continent home. Jefferson had no illusions
about the profound injustice of racial slavery. Yet it is striking that he
apparently worried so little about the wrong done to individual slaves,
including the many hundreds of human beings he owned and exploited
over the course of his long life. In chapter 5 I suggest that Jefferson was
much more troubled by the injustice to enslaved Africans as a people.
Stolen from their own country, the captive nation of slaves could only
look at their captors as enemies. At the same time that Americans proclaimed their own existence as an independent people, they thus encountered an internal enemy, determined to overthrow the rule of their
masters and prepared to ally themselves with the British tyrant. For the
sentimental Jefferson the new republic would be a community of love;
but blacks, never forgetting "the injuries they have sustained," and
whites, with their "deep rooted prejudices," could only hate one another—until the captive nation was sent away, to a country of their own,
where the captors would "declare them a free and independant people."
Only then could full justice be done. Only then could these two nations, each in possession of its own country, claim its "separate and
equal station" among "the powers of the earth."[33]

Jefferson argued that slavery had a demoralizing effect on white masters as well as black slaves. The despotic rule of master over slave was
hardly a model of social relations for impressionable young republicans.
Perhaps even more troubling, I suggest, was the fact that the presence of
this enslaved people, coerced into working the land for their masters'
benefit, denied Virginians the direct, unmediated relationship with
their "country" that they sought to vindicate in their struggle for inde-

pendence against Britain. The virtuous farmer is an American icon; his virtue consists not only in his vaunted independence but in his patriotism, for his relation to his own land is a microcosm and metaphor for the people's love of their country. Jefferson's conception of the new American nation dictated, or rationalized, the expatriation and colonization of enslaved blacks; it also led this great planter to celebrate the agrarian virtues of nonslaveholding yeoman farmers. It was with these hardy patriots in mind that the imperial Jefferson looked westward in his Inaugural Address, to the "chosen country" beyond the frontiers of settlement where there was "room enough for our descendants to the thousandth and thousandth generation."[34]

Jefferson's hyperbole here is astonishing. But he was not really talking about boundless spaces: at this point the Louisiana Purchase was not even a speck on his horizon. Talk about thousands of generations was instead a paean to the immortal nation, an exultant leap into futurity for a people who had barely survived the transit from the first generation to the second. But obstacles had to be overcome before the nation could fulfill its destiny. Early American policy makers could not overlook the presence of Indian peoples. For the philosophic observer it might be only a matter of time—a very few of the thousands and thousands of generations Jefferson had in view—before the Indians faded away, in futile resistance to the inexorable advance of republican civilization or by assimilation with the Americans. Yet the Indians remained a formidable threat throughout the first decades of national history. During the Revolution, as Jefferson wrote in the Declaration, George III had unleashed "merciless Indian Savages," vicious remnants of once proud nations, against the American frontiers.[35] As tools of counterrevolution, these "Savages" threatened to deny the rising generation its birthright, preempting the formation of new self-governing republics within the new nation's imperial domain.

Jefferson's empire was threatened on all sides, at home and abroad. To counter those threats, Jefferson imagined a new nation, a people "with one heart and one mind," the living embodiment of his imperial ideal. American nationhood was supposed to be the first great step toward the republican millennium, when self-governing peoples across the world would join in peaceful, prosperous, harmonious union. Enslaved

Africans had to be repatriated to their own country, so that they too could participate in this progressive development—and so that the new nation could be freed from a chronic and demoralizing state of internal war that threatened to subvert its republican institutions. Indian nations, remnants of an earlier, savage stage in human history, either must accept the gifts of civilization and become part of the American nation, or they must face removal and extinction. The western hinterland constituted a single country, the future home of one great people.

Jefferson's imperial vision is most conspicuous to us now in the history of a federal union that would be destroyed in a civil war, thus finally sharing the fate of the British empire itself, the original inspiration of his vision. But if the constitutional form of Jefferson's empire of liberty collapsed, it left an enduring legacy in the language of American nationhood. Jefferson believed that the continuing existence and future prosperity of the new federal republic—an empire without a metropolis, a regime of consent, not coercion—lay in the character of the people, the source of all legitimate authority. In effect, the nation was conjured into existence in order to secure and sustain a new and improved republican empire. Yet when the imperial superstructure collapsed, the national foundation survived. By 1861, the idea that Americans constituted a single people was powerful enough to justify a massive war against supposedly misguided Americans who wanted to take their states out of the union. For those who would preserve the union at any cost, the Revolutionaries' vision of perpetual peace in an expanding republican empire was mere delusion, the archaic fantasy of another age.

Can we conclude that Jefferson's great invention, his conception of American nationhood, ultimately subverted his great hope, his vision of republican empire? Though such a formulation resonates with Jefferson's despair during successive crises of the union, it seems much too neat. The juxtaposition between "empire" and "nation" that I elaborate throughout this book obscures the flow of meaning from one term to the other. Something of what Jefferson and his fellow founders hoped for in their new republican dispensation is still discernible in our self-understanding as a people.

Nationalists are now often depicted as advocates of essentialism, exclusivism, and hatred of alien others. Yet it remains true today, as it was in American Revolutionary days, that national self-determination is the threshold of political modernity, of full participation in international society; and if cosmopolitans now eschew the crude ways in which nationalists have defined nationhood—evoking as Jefferson did a mystical identification of land and people through time and across space—they generally acknowledge the need for affective and effective communities of some sort, "nations" at a more highly evolved state of political "civilization." And for peoples seeking to determine their own political destiny and so to participate in the democratizing modern world, nationhood is clearly a great boon, not a source of agonized ambivalence. For these new nationalists, Jefferson remains a powerful icon.

Yet in Jefferson's own country—in this no longer new nation—we have come to recognize that civilization is not necessarily an unmitigatedly good thing. For Americans, the protracted and destructive assault on Indian peoples in which Jefferson played such an important role, like the trade in human beings that made Jefferson and the new nation so prosperous, raises acutely discomfiting questions about both "progress" and "civilization." At the end of the "American Century," we may also wonder if the universal values that American policy makers espouse have not sometimes, too often, been the cover or pretext for the projection of less laudable national interests. It is a nice irony that foreign policy critics have decried American "imperialism," thus identifying the United States with other "great powers"—and, implicitly, with the British imperial regime that the American Revolutionaries thought they had demolished. For the central premise of the Jeffersonian creed was that the Revolution had given rise to a new dispensation, a republican empire that was the very antithesis of the Old World balance of power. This republican "imperialism" survives both in the professions of American foreign policy makers and in the skepticism of their critics.

The modern dialogue about professions and practices is itself the legacy of the Enlightenment, signifying our sense of ourselves as reaching toward a higher stage of moral and political development. This is where we begin with Jefferson, optimistically looking toward the progress of civilization in his new world, yet fearing that the new nation might forfeit its historic opportunity. We may see things differently, or think we do, but we find ourselves in much the same place. And we are still speaking the language of American nationhood.

CHAPTER I

"We Shall All Be Americans"

❧

IN EARLY JUNE 1781, in one of his last official acts as governor of
Virginia, Thomas Jefferson thanked his "brother," Jean Baptiste
Ducoigne, the leader of the Kaskaskias, for his visit to Virginia and
called for continued peace and friendship between their peoples. Three
years earlier George Rogers Clark had seized the old French settlement
at Kaskaskia, effectively extending Virginia's jurisdiction through the
Illinois country. An aggressive British presence in Detroit jeopardized
Virginia's control, however, forcing the Americans to enlist as many Indian allies in the region as possible. "I have joined with you sincerely in
smoking the pipe of peace," Jefferson told Ducoigne. "It is a good old
custom handed down by your ancestors, and as such I respect and join
in it with reverence. I hope we shall long continue to smoke in friendship together. . . . We, like you, are Americans, born in the same land,
and having the same interests." The most compelling interest of all true
Americans was the elimination of British influence in the backcountry.[1]

Shortly after meeting with Ducoigne, Jefferson retired from office
and began writing his *Notes on the State of Virginia*. Celebrating his
state's glorious prospects, the *Notes* offered a powerful rebuttal to the
claims of the comte du Buffon and other European natural philosophers
that the New World's inferior natural endowment inevitably led to the
degeneracy of animal species, including humans. Toward the end of a
long section on Virginia's "Productions, Mineral, Vegetable, and Animal" (Query VI), Jefferson described the natural genius of the continent's indigenous peoples, echoing the benevolent sentiments of his address to the Kaskaskia chief.

Uncorrupted by civilization, Native Americans reflected man's true nature. Their "keen" sensibility, affection for their children, capacity for "strong and faithful" friendship, and unsophisticated "moral sense of right and wrong" preserved social order without compulsion or coercion.[2] For Jefferson, the Indians were natural republicans who showed that society did not depend on submission to the authority of a governing class but was instead the spontaneous expression of man's sociable nature.

Despite the implied invitation to Ducoigne and other Indian leaders, Jefferson's generous assessment of the human potential of Indians did not lead to the construction of a durable multiracial, multicultural political order in the New World. On the contrary, Jeffersonian philanthropy provided the moral and intellectual rationale for the removal of Indians across the Mississippi under President Andrew Jackson.[3] When Jefferson celebrated the human potential of native peoples, he embraced the binary opposition of savagery and civilization, situating Indians at an earlier stage of historical development and displacing them from the present moment. In fact, the Indian population of the settled region of Virginia was at its lowest ebb since the advent of English settlement: receding across space, Indians—like the artifacts that Jefferson so assiduously collected—seemed like relics of a distant past, or perhaps of his own childhood.[4] For the time being, of course, native peoples such as the Kaskaskias remained a vital and strategically important presence in the hinterland. But Jefferson anticipated that the same historical drama would be enacted in the West that he and his forefathers had witnessed in Virginia.

In stipulating a universal human nature, Jeffersonians explained cultural differences in terms of a grand historical narrative, with mankind moving progressively from a savage to a civilized state. In September 1824, less than two years before his death, Jefferson looked back on the "march of civilization advancing from the sea coast" westward. This was a movement that would inevitably consign Indians to the dustbin of history—unless they embraced white civilization:

> Let a philosophic observer commence a journey from the savages of the Rocky Mountains, eastwardly towards our seacoast. These he would observe in the earliest stage of association living under

no law but that of nature, subsisting and covering themselves
with the flesh and skins of wild beasts. He would next find those
on our frontiers in the pastoral state, raising domestic animals to
supply the defects of hunting. Then succeed our own semi-bar-
barous citizens, the pioneers of the advance of civilization, and so
in his progress he would meet the gradual shades of improving
man until he would reach his, as yet, most improved state in our
seaport towns. This, in fact, is equivalent to a survey, in time, of
the progress of man from the infancy of creation to the present
day.[5]

In this philosophic vista sentimental bonds of "friendship" predicated
on a universal human nature gave way to the inexorable and impersonal
forces of historical change. Indeed, the Indians' natural gifts—their human potential—made them responsible for either falling in step with
the march of civilization or falling by the wayside.

There was "room enough" in this "chosen country," Jefferson told his
countrymen in his First Inaugural Address, "for our descendants to the
thousandth and thousandth generation."[6] But there was no room for
the "aboriginal inhabitants" who resisted the tide of settlement and civilization, Jefferson explained in his Second Inaugural four years later.
Progress exacted human costs that the sentimental Jefferson was prepared to acknowledge "with the commiseration their history inspires,"
for the Indians, "endowed with the faculties and the rights of men," remained a model for American republicans, even as they resisted white
encroachments:

Breathing an ardent love of liberty and independence, and occupying a country which left them no desire but to be undisturbed,
the stream of overflowing population from other regions directed
itself on these shores; without power to divert, or habits to contend against, they have been overwhelmed by the current, or driv-
en before it; now reduced within limits too narrow for the
hunter's state, humanity enjoins us to teach them agriculture and
the domestic arts; to encourage them to that industry which
alone can enable them to maintain their place in existence, and to
prepare them in time for that state of society, which to bodily
comforts adds the improvement of the mind and morals.[7]

Of course, civilization of the natives proved to be an elusive goal. Indeed, Jefferson suggested that the Indians best expressed their true nature—their fundamental equality with Europeans—by resisting and falling before the torrent of white migration, a great natural force that cleared the way for civilization.

The American Revolution was pivotal in the grand sweep of Jefferson's historical narrative. It gave birth to a new American people who were entitled, as Jefferson proclaimed in the Declaration of Independence, "to assume among the powers of the earth" a "separate and equal station" and who could rightfully claim the lands bartered away by Indian peoples.[8] "You find us, brother, engaged in war with a powerful nation," Jefferson informed Ducoigne in 1781. The war started as "a family quarrel between us and the English, who were then our brothers." We began as a single people, for "our forefathers were Englishmen, inhabitants of a little island beyond the great water." "Being distressed for land," the first Virginians exercised their natural right of emigration "and settled here." "As long as we were young and weak," Jefferson explained, "the English whom we had left behind, made us carry all our wealth to their country, to enrich them; and, not satisfied with this, they at length began to say we were their slaves, and should do whatever they ordered us." The Revolution was set in motion by this betrayal of familial ties. Although the Americans were "grown up and felt ourselves strong," they resisted the final break. But when the English made war on them, Americans could only declare their independence. "We knew we were free as they were," Jefferson told Ducoigne. The very act of coming to the New World was itself the act of a free people: "We came here of our own accord and not at their biddance, and were determined to be free as long as we should exist."[9]

Jefferson's conception of Virginian and American nationhood assumed a fundamental relationship between a particular people and its territorial domain. As Jefferson explained in his *Summary View of the Rights of British America* (1774), royal assaults on Virginia's charter boundaries and changes in land policy that retarded the transfer of crown lands to private hands had been major causes of discontent in the Old Dominion. Paradoxically, Jefferson and his fellow Virginians invoked the inviolability of the 1609 Virginia charter, a grant from the

English king James I, in resisting later encroachments of English kings on their territorial rights. The premise of their reading of the old charter, which had long since been vacated, was that it definitively gave this vast domain to the first settlers and their descendants.

Virginians argued that if their charter rights were subject to amendment or revocation through subsequent grants, then they were not, properly speaking, rights at all. The territorial issue was thus defined in dichotomous terms: either the king was completely free to distribute property and establish governments where property had not yet been vested in private individuals and where no existing colony government exercised effective jurisdiction; or he was bound to respect the corporate rights of colonies under charters, construed as contracts or constitutions, and therefore could not exercise his authority within those charter limits in any way that violated the people's present rights or legitimate future expectations. Jefferson made the point succinctly in the *Summary View:* "Kings are the servants, not the proprietors of the people." George III did not own Virginia, even if ungranted lands in the colony were crown lands and were customarily distributed through the agency of royal government. "He has no right to grant lands of himself," declared Jefferson. "From the nature and purpose of civil institutions, all the lands within the limits which any particular society has circumscribed around itself, are assumed by that society, and subject to their allotment only."[10]

The gravamen in Jefferson's argument was that Virginians constituted a "people" in history, having in the past entered into a contractual agreement with the king and looking to the fulfillment of the contract's terms in the future. The king virtually disappeared in this formulation. Indeed, it was the Virginians who, by assenting to the charter, set their own limits and so perfected their claim to "all the lands within." So interpreted, a charter constituted a claim to nationhood, giving Virginia a historic pedigree that justified (or disguised) its Revolutionary act of self-creation. Sublimated in a myth of national origins, this idealized and radically limited conception of monarchical authority provided Jefferson and his republican colleagues with a compelling standard against which the king's abuses could be measured. The charter could then be read as a kind of constitution in which a people secured royal recognition of its preexisting rights. Jefferson's story of voluntary expatriation, whereby Englishmen came to the New World at their own expense and without sacrificing any of the rights they had enjoyed at home, made Virginia's founders a "people" even before they found Virginia. Thus the vast territory defined by the charter became the Virginians' "country," with the claims of native proprietors disappearing along with those of the king. This was no coincidence, for Jefferson and his fellow Virginians saw the pretensions of George III and his native allies as corruptly interdependent and inimical to their new republic's vital interests.[11]

NATURAL REPUBLICANS, UNNATURAL ARISTOCRATS

Late in life, Jefferson still cherished childhood memories of visits by the "great Outassete [i.e., Outacity], the warrior and orator of the Cherokees" to his father's home and later to Williamsburg when Jefferson was studying at William and Mary. Outacity's "sounding voice, distinct articulation, animated action, and the solemn silence of his people at their several fires, filled me with awe and veneration," Jefferson told John Adams in 1812, "altho' I did not understand a word he uttered." Jefferson then "acquired impressions of attachment and commiseration for them which have never been obliterated."[12] As he matured, Indian eloquence acquired new meanings for Jefferson, most famously in the lament of the Mingo chief Logan, whose family allegedly had been "murdered . . . in cold blood" by Colonel Michael Cresap in the spring of 1774. Logan's speech, addressed to Governor Dunmore and memorialized in Jefferson's *Notes,* struck the tragic note that shaped Jefferson's understanding of the Indians' fate. Logan (speaking of himself in the third person) had been "the friend of white men" but was now resigned to his own imminent death. "He will not turn on his heel to save his life. Who is there to mourn for Logan?—Not one."

Jefferson, for one, would remember Logan. As much as the Virginian cherished the classic authors of antiquity, he would "challenge the whole orations of Demosthenes and Cicero, and of any more eminent orator, if Europe has furnished more eminent, to produce a single passage, superior to the speech of Logan." The chief's oratorical gifts surely marked him as a natural republican, whose eloquent appeal went straight to the heart. But it was the content of Logan's speech, lamenting his family's and his people's displacement and demise, that moved Jefferson. When he "commiserated" the Indians' sad destiny, he mourned the passing of an "uncultivated" people who exemplified the natural virtues of the human race in its "childhood." So, too, Jefferson would remember his own childhood, before the arduous process of self-cultivation made him a republican Revolutionary.[13]

As governor and president Jefferson addressed Indian leaders as "brothers" or "children," so invoking the traditional language of frontier diplomacy. Fictive kin relationships integrated European and American sovereigns into the complex and shifting system of alliances and obligations that linked Indian peoples. The paternalistic Jefferson was less sensitive to the diplomatic dimension of "family" ties in Indian country than to the way that reliance on such ties demonstrated the natives' prepolitical, childlike condition.[14] Jefferson's celebration of Indian virtues in the *Notes* was predicated on "the circumstance of their having never submitted themselves to any laws, any coercive power, any shadow of government." Because, without recourse to laws and government, Indian societies remained small, they also remained virtuous: "Their only controuls are their manners, and that moral sense of right and wrong, which, like the sense of tasting and feeling, in every man makes a part of his nature." Among the Indians offenses could only be "punished by contempt, by exclusion from society, or, where the case is serious, as that of murder, by the individuals whom it concerns." Yet the result was not the anarchy—the imagined war of all against all—that social contract theorists invoked to justify the coercive authority of the early modern state. On the contrary, Jefferson suggested, the natural affection and sociability that sustained peace and harmony in "lawless" Indian communities constituted an attractive alternative to coercive state power. It might well be asked "whether no law, as among the savage Americans, or too much law, as among the civilized Europeans, submits man to the greatest evil." As "one who has seen both conditions of existence," Jefferson voted for lawlessness: "The sheep are happier of themselves, than under care of the wolves."[15]

The logical corollary of Jefferson's familial conception of Indian society was that it could not survive over an extensive domain. "The Savages" recognized instinctively "that great societies cannot exist without government" and "therefore break them into small ones."[16] But these small, self-contained family-societies were poorly equipped to resist the encroachments and seductions of powerful European and American neighbors. The Indians could only sustain their way of life as long as they had access to the vast supply of undeveloped land that a primitive hunting economy required and that isolated them from each other and the world. Jefferson's Edenic view of indigenous societies thus reinforced his sentimental identification with the Indians even as it explained and justified their displacement.

But there was trouble in paradise, and not simply because of the encroachments of the modern world. Jefferson's idealized account of the Indians' society-without-government reflected the profound ambivalence at the core of his sentimental politics. First, the choice between "too much law" and "no law" was not a genuine one for Americans, who were supposed to submit happily to laws of their own making under their new republican governments. As an enlightened, republican imperialist, Jefferson was the great enemy of despotic rule, where law was the command of supposedly superior beings, but not of "great societies." The Revolutionary challenge was to perfect republican governments that would preserve liberty—and the sanctity of republican families— while enabling Americans to participate in, and contribute to, the progress of civilization. This meant establishing ever more perfect unions, thus expanding the sphere of their republican empire, not retreating into a more primitive, isolated, and lawless state. Under republican governments the rule of law defined and protected the domestic sphere, securing the ambit of natural virtue and sociability that proved so vulnerable for the Indians.

Indian lawlessness did not reflect any natural incapacity. As Jefferson assured his friend Chastellux, the Indian was "in body and mind equal to the whiteman."[17] Yet, despite their natural genius, Indian men would resist the regime of law because of their profound attachment to male prerogatives. If Indian men were natural republicans, exhibiting in their dealings with one another the manly virtues Jefferson celebrated in the *Notes,* the tyranny they exercised over their women made them natural aristocrats of the most brutal sort.[18] The very premise of Indian culture, the regime of the "manners" that preserved order in their lawless societies, was male supremacy, a "perversion" of the consensual conjugal union that constituted the foundation of a just and lawful social order.[19] Jefferson's belief in the capacity of individual Indians for civil life thus justified his unwillingness to recognize the collective rights of Indian communities, for these communities were based on force, not consent. Tragically, brave Indian men demonstrated this capacity for reason and choice in their willful resistance to white civilization. The tragedy was not simply that such resistance was hopeless, but that Indians chose to defend unnatural prerogatives, not natural rights.

Indian men could only be virtuous, and only then in their relations with one another, when they were left alone. In Jefferson's view any form of social or political organization among the Indians that American Revolutionaries encountered could only reflect the demoralizing effects of contact with Europeans. Far from promoting the progress of their civilization, adaptations to European diplomacy and warfare stripped Indians of their natural virtues, transforming them into the "merciless Indian Savages" Jefferson excoriated in the Declaration. The natives' moral degradation was a function of their unnatural dependency on an English "father" who had betrayed his children, red and white. But while American patriots resisted George's tyranny, standing up for their rights and assuming the "separate and equal station to which the Laws of Nature and of Nature's God entitle them," their native "brothers" served as the mindless instruments of the king's wrath, rioting in "an undistinguished destruction of all ages, sexes and conditions."[20]

Jefferson's rage against the Indians proceeded from sentimental identification.[21] These "wretches" were not ordinary enemies to be treated with the moderation and restraint that the law of civilized nations enjoined. The Indians were at once too close, "brothers" born in the same land, indistinguishable from whites in their "uncultivated" state, and, in their perverse and obdurate opposition to the progress of civilization, too different to be welcomed into the family of nations. In more benign moments Jefferson could nostalgically evoke childhood attachments or project paternalistic solicitude for his childlike charges. But when Indians made war on the Americans, it was as if they had violated some taboo. Now that they had "commenced war" against us, Jefferson told his childhood friend John Page in August 1776, Congress was justified in "pushing the war into the heart of their country." But Jefferson would not be satisfied with a mere reprisal that was proportionate to the original injury. "I would never cease pursuing them while one of them remained on this side the Misisippi."[22]

Like their loyalist counterparts, Indians who served as pawns of British power forfeited their natural place in the new republican dispensation. As fellow "Americans" they should have joined the resistance against despotic, monarchical authority, eschewing the corrupt enticements of treaty agreements that deepened their dependency on English weapons and trade goods. Under the bastard political forms that flourished in Indian country during a century of conflict between European imperial powers, Indians had failed to develop the civil institutions that would have sustained their collective moral development. The history of the Indians thus offered a dark counterpoint to Jefferson's grand narrative of the progress of white civilization across the continent: their trajectory moved in the opposite direction, from a regime of natural virtue and sociability to the degradation and dependency that contact with European powers entailed. When they looked westward, Americans therefore did not simply encounter an earlier version of themselves: they met instead the perverse and corrupt forms that "civilization" took under the aegis of despotic power, an image of their own future should their struggle for independence fail.[23]

Jefferson thus offered a counternarrative to the story of New World degeneracy told by Buffon and Raynal that vindicated the Indians' natural potential as fellow human beings, condemned the corruption of despotic imperial regimes, and identified the fatal weaknesses of Indian societies. The degraded condition of indigenous peoples in Spanish America who had "passed through ten generations of slavery" offered the most poignant testimony to the human costs of despotic rule. Insult compounded injury when natural philosophers such as Buffon, basing their judgments on reports of recent travelers, mistakenly concluded that humans, like other species, degenerated in the New World. Species did not degenerate on this side of the Atlantic because of the debilitating effects of the environment; they were sustained, as Jefferson showed in the *Notes,* by an extraordinary natural abundance. If the native inhabitants were in such a degraded condition, it was because of their contact with European "civilization." As Jefferson told Chastellux, it was "very unfair . . . to judge of the natural genius of this race of men" on the basis of such a corrupted "sample" adduced by Buffon. "It is in N[orth] America we are to seek their original character: and I am safe in affirming that the proofs of genius given by the Indians of N. America, place them on a level with Whites in the same uncultivated state."[24]

To penetrate beyond Buffon's misrepresentations to a proper assessment of the "natural genius of this race of men," Jefferson recalled his own observations, studied the literary artifacts of earlier encounters, sponsored expeditions into the yet-uncorrupted regions beyond the frontier, and assembled a vast collection of word lists that could provide philological clues to Indian beginnings.[25] Jefferson's vindication of the natives' natural equality began with a refutation of Buffon's assertion that "the savage is feeble, and has small organs of generation; he has neither hair nor beard, and no ardor whatever for his female." In fact, Jefferson retorted, the Indian "is neither more defective in ardor, nor more impotent with his female, than the white reduced to the same diet and exercise." Nor was the Indian woman less fertile than her European counterpart. Birthrates were low because of periodic famine, the exploitation of female labor, and the voluntary abortions that preserved a rough balance between population and resources in hunting societies. Indian women "produce and raise as many children as the white women," Jefferson reported, "when married to white traders, who feed them and their children plentifully and regularly, who exempt them from excessive drudgery, who keep them stationary and unexposed to accident."[26]

That Indian country was so lightly populated was a function both of environmental constraints and cultural choices, not of the natives' sexual deficiencies. These choices, most notably the preference for hunting over agriculture, made Indian societies weak and vulnerable to European and American encroachments. As president, Jefferson never tired of preaching to his Indian "children" the great advantages of a settled, agricultural regime that would enable them to have more children and thus counter the devastating effects of population loss. For Indian men who were, by Jefferson's account, affectionately devoted to their families, this should have been sufficient incentive to abandon their primitive ways, liberate their women from "drudgery," and make farms. Indian men in their natural state were far from unthinking brutes, incapable of reasoned choices. Quite the contrary, Jefferson told Chastellux, Indians exhibited "a male, sound understanding."[27] They were brave and stoical when the occasion required but, in stark contrast to the supposedly "civilized" Europeans, preferred "finesse" to the exercise of force. Developing these themes in the *Notes,* Jefferson offered one of his characteristic paeans to human nature. To him it was important for his readers to know that the Indian "meets death with more deliberation, and endures tortures with a firmness unknown almost to religious enthusiasm with us: that he is affectionate to his children, careful of them, and indulgent in the extreme: that his affections comprehend his other connections, weakening, as with us, from circle to circle, as they recede from the center: that his friendships are strong and faithful to the uttermost extremity: that his sensibility is keen, even the warriors weeping most bitterly on the loss of their children."[28]

Indians were fully the equal of Europeans in possessing and expressing the social virtues that formed the foundation of the new republican social order. But living in small familial societies, these natural republicans had never developed the legal institutions or cultivated the respect for the law that enabled civilized republicans to extend their empire across the continent. The greatest obstacle to their civilization was the Indians' exploitation of their women. Although they happily lacked the means for tyranny that characterized the despotic regimes of the Old World, Indian men inflicted an "unjust drudgery" on their women. In this crucial respect, among "every barbarous people . . . force is law." As a man who admired the natives' manly virtues, Jefferson might well prefer a regime of "no law" where "the stronger sex . . . imposes on the weaker" to the universal oppression of "too much law." But Jefferson recognized the injustice of this primal form of domination. "It is civilization alone which replaces women in the enjoyment of their natural equality," he wrote in the *Notes.* If the absence of despotic government over men made Indian societies seem more "natural" to Jefferson, the oppression of Indian women clearly violated the women's natural rights and showed why the progress of civilization was a moral necessity. "Women are formed by nature for attentions," he later asserted, "not for hard labor." By this exalted standard Indian societies, despite their apparent virtues, were fundamentally flawed.[29]

Jefferson's account of gender relations provides the crucial pivot in his broader discussion of the future of native peoples on the American continent. When Jefferson shifted his gaze from manly virtues to female oppression, the terms of his analysis reversed: it was native, not European, societies that exhibited the most fundamental reliance on the rule of force. Indeed, from this perspective the rough equality that prevailed among Indian men was merely adventitious: lacking the political means to enforce their will on one another, they were forced to act as if they respected each other's rights. If under such circumstances Indian men developed "a male, sound understanding" that counseled prudence and circumspection in their dealings with other men, however, their moral capacity remained radically undeveloped, for it was the women who served as moral exemplars and arbiters in civilized societies. Civilization "teaches us to subdue the selfish passions," Jefferson asserted. By restraining their licentious impulses to exploit powerless dependents, civilized men learned "to respect those rights in others which we value in ourselves." Jefferson's celebration of Indian society and his moral indictment of European despotism thus gave way to his more profound identification with the great struggle of civilization against savagery. "Were we in equal barbarism" with the Indians, Jefferson concluded, "our females would be equal drudges." This was not only a contest for possession of a continent but a struggle for the "natural equality" of the sexes in a virtuous republican regime that would foster mankind's moral development.[30]

Indian societies were like republican families in their reliance on persuasion and affection to sustain harmonious social relations. But it was the radically defective constitution of Indian families, with men exercising brute force over women, that stunted the moral and political development of Indian societies. Lacking a sense of the "rights of others" that for civilized Europeans began at home, Indians were incapable of looking beyond the local, immediate, and particular to see themselves as part of a great society that could secure reciprocal rights and benefits for an expanding population. Habituated by their domestic tyranny over women to confuse force and law, Indian men could not imagine their own submission to a regime of law as anything less than dishonorable and degrading, even if it was based on consent.

The proud independence of Indian men constituted the most formidable obstacle to the assimilation of indigenous peoples in republican society. Those cultural traits that some Americans professed to admire in the natives—the "ardent love of liberty and independence" that Jefferson memorialized in his Second Inaugural—were, paradoxically, those traits that guaranteed their demise. With "no desire but to be undisturbed," natives resisted those changes—from hunting to agriculture, from recognizing the just claims of their oppressed women—that would have promoted not only the growth of population but, more importantly, the moral and political development needed for them to participate as equal partners in the expansion of the Americans' new empire of liberty.[31] Thus, while the Americans declared their independence from Europe in order to promote the progress of civilization, Indians fought a hopeless rearguard action against the future, identifying their own independence with a barbarous regime that retarded the population and prosperity of the Western world. The tragic outcome of this struggle was predetermined by willful Indian men who refused to allow their peoples to fulfill their human potential.

The whites' great advantage in displacing Indians from their aboriginal homes was demographic. With every succeeding generation the American population doubled, increasing the pressure of settlement to the west even as the Indians' numbers—and their ability to resist—dwindled. But this progress, however certain in the long run, was subject to obstacles and reverses, particularly during the Revolutionary era when Britain mobilized Indian allies in assaults on the new nation's frontiers. The very weaknesses that Jefferson believed ultimately would guarantee the Indians' demise made them dangerous enemies in war. Their bellicose hunting culture may have oppressed women, retarded population growth, and prevented moral and political progress in Indian societies, but it also produced formidable warriors. Insufficiently domesticated by female influence, impatient with and contemptuous of the rule of law, Indian men were vulnerable to European corruption. As they exchanged their services as mercenaries for essential material support, these wilderness aristocrats—a leisured warrior class that traditionally lived off the labor of oppressed women—became increasingly dependent on their European masters. Proud and independent Indians thus were transformed into Jefferson's "merciless Indian Savages," ruthlessly efficient tools of ministerial corruption.

When Jefferson contemplated Indians at war, as he did throughout the Revolution and its protracted aftermath, the image of wilderness aristocrat obliterated the natural republican he had invoked in his polemic against the degeneracy thesis of Buffon and Raynal. This degradation was cultural and historical, Jefferson insisted, the final sad effect of the "barbarous perversion of the natural destination of the two sexes" in Indian societies. As long as the Indians remained immune to Europe's corrupting influence, the effects of this "perversion" were mitigated by the small scale of their societies and the inability of savage men in their natural state to tyrannize each other systematically. But competing European imperial powers solved the problem of scale for Indian warriors, providing both the armaments that only advanced commercial societies could produce and the political resources of "great societies" that could exercise authority over extensive empires. As Jefferson wrote in April 1788, while traveling in the French countryside, "Every Indian man is a soldier or warrior, and the whole body of warriors constitute a standing army, always employed in war or hunting. To support that army, there remain no laborers but the women. Here, then, is so heavy a military establishment, that the civil part of the nation is reduced to women only."[32]

American patriots could extol the bravery of Indian warriors, in retreat before the inexorable torrent of white settlement, desperately fighting to preserve their traditional way of life.[33] Then, as in Jefferson's apotheosis of Chief Logan, Indian resistance could be compared to the patriotic mobilization of citizen-soldiers in defense of their own families and communities. For Jefferson, the "half-way pacifist," defensive war was always legitimate, especially when republican men fought to protect their women and children.[34] But for Jefferson and fellow patriots who drew deeply on the English libertarian tradition, there was a fundamental difference between citizens who became soldiers in times of local and national emergency and a "standing army," hireling soldiers such as those "foreign Mercenaries" George III had sent to America "to compleat the works of death, desolation and tyranny." When "merciless Indian Savages" served as mindless tools of British despotism, the worst of two worlds converged, threatening to retard and reverse the progress of republican civilization across the continent.[35]

For Jefferson the familial forms that governed Indian diplomacy and made European sovereigns into "fathers" of dependent native peoples represented another more dangerous manifestation of the fundamental flaw of Indian societies: the tyranny of Indian men over their women. Where later generations of historians have recognized that the elaboration of these kinship connections constituted creative intercultural adaptations to the changing balance of power in Indian country, Jefferson could see only the debasement and corruption of family values.[36] Indians were bound to transgress the sacred boundaries of family life, the moral foundation of civilized societies, precisely because their families were founded on the rule of force, not love. Thus, at the very moment that patriotic Americans were overthrowing monarchy and aristocracy—the perverted forms of familial rule that retarded the progress of political civilization in the Old World—Indian peoples embraced new, more degrading forms of dependency as the "children" of European despots.

THE FUTURE OF THE WEST

During wartime Jefferson's most immediate and compelling concern was with the military threat that Indian enemies presented to vulnerable frontier settlements. But his apparently paradoxical account of Indian strength and weakness—a formidable fighting force that lived off the dwindling resources of demoralized and depopulated communities—pointed to a more pervasive threat. The Indians' ultimate removal may have been inevitable, but the actual sequence of events that led to that outcome would leave an indelible imprint on the western landscape. The great fear shared by Jefferson and his colleagues was that, like the bidding for Indian auxiliaries in wartime, competition for Indian lands among the American states and private land companies, as well as between the new nation and its imperial neighbors, would foster dangerous concentrations of property and power. If fertile western lands offered a vision of prosperity for "our descendants to the thousandth and the thousandth generation," they also dazzled speculators with the possibility of landed properties that would support their aristocratic pretensions.[37] The uncertain future of the vast domain the Indians relinquished hinged on the transactions, violent or peaceful, that led to their removal. The question for Jefferson and his followers was not whether, in the process, justice would be done to native proprietors but rather whether the Americans, in resolving their own conflicts over jurisdiction and property rights, would lay the groundwork for the expansion of republican institutions or a counter-Revolutionary, aristocratic revival.[38]

The future of the West posed a series of related problems. First, the new American union had to resolve the conflicting jurisdictional pretensions of its members, potentially the most divisive and destructive legacy of the imperial old regime. Jefferson and his fellow Virginians insisted that the other states would have to recognize the integrity and inviolability of their Commonwealth's colonial charter claims, the same demand they had made on George III; for their part, the Virginians "ceded, released, and forever confirmed" to the peoples of neighboring states the Virginian territory that had been granted to them by subsequent charters.[39] To the consternation of Virginia's delegates, this apparently straightforward demand was rejected in 1781 when they tendered their state's offer to cede the region north and west of the Ohio River to the United States in exchange for confirmation of its remaining claims. The impasse jeopardized union at the very time the new nation's military and diplomatic success most depended on cooperation among the states.

Virginia's leaders had a simple explanation for the obduracy of the "landless" state bloc in Congress: land speculators who based their claims to western property on treaties or private purchases from the Indians that disregarded Virginia's charter rights distributed company shares to corrupt politicians in Maryland, Pennsylvania, New Jersey, and other states. To advance their own selfish interests, aspiring aristocrats would recklessly put the Revolution itself at risk. But this was not surprising, after all, for all of the great land speculations could be traced back to the colonial era, when prominent politicians on both sides of the Atlantic combined forces to grab large chunks of Indian country. Perhaps these silent English partners lurked in the background, exercising a covert, corrupt influence that was manifest in land company machinations. Perhaps the ostensible patriots who claimed to lead the companies would benefit from the failure of the Revolution, particularly if Virginia and the other landed states succeeded in vindicating their charter claims, thereby disallowing prior grants and purchases and preempting future encroachments.[40]

The western lands controversy thus reinforced the Virginians' fundamental understanding of the Revolution as the vindication of the corporate rights of the peoples of British America, defined by their charters, against the assaults of a corrupt metropolitan government that was beholden to the selfish private interests of speculators and financiers. As the controversy unfolded, however, the implications of that understanding became increasingly complicated and confusing. In 1776 enthusiastic patriots might well imagine that "killing the king" would inaugurate the republican millennium. But such hopes were all too soon dashed: the removal of the king simply meant that corruption took on new, more insidious forms. Under the influence of the land companies, corrupt congressmen argued that the United States should assume title to the crown lands in the West, disregarding state charters.[41] In a sharply worded remonstrance of December 1779, the Virginia assembly warned:

> Should Congress assume a jurisdiction, and arrogate to themselves a right of adjudication, not only unwarranted by, but expressly contrary to the fundamental principles of the confederation; superseding or controuling the internal policy, civil regulations, and municipal laws of this or any other State, it would be a violation of public faith, introduce a most dangerous precedent which might hereafter be urged to deprive of territory or subvert the sovereignty and government of any one or more of the United States, and establish in Congress a power which in process of time must degenerate into intolerable despotism.[42]

By this jurisdictional legerdemain Congress would take the place of the king, using its property to spread its influence among a new class of supposedly republican courtiers and retainers; a new metropolis would emerge, subjecting the American provinces, stripped of their rights, to its despotic rule. In resisting these assaults on their vital interests, Virginians learned that counter-Revolutionary threats were pervasive, even among those Americans who most loudly professed their patriotism. It was a lesson that would shape the responses of Jefferson and like-minded Virginia patriots to the dangers of "consolidation" in decades to come.

Concerns about the consolidation of power at the center were inextricably linked to anxieties about how that power would be exercised on the peripheries of the new republican empire. To prevent an aristocratic revival, it was essential that republican governments act as careful stewards of the public domain. The great challenge was to liberate landholdings from the incubus of feudal tenures, enabling free men to enjoy genuine independence on their own properties. Looking back on the headright system of early Virginia (under which, supposedly, land had been distributed to free white settlers) and looking forward to rising generations of young republicans spreading across the hinterland, Jefferson saw the West as a vast reservoir of free land, unencumbered by the fraudulent titles that proliferated under a corrupt ministry. Jefferson's hostility to feudal tenures and the aristocratic rule that they supported provided the ideological justification for overlooking the imperfect and conflicting property claims that covered the West in the wake of imperial rivalries, land speculation, and the opportunism (or desperation) of native peoples. His vision of a "fee simple empire" was the radical republican counterpoint to a British imperial regime that threatened to transplant feudal corruption to the New World and so reverse the proper course of world history.[43]

The British empire in North America was an incoherent complex of discrete jurisdictions, each standing in a distinct, though not often clearly defined, relationship to metropolitan authority. Jurisdictional confusion in the West was exacerbated in the last decade of imperial rule by a diplomatic revolution, ratified by the Peace of Paris in 1763, that destroyed the balance of power that Indian tribes, most notably the Iroquois, had successfully exploited for decades. Anxious to curb the costs of their newly extended empire, British authorities reduced their "gifts" or subsidies to Indian clients even as they sought to exploit new sources of revenue in the coastal colonies. Meanwhile, settlers and speculators pushed aggressively against the successive boundaries—beginning with the Proclamation line of 7 October 1763—that were supposed to restrain westward settlement. The escalating costs of negotiating and enforcing these boundaries led imperial authorities to delegate increasing responsibility to the colonial governments, subverting any possibility of effective, centralized rule in Indian country. It was against this background of imploding imperial authority and proliferating claims in Indian country that Virginians projected their own exclusive territorial rights to the vast domain defined by the 1609 charter.[44]

To secure Virginia's territorial integrity, Jefferson and his colleagues asserted their state's monopoly over Indian purchases in the 1776 constitution.[45] Threats to Virginia's essential rights and vital interests ultimately derived from the "detestable and insupportable Tyranny" of George III, but the king's corrupt influence was most immediately and dangerously present in the machinations of royal officials in America and their Indian clients. For republican Virginians the "covenant chain" that linked the English king to his native children was recast as a chain of corruption, which was the epitome of an unnatural aristocracy. In exchange for patronage and protection, servile and dependent Indians bartered away their dubious or at best imperfect rights to western lands, providing the putative source for the myriad title claims that threatened to deprive future generations of Virginians of their patrimony. Conspiring against the property rights of a free and independent people, the king and his Indian clients, the highest and the lowliest, were slavishly interdependent. When the war came and the king's character and intentions stood revealed, it was hardly surprising to Jefferson that the English tyrant's "Savage" tools should descend on the American frontiers in a frenzy of "undistinguished Destruction."[46]

Jefferson's language in the Declaration seems intemperate to modern commentators, striking a note that hardly resonates with the philosophical and philanthropic views eloquently expressed in the *Notes* and in his addresses to Indian leaders. But the animus in the Declaration was directed against a corrupt imperial regime that had reduced so many natives to their present pathetic state, not against the Indians who might still be found in their "natural" condition or in their reformed state if they submitted to the new republican dispensation. The frightening scenes Jefferson conjured up in the Declaration revealed profound anxieties about the king's awesome power to mobilize so many auxiliaries in his assault on American liberties: from "large Armies of foreign Mercenaries" to "merciless Indian Savages," and, moving still closer to home, "fellow-subjects" allured by the prospect of the "forfeiture & confiscation of our property," and finally and most frighteningly the enslaved Africans who labored on Virginia's plantations. This ever tightening circle of despotism, culminating in George III's instigation of murderous slave revolts, shaped Jefferson's dark image of the British empire on the eve of American independence.[47] Whatever Americans might declare, this empire was not about to wither away. British influence was pervasive, reaching through porous frontiers into the neighborhoods of treasonous fellow citizens and the homes of patriot planters.

In some fundamental sense Jefferson may have been expressing anxiety about his own virtue or, more plausibly, about the virtue of his countrymen. How else could the toryism of so many Americans be explained? But Jefferson was less concerned with character defects than with the corrupt foundation of the imperial constitution: the inequality of persons, classes, and communities that fostered dependency and servility and produced so many willing tools of despotic rule. Thus for Jefferson the crucial republican premise was equality. Within Virginia this meant the dismantling of primogeniture and entail, the legal props of a landed aristocracy, where families—and generations—were unequal; it also meant that the new state's public domain should not be encumbered by the claims of court favorites, speculators, or their Indian clients but should be broadly distributed on equal terms to all of Virginia's families.[48] The integrity of Virginia's public domain depended in turn on the constitution of a new American union that was purged of all monarchical forms and influences. The new states all must be republican, independent of each other and the world yet bound together in a perfectly harmonious and consensual union. Just as consent among individuals was only possible where they were truly equal, so too states in union must be equal. The British imperial regime prior to independence seemed deeply flawed not only because of the dangerous concentration of power in the metropolis but equally because of the wide diversity of colonial governments and jurisdictions through which Britain ruled America. "Divide and rule" was the ministry's motto: distinctive constitutions, overlapping boundaries, and competing interests would keep provincial Americans at each other's throats—and guarantee the continuing supremacy of a corrupt ministry.

Jefferson and fellow defenders of Virginia's claims insisted that the states must enjoy a territorial monopoly in the union, precluding any jurisdiction by a less than equal, less than fully republican government that would concentrate power dangerously in the central government. Provision for the creation of new and equal republican states in the hinterland, as required by the state land cessions to Congress, meant that the federal government would never be able to develop a system of colonies or client states in the West that could be mobilized against the original members of the union.[49] This determination to prevent the emergence of a powerful metropolitan government meant that there was no political space for native peoples within the new American empire.[50] Adroit negotiators in the diplomacy of the imperial old regime, Indians were too prone to seek corrupt, unequal advantages—"gifts," subsidies, and military aid—that would make genuine union impossible; lacking the attainments of political civilization, native peoples were incapable of forming true republican governments and therefore of meaningfully consenting to any durable engagements.

The ultimate victory of Virginia and the other landed states in the protracted western lands controversy set the framework for Indian diplomacy in the early republic. Had Congress been able to assert its own title in the West without depending on the cession of state claims, it would have been, as successor to the crown's prerogatives, better situated to enter into political engagements with native peoples.[51] But Congress's title in the new national domain would be both derivative and conditional: the vast western hinterland was to be held in trust for future white settlers who, as the Northwest Ordinance of 13 July 1787 promised, eventually would be entitled to draft their own republican constitutions and claim admission to the union on equal terms. In other words, Congress announced that any political arrangements short of statehood would be temporary: direct rule by Congress in the territorial phase would give way to republican self-rule; implicitly, any recognition of Indian rights under treaties also was understood to be provisional, subject to future negotiations that would guarantee the land's highest use and the ultimate establishment of republican government, the most civilized form of rule.[52]

Congress's reliance on state titles logically culminated in the "conquest theory," first set forth in negotiations with the Indians at Fort Stanwix, New York, in 1784. According to the congressional commissioners, the tribes by choosing to be wartime allies of the British had forfeited any legitimate claims within the limits of the United States as recognized by the recently concluded Peace of Paris and therefore could only continue to live in their ancestral homes at the new nation's sufferance: "You are a subdued people; you have been overcome in war which you entered into with us, not only without provocation, but in violation of most sacred obligations."[53] Congress now pretended to much more authority in Indian country than the British "father" had ever claimed before American independence. But Congress did not stake out this ultimately untenable position on its own behalf. On the contrary, because the conquest theory was premised on the sufficiency of the state titles, it preempted politically controversial counterclaims from other sources, most notably from Congress itself as the successor to the British crown's jurisdiction in the West. Accepting all state cessions, regardless of their defects and mutual contradictions, Congress would not challenge the territorial integrity of the states within their still extensive remaining claims; in dealings with the Indians, Congress would act as the agent of the respective states within their recognized boundaries or of the states collectively in the new national domain. The conquest theory fully accorded with these political imperatives. In effect, the Confederation government promised not to pursue an independent policy with the Indian tribes that, through the process of treaty negotiations, could provide a plausible foundation for its own title claims, which could then be turned against the states.[54]

The peace and stability of the American union depended on the definitive resolution of jurisdictional issues, not the perpetual conflict and negotiation that historically characterized Indian diplomacy. The need for a settlement offered eloquent testimony to the weakness of an "imbecilic" union teetering on the verge of collapse. But if the resolution of the land controversy kept the United States from falling apart and offered the wise men at Philadelphia their historic opportunity to frame a still "more perfect" union, it defied geopolitical realities in Indian country. Abandoned by their British protectors, the tribes had not been represented at the Peace of Paris in 1782 and their concerns were not heard in Congress when the states resolved their differences and charted the future of the West. The Indians' absence was no coincidence but rather the essential condition for bringing these negotiations to a successful conclusion. For it was only by ignoring the indigenous peoples that the American states could assert their collective claims against the other sovereignties of the world and simultaneously reconcile their own conflicting claims without risking a dangerous concentration of power in Congress. Not surprisingly, the logic of these settlements was lost on the Indians. Indeed, the combination of extravagant American pretensions, articulated in the conquest theory, and the new nation's obvious weaknesses as a military power set the stage for a series of disastrous and humiliating setbacks. The Americans could not have devised a surer means to promote a belligerent, pan-Indian mobilization, even among tribes that had allied with them or remained neutral during the Revolution.

Historians of early American Indian policy have lavished upon the conquest theory all the contempt it deserves.[55] Pacification of the frontier depended both on mobilizing a more credible force than the Americans could at first muster and on negotiating with the natives in good faith, according to the traditional conventions of Indian diplomacy. The new Washington administration learned these lessons quickly, although it took several years before Anthony Wayne's decisive campaign against the Ohio Indians prepared the way for a return to more conventional treaty making. Carrying a much bigger stick than the old Congress, the Federalists negotiated reasonable treaty settlements with the Indians, one of their most important achievements in consolidating the new nation's tenuous position in a dangerous world.[56] But the emerging Republican opposition was skeptical about Federalist Indian policy, and not simply because early military setbacks offered plausible targets for partisan sniping. Sniffing "consolidation" in every shifting breeze, Republicans feared that the administration would make unacceptable concessions to the tribes and their British sponsors in order to pacify the frontier: recognizing Indian rights through treaties could subvert the carefully crafted territorial settlement on which the federal union itself was grounded.

The thrust of Republican polemics through the 1790s was to show that Alexander Hamilton and his accomplices were intent on transforming the new national government into a corrupt, British-style aristocracy, covering their tracks through loose misconstructions of the federal Constitution.[57] A properly strict interpretation of the Constitution would respect the states' territorial rights as they were confirmed in the settlement of the western lands controversy. Instead, as the opposition's leading ideologue, John Taylor of Caroline, explained, the administration's misguided efforts to placate the Indians violated the conditions of cession compacts in the Northwest and "dismembered" states to the south.[58] For a Jeffersonian who remembered why Virginians had fought the Revolution in the first place, history seemed to be repeating itself. In blatant disregard of colonial charter rights, a corrupt imperial government had sought to block western settlement and cultivate Indian clients, the "merciless" savages whom the ministry proceeded to unleash on defenseless frontiers. As they jettisoned the conquest theory and negotiated new treaties with the tribes, Federalists pursued a similar policy, buttressing the consolidation of power in the central government by promoting the pretensions of native auxiliaries on the new nation's periphery. For Taylor, this arrangement was the very image of imperial corruption and the antithesis of the republican union of equal states that Americans had sought to create in 1776 and had perfected through the resolution of the western lands controversy.

The Federalists had no intention of winning the war in the West. Invoking a favorite theme in Republican rhetoric, Taylor juxtaposed the effectiveness of citizen-soldiers, fighting for their homes and families, with a corrupt and dangerous "standing army." Frontier self-help, a few "incursions of mounted riflemen," and the rapid distribution of the public lands would have cleared the Ohio country of Indians without any assistance from a "military *establishment*." But it was in the Federalists' interest to keep the frontiers aflame. "An expensive and unsuccessful war," Taylor wrote, "may cultivate the public mind into a willingness to treat away this territory to the Indians." As a result, the conditions of Virginia's 1784 land cession, the model for subsequent state cessions, would not be fulfilled. Public lands would not be sold at reasonable prices to industrious settlers, thus helping to discharge the nation's Revolutionary debts, nor would frontier settlements be formed into new states "in faithful compliance with the solemn compacts long since entered into with the ceding states." Scarcely a financial boon, the national domain would instead be a constant drain on the Treasury and a justification for higher taxes. "Nothing is wanting to consummate the system," Taylor concluded, "but a relinquishment of the right of pre-emption to the Indians, beyond the Ohio. So that the Indians and British may mount guard over the growth of republicanism in that quarter."[59]

The shape of things to come could be seen in the western reaches of North Carolina and Georgia, where federal treaties with the Creeks (1790) and Cherokees (1791) recognized Indian property rights within state boundaries as defined by colonial charters. If transactions with the tribes, duly confirmed by the Senate, were to enjoy the exalted status of treaties, there was nothing to stop the administration from "dismembering" the states: "From the power of making treaties, a power of dismembering a state has been deduced and exercised. And a power of dismemberment, is evidently equivalent to a power of annihilation." Indian treaties subverted the union—by encroaching on the states' territorial rights or violating the "solemn compacts" in state land cessions that provided for the creation of new states—and invested the tribes with political and property rights under the law of nations. Before the Revolution imperial officials had sought to establish "a *perpetual* boundary" with the Indians that would have given them similar standing as client states under British protection. The Federalists apparently "forget," Taylor concluded, "that a violation of charters, and an endeavour to prevent population, were of late two articles of impeachment against the king of England."[60]

Of course, Taylor well knew that the cunning Hamilton and his corrupt allies forgot nothing. Taylor's polemics were designed to arouse the great Republican majority from its forgetful slumbers, teaching vigilant voters to see dangerous patterns in apparently disconnected policies: Americans should be prepared to play their patriotic part when a "long train of [Federalist] abuses" finally forced them to reenact the Revolution. Taylor exposed the nefarious initiatives of the "paper junto," the incipient aristocracy of security holders—"the 5000"—who sought to exploit and impoverish the great mass of the people—"the 5,000,000." "A paper junto can find an interest in restraining population, even at the expence of the constitution. The danger and difficulty, with which our frontier are extended, invariably engenders an intrepid republican spirit. The enmity of this spirit to an intriguing junto, is so constant, that it is already regarded as a deadly foe. Besides, an aristocracy for ever obstructs mankind in the pursuit of competency and happiness, because by compressing them within the locality of their devices, they are more easily brought to the magical mint, and coined into money."[61] Federalist "aristocrats" promoted a standing army, opposed the formation of new states—potential "recruits for the 5,000,000"—and sought allies among Indian clients whose "rights" they recognized.

Taylor's denunciation of Federalist Indian policy echoed Virginia's complaints against the king during the Revolutionary crisis. "Instead of encroaching upon the barbarians," the Federalists were encouraging "the barbarians to encroach upon us"; "instead of procuring safety," so-called treaties of peace proved to be little more than "annual supplies of arms, ammunition and clothing to the enemy; . . . instead of securing the territories, acquired in a time of comparative weakness and distress," the administration was "surrendering [them] . . . to a despicable banditti."[62] These would-be aristocrats had the same antirepublican vision of the West's future that had inspired land speculators before the Revolution: they hoped to acquire "principalities out of the national territory for themselves." To do so, Taylor predicted, "those who call themselves federal" would "league with Indians and foreigners, to remove the land marks of union, and to revoke a fundamental stipulation for the security of independency itself."[63]

In the short run Taylor proved a poor prophet. Federalist campaigns in Indian country culminated in treaties that opened up vast new territories to settlement while pacifying the tribes. Meanwhile, the administration negotiated treaties that promised the removal of British forts from American territory (the Jay Treaty) and opened the Mississippi to American commerce (the Treaty of San Lorenzo), ratified in 1795 and 1796 respectively. Under these new circumstances it was no longer clear that the "intrepid republicans" of the new settlements, the chief beneficiaries of these diplomatic successes, would rally behind the Republican opposition. But Taylor's evocation of an aristocratic conspiracy against states' rights and republicanism would leave its imprint on the "Jeffersonian Persuasion," both in the dark days immediately ahead and in the party's triumphant revival in the election of 1800. The lurid details of Taylor's dire predictions about the future of the West were less important than the underlying conception of the union that he drew from Jefferson and his fellow Virginia patriots.

Jefferson's vision of republican empire, an empire without a powerful metropolis or an aristocratic ruling class, provided the conceptual framework for Taylor's gloomy scenario of corruption and loss. Growing out of the defense of Virginia's charter claims, Jefferson's ideas about states' rights and union had always been subject to challenge, whether from the British crown, "merciless Indian Savages," land speculators, or corrupt congressmen; in the 1790s the ascendant Federalists showed how an energetic central government, raising the cry of national security, could so easily subvert federal union and republican liberty. Yet the people came to their senses in the epochal election of 1800, rehabilitating republicanism by routing the aristocratic Federalists.

Liberated at last from the incubus of aristocracy, the empire of liberty would expand westward. "Kindly separated by nature and a wide ocean from the exterminating havoc" of the Old World, Americans would take possession of their "chosen country." The Indians who had loomed so large in Taylor's vision of a shrinking West, dismembered by treaties and parceled out in corrupt new "principalities," simply disappeared in Jefferson's optimistic account. But this was precisely the point: however formidable their warriors might be, Indian "nations" were mere shadows, the tools of corrupt European paymasters, incapable of exercising any real power of their own. Without the artificial support of the British empire or of Federalist administrations, the Indian threat would quickly dissipate. Like Federalist leaders who had been abandoned by enlightened voters, the Indians were suddenly rendered impotent and harmless; like a standing army, deprived of royal patronage, the "barbarians" could only retreat. They were no match for "the strongest Government on earth . . . where every man, at the call of the law, would fly to the standard of the law, and would meet invasions of the public order as his own personal concern."[64]

Jefferson could afford to ignore the Indians because of the diplomatic and military successes of Federalist administrations, not because voters had finally come to their senses and purged the federal republic of dangerous aristocratic and monarchical tendencies. Americans owed their reprieve from diplomatic and military entanglements to a brief interval in the European wars, not to the irresistible power of citizen-soldiers. But Jefferson struck a responsive chord when he congratulated his fellow Americans on the vast arena open to their enterprise. The absence of Indians in his account was testimonial to a powerful new sense of the new nation's manifest destiny, held in check throughout the 1790s by the ascendancy of aristocratic Federalists.

Jefferson's vision of continental greatness represented the convergence of two distinct but interdependent historical narratives. By redeeming their republican experiment in the "revolution of 1800," Americans rejoined the story of their Revolutionary struggle against British tyranny with the larger story of civilization's westward progress. If the Revolution failed, a possibility that seemed increasingly likely to Republicans during the 1790s, civilization necessarily would take a radically different course. Keen students of the new science of politics, republican theorists recognized that there was a dangerous discrepancy between the progress of civilization generally and the development of enlightened political regimes: aristocratic and monarchical elements constituted archaic survivals in European regimes that jeopardized their stability and prosperity. Through the degradation and enslavement of native peoples, these regimes could extend their sway through the American hemisphere, throttling the natural development of republican institutions.

In both of Jefferson's stories, converging in the Inaugural Address's triumphant vision of a dynamic and expansive republican empire, Indians played roles that disgraced and dishonored their natural gifts. The only hope for the individual Indians was that they follow the arduous path toward republican civilization; they must abandon political pretensions that made them dependent on corrupt imperial patrons and retarded their moral development. With the war for the West apparently won, the philanthropic Jefferson was prepared to teach his Indian children how they too could become Americans.

PHILANTHROPY

Jefferson did not hate Indians. Instead, he hated their degraded condition under the pernicious influence of America's antirepublican enemies; it was George III, after all, who turned the natives into savages. After his inauguration in 1801, the new president rarely expressed hostile sentiments toward the Indians. The balance of power now decisively favored the Americans; with European powers no longer offering critical support, dwindling numbers of Indians were no match for the rapidly growing American population. "You see that we are as numerous as the leaves of the trees," Jefferson told one Indian leader in 1808, "strong enough to fight our own battles, and too strong to fear any enemy."[65]

The Americans' numerical preponderance was so great that the Indians would never again be able to intervene in the new nation's conflicts with neighboring imperial powers. Toward the end of his second term, when chronic conflict over maritime rights threatened war with England, Jefferson told the northwestern Indians that though the English were "strong on the water," they were "weak on the land." The Indians should play no role in this looming conflict: "We do not ask you to spill your blood in our quarrels," nor, he added ominously, "do we wish to be forced to spill it with our own hands." His meaning could not be mistaken: "The tribe which shall begin an unprovoked war against us, we will extirpate from the earth, or drive to such a distance as that they shall never again be able to strike us." Jefferson's chilling warning recalled his Revolutionary rage against the "Savages" and undoubtedly betrayed similar anxieties. But the message's tone was calculated and confident, with professions of friendship balancing threats. Jefferson presented a stark choice to his native "children" so that they would learn an important lesson: Indians must abandon war if they ever hoped for the peace, prosperity, and population growth that would make them a "great nation."[66]

The British were responsible for chronic warfare in the Northwest, Jefferson told another group of chiefs. "While we were under that government," before independence, "we were constantly kept at war with the red men our neighbors." Then many tribes fought against us in the Revolution, leaving a legacy of "ill blood . . . after we had made peace with the English," and the English had abandoned their Indian allies; "it was not till the treaty of Greeneville that we could come to a solid peace and perfect good understanding with all our Indian neighbors," he wrote.[67] According to Jefferson, wars between Indians and Americans were unnatural; they could only be explained by outside interference.

Their British allies and patrons were not the Indians' true friends, for they fomented the chronic conflicts that led directly to the depopulation and demoralization of their communities. "Now, my children," the paternalistic president exhorted, "if we wanted to diminish our numbers, we would give up the culture of the earth, pursue the deer and buffalo, and be always at war; this would soon reduce us to be as few as you are, and if you wish to increase your numbers you must give up the deer and buffalo, live in peace, and cultivate the earth."[68]

Constant warfare led to a massive sacrifice of Indian peoples, not only of the young warriors wasted in battle but of future generations as well. Indians need only look across the frontier, to the rising tide of white settlement, to see the future they were forfeiting by holding fast to their savage way of life. "What a brilliant aspect is offered to your future history, if you give up war and hunting," exclaimed Jefferson, and "adopt the culture of the earth and raise domestic animals; you see how from a small family you may become a great nation by adopting the course which from the small beginning you describe has made us a great nation."[69] Jefferson invoked two related themes as he urged his native "children" on toward civilization. Only by turning to agriculture would Indians be able to sustain an enduring relation to their country, "the earth which covers the bones of your fathers," and therefore to their own past; only by making farms, by growing instead of wasting children, could they hope for a future.[70] The choice lay with the present generation and its leaders:

> It depends on yourselves alone to become a numerous and great people. . . . Nothing is so easy as to learn to cultivate the earth; all your women understand it, and to make it easier, we are always ready to teach you how to make ploughs, hoes, and necessary utensils. If the men will take the labor of the earth from the women they will learn to spin and weave and to clothe their families. In this way you will also raise many children, you will double your numbers every twenty years, and soon fill the land your friends have given you, and your children will never be tempted to sell the spot on which they have been born, raised, have labored and called their own.[71]

If the Indians rejected Jefferson's advice, they would "disappear from the earth."[72] Demographic disaster was the real enemy, not American armies or the legions of white settlers that followed in their wake. And if the Indians should succumb to this enemy, if these refractory "children" should spurn their father's teaching, it would be their own responsibility.

Jefferson's presidential addresses to the Indians offered a righteous justification for an expansionist territorial policy that would set the stage, within less than two generations, for Andrew Jackson's removal policy. The inexorable progress of civilization—self-evidently a good thing—absolved Americans of agency or moral responsibility for the displacement of indigenous peoples; in stark contrast, the Indians did face choices and were responsible for their own fate. Professing solicitude for the welfare of his red children, the white father could offer them little protection from the expansion of settlements and the penetration of market forces. Jefferson argued that Indian peoples could only benefit by submitting to the discipline of the market, paying their debts to merchant creditors, exchanging portions of their vast land reserves for the capital needed to make farms. White settlers' land hunger thus was not a threat but a resource Indians should exploit. "Our people multiply so fast that it will suit us to buy as much as you wish to sell," Jefferson told the Chickasaw chiefs in 1805, and "if at this time you think it will be better for you to dispose of some of them to pay your debts, and to help your people to improve the rest, we are willing to buy on reasonable terms."[73]

The self-serving logic of these addresses provided the ideological rationale for an expansive republican empire. But Jefferson did not consciously seek to deceive or defraud his native charges, and if he was manipulative in his dealings with them, he was equally so with his own children.[74] Everything he said in his messages to the Indians was meant for their own good: by giving up land they could not use, they might improve and secure the remainder. Becoming good husbands, Indian men would reap bountiful harvests of crops and father many children; learning to live under laws of their own making, Indian communities would become true republics, ultimately merging with white Americans in a single "great nation." If all of these adaptations to republican civilization served the interests of land-hungry white farmers, this was only as it should be in a peaceful and harmonious union of peoples. After all, Jefferson insisted, the assumption of a natural enmity between Indians and white settlers was false, an ugly image from the old regime fostered by generations of imperial warfare and diplomacy. The New World, purged of Old World corruption that had fostered Indian savagery, presented a different picture. If they did not disappear from view altogether, the Indians would be a part of this picture. This was Jefferson's promise to Captain Hendrick, an Indian leader, in December 1808: "Unite yourselves with us, join in our Great Councils and form one people with us, and we shall all be Americans; you will mix with us by marriage, your blood will run in our veins, and will spread with us over this great island."[75]

Jefferson knew that the choice would be difficult. "Are you prepared for this?" he asked the Upper Cherokees when they sought assistance in civilizing themselves. "Have you the resolution to leave off hunting for your living, to lay off a farm for each family to itself, to live by industry, the men working that farm with their hands, raising stock, or learning trades as we do, and the women spinning and weaving clothes for their husbands and children?"[76] For Jefferson the choice itself, not federal patronage, was crucial. The real American Revolution would come to Indian country when Indian men renounced their "aristocratic" prerogatives, elevated women to their naturally equal position, and provided for the welfare of future generations. The first challenge was to have children at all: Indian men should know that their savage way of life was a form of generational murder against unborn children, a criminal waste of the male potency and female fertility Jefferson celebrated in his *Notes on Virginia*.

Jefferson's addresses to the Indians revealed powerful emotions. Far from cynical productions of a manipulative diplomacy, these addresses were heartfelt testimonials to the principles on which, he believed, the new American regime was founded. As they asserted their rights and declared their independence, Americans acted as moral agents, following the precepts of natural law. The Revolution was lawful, not licentious; republicanism represented the high achievement of a civilized people, not a regression to savagery. Jefferson and his fellow patriots had provided freedom and prosperity for future generations by liberating a great continent from monarchy and aristocracy. This great boon, "our country," had required great sacrifices in years of bloody warfare. Indians who would share in this magnificent legacy had to change themselves into civilized republicans and good Americans. Their arduous progress, recapitulating the progress of civilization itself, must begin at home.

"YOUR BLOOD WILL MIX WITH OURS"

Jefferson's sentimental republicanism also began at home, in the idealized domesticity constituted by consensual conjugal union. In his most extravagantly optimistic moments, he could envision unions of unions, spreading circle upon circle, layer upon layer, until the whole enlightened world was transformed and redeemed. This republican millennium would be both the culminating moment in the progress of world history and a return to the wholeness and perfection of the family circle. The same pattern of thought can be traced through Jefferson's Indian addresses. When he imagined the reconciliation of the races, the merging of nations into "one people," the old language of Indian diplomacy took on new life for him: Jefferson was no longer a "father" by courtesy or convention, nor were the Indians "children" who would opportunistically adopt and dispose of "fathers" as the balance of forces in Indian country changed. Instead, Jefferson foresaw white Americans and their "red brethren" forming a single great family, connected by the most intimate ties of consanguinity. For the Indians this merging of the races would be at once the moment of their restoration—"peace and agriculture will raise you up to be what your forefathers were"—and their rebirth as Americans. Once "you . . . possess property" and "live under regular laws," Jefferson told the Indians, they would be prepared "to join us in our government, to mix with us in society, and your blood and ours united will spread again over the great island."[77]

In becoming Americans, the Indians would regain the continent that their forefathers had recklessly forfeited. Through this same process the new nation's title to its imperial domain would become perfect: any lingering misgivings about the Americans' claims to their country would be allayed. When, for instance, Jefferson told the Mandan that "we consider ourselves no longer of the old nations beyond the great water, but as united in one family with our red brethren here" or declared to the

Osage that "it is so long since our forefathers came from beyond the great water, that we have lost the memory of it, and seem to have grown out of this land, as you have done," he acknowledged that native peoples had a prior, and in some sense more legitimate, claim to the land.[78] But as the two peoples merged into one, their common patrimony would be a bond of union, not a source of strife.

It is tempting to dismiss Jefferson's vision of interracial nationhood. Invoking his own experience and observation of Indian culture and politics, he emphasized the formidable obstacles to its fulfillment in his Indian addresses. Perhaps Jefferson was simply setting the stage for experiments that he knew were bound to fail; he was full of "commiseration" for the Indians but free of any sense of moral responsibility. Yet Jefferson's Indian addresses did speak powerfully to some of the central concerns of his public career and private life. How could the Americans justify their claim to being a distinct people? By what right did they claim the continent as their own? How did native peoples figure in his understanding of the American Revolution? What place could these peoples claim for themselves in the new republican empire?

Jefferson never betrayed feelings of guilt about the fate of the Indians. He was more likely to be righteously enraged at their savagery or, in times of peace, philosophically resigned to their cultural resistance. But running through all of his responses was a sense of personal identification, the "attachment and commiseration" evoked by childhood memories that were still vivid in his old age. Perhaps, reasonable men would be inclined to agree, the Indians were doomed to "disappear from the earth." The wish for a different fate for the Indians, the fantasy of a "great island" redeemed from European corruption and the savagery it fostered, and nostalgia for lost childhood innocence—all were palpable in Jefferson's romantic image of the millennial moment when, he told the Indians, "your blood will mix with ours" and a truly new nation would emerge.

CHAPTER 2

Republican Empire

✖✖✖

W HO CAN LIMIT the extent to which the federative principle may operate effectively?" asked Thomas Jefferson in his Second Inaugural Address in March 1805. The Louisiana Purchase had added a vast new domain to the United States, leading less optimistic observers to fear "that the enlargement of our territory would endanger its union."[1] But Jefferson looked forward to the proliferation of free republican states, bound together by ties of common principles and harmonious interests. The Enlightenment vision of a benign imperial order, predicated on the reciprocity of benefits and the security of natural rights, would be fulfilled with the union's progressive expansion. Power would be diffused and decentered in the federal republic: the Americans would no longer be subject to the domineering rule of a distant metropolis, as they had been before declaring and securing their independence. Their new regime would be imperial in scope, far exceeding the most ambitious designs of a corrupt and despotic British ministry. As Indian nations faded from view, overwhelmed by the rising tide of American settlement—and deprived of crucial support by European patrons—the republican union would spread westward, irresistibly.

Once its independence was firmly established, Jefferson's new nation would be invulnerable. Its strength could not be measured in conventional military terms but rather in the loyalty of the patriotic citizens who would rise up in defense of their own liberties and their country's independence whenever they were threatened. It was strong precisely because it had not concentrated authority and resources in a single central place, so inviting the assaults of hostile, counter-Revolutionary powers. Jefferson's "federative principle" was based on the equality and independence of its members. Because their union was consensual, the exercise of coercive force (the despotic principle) was unnecessary to its survival and prosperity. Like the "honest patriot[s]" who constituted the nation, the separate state-republics would rally to each other's defense in time of emergency.[2] For Jeffersonians, the American Revolution was the prototype for the spontaneous popular mobilization that made a strong central government unnecessary and dangerous. Within the community of sentiment and interest that defined the new republican empire, a self-governing people would mobilize men and resources much more effectively than any despotic regime. Banishing metropolitan power from the New World, Jefferson imagined a great nation, a dynamic and expansive union of free peoples.

Montesquieu, author of the influential *Spirit of the Laws*, taught his readers that republics must be small to survive, that virtue, the animating principle of republics, could flourish only in closely knit civic societies. In opposing ratification of the federal Constitution, Antifederalists had invoked Montesquieu's authority in arguing against a more powerful, "consolidated" regime that they feared would subvert the state governments and destroy civil liberties.[3] But Jefferson, drawing inspiration from James Madison's *Federalist* No. 10, came to believe that Montesquieu's "doctrine, that small States alone are fitted to be republics, will be exploded by experience." The Revolution had shown that the American people could transcend "local egoisms," evincing the most exalted patriotic sentiments on a continental scale. Indeed, as Jefferson suggested to his Genevan friend François d'Ivernois in 1795, it would be much easier to discover a majority "free from particular interests" in the nation as a whole than in the respective states: "The smaller the societies, the more violent and more convulsive their schisms."

Under the new constitutional regime, Americans could become conscious of themselves as a people in their common dedication to "principles of justice"; having overthrown the despotic power of a distant metropolis, they would also avoid the tyranny of evanescent majorities in local assemblies. "We have chanced to live in an age," Jefferson told d'Ivernois, "which will probably be distinguished in history, for its experiments in government on a larger scale than has yet taken place." In the Old World, as the French Revolution showed, such experiments "will be accompanied with violence, with errors, and even with crimes."⁴ But freedom would prosper in the New World, Jefferson promised in his inaugural addresses: Americans would enjoy the benefits of "government on a larger scale" that the Revolutionaries had sought to secure first within the British empire and then as an independent people. Jefferson's conception of republican empire, an idealized vision of the old regime purged of corruption, thus provided the framework for his inspiring vision of a new national identity. An empire without a metropolis would be sustained by the patriotism of a free and united people.

Jefferson's conception of a new republican empire in the American hemisphere met with considerable skepticism in his own day (the "candid apprehension" of antiexpansionist critics that he acknowledged in his Second Inaugural) and derision in our own. The thrust of the criticism then and now has been that Jefferson did not have a firm grasp of geopolitical reality, and that his penchant for ideological posturing and empty abstractions led him dangerously astray. Federalists warned against the centrifugal effects of an overextended polity, invoking the teachings of contemporaneous political science. They were not always opposed to expansion: national security might dictate an aggressive, expansionist policy, as when Federalists urged a preemptive strike against New Orleans—before Jefferson's diplomacy (and good luck) gained the prize by peaceful means. The premise of Federalist foreign policy was that there should be a correspondence between military force and strategic objectives, that the expansion of the union should never run ahead of the federal government's ability to enforce its authority against foreign and domestic threats. The annexation of New Orleans might be imperative, but Federalists were equally certain that the acquisition of the Louisiana Territory would be a disaster. The disproportion between its present extended domain and its pathetically inadequate military force already put the new nation at serious risk: further expansion would weaken the bonds of union, exposing and exacerbating interregional conflicts of interest.⁵

The Federalist critique of Jeffersonian expansionism asserted that a polity of imperial dimensions could survive multiplying external challenges to its extended frontiers and corresponding centrifugal pressures from within only by modeling itself on the powerful nation-states with which it must necessarily contend. The visions of universal monarchy that had once inspired European imperialists could not be sustained in the modern era of great-power politics; nor, as the American Revolution surely had demonstrated, was it possible to sustain a less autocratic, more liberal imperial regime, dedicated to the pursuit of common interests and reciprocal benefits. Antiexpansionist Federalists concluded that the very idea of "empire" itself was an anachronism in the modern age, that the Republican quest for an "empire for liberty"—an empire that would dispense with concentrated power and metropolitan rule— would leave the new nation hopelessly ill equipped to deal with pressing and pervasive threats to its vital interests and even to its survival.

The United States should become a stronger nation, consolidating authority in a central government that commanded the resources of the continent, before it recklessly risked the enmity of the great European powers. Federalists thus saw the new nation operating as a weak secondary power in a postimperial balance of power. Embracing the logic of national sovereignty and the competitive struggle for relative advantage, they saw Britain as the exemplar of an effective, modernizing nation-state that could best secure and project its vital interests. Federalists were most characteristically anti-imperial and therefore "modern" on the question of size, for they were convinced that an overextended union could never achieve a sufficient degree of national integration to function effectively in a dangerous world.

Jeffersonian expansionists, by contrast, rejected the consolidation of authority that they believed had destroyed the British empire and that Federalists persisted in advocating precisely because they continued to think and act within an imperial framework. As reform-minded proponents of an idealized world order, made fully and finally compatible with natural rights, free exchange, the progressive diffusion of civilization, and the rights of self-government within and among confederated states, Republican imperialists looked backward. Under the republican aegis the New World would be redeemed from the destructive struggles of European powers for dominion: the expanding American union would become an "empire for liberty." Jeffersonian avatars of the new dispensation thus invoked the most enlightened and advanced thinking of the modern age on behalf of an antique imperial vision.[6]

EMPIRE

The conceptual framework within which Jefferson and his fellow republicans operated was provided by the idealized version of the British empire that emerged in the whigs' patriotic resistance to British authority in the years before independence.[7] Throughout the imperial crisis provincial patriots resisted divide-and-conquer tactics that were meant to illuminate and exploit the colonies' conflicting interests: the assault on Massachusetts in the Intolerable Acts of 1774 was, by this imagined identification, an attack on the entire continent. More fundamentally, punitive policies—whether aimed at particular provinces or at all of them—challenged the patriots' increasingly idealized and abstract conception of the empire as a regime of equal rights, reciprocal benefit, and progressive improvement. The higher resistance leaders raised the bar—from repeal of specific legislation, to a general rollback to the status quo in 1763, and finally to demands for explicit guarantees in a new intraimperial treaty or constitution—the more they suppressed and denied differences among themselves. The imperial crisis thus worked to reinforce provincial Americans' sense of a transcendent collective identity in the empire.[8]

The imperial idea persisted in America well past independence. In 1783 George Washington called on his countrymen to lay the "foundation of our empire." "Behold!" enjoined the poet Francis Hopkinson, "Behold! an Empire rise."[9] Until the French Revolution and the party battles of the 1790s fostered a more indiscriminate Anglophobia, it sufficed for American patriots to denounce monarchy, aristocracy, and their associated corruptions: they happily linked their own imperial project to its British antecedents. Ezra Stiles's 1783 oration *The United States Elevated to Glory* thus called on Britain's "American sons, inheriting thine ancient principles of liberty and valour, to rescue & reinthrone the hoary venerable head of the most glorious empire on earth!"[10]

Historians have seen such effusions as premonitions of the "manifest destiny" for continental expansionism and pretensions to hemispheric hegemony—and world power—that characterized later periods of

American history. Stiles's evocation of the Anglo-Saxon genius for liberty and self-government also previews the racialist ideology of later proponents of imperialism, determined to take on their fair share of the white man's burden.[11] But as Anthony Pagden has shown, before the American Revolution "empire" did not have these ominous associations for admirers of Britain's enlightened colonial and commercial policy.[12] Before independence, Anglicizing provincial elites were irresistibly drawn toward the ideas of radical reformers in the metropolis who advocated a greater degree of equality and reciprocity in a more enlightened imperial political economy. Revolutionaries imagined that their own decentralized regime, a federal union of self-governing republics, was a worthy successor to Britain's empire in America: indeed, the two terms could be used interchangeably, as when a writer in the *United States Magazine* in 1779 referred to the "several states in the union of the empire."[13]

Having identified the radical, constitutional defect in imperial governance—a corrupt and grasping administration that was determined to enrich the metropolis while beggaring its distant provinces—Americans could embrace an improved, republicanized version of the imperial ideal in projecting the prosperity and freedom of their expanding union of states. "Empire" conjured up positive images for an enterprising generation; in the words of a New Jersey poet, "This rising empire of the west, / May be with peace and honors blest."[14] At the same time, empire evoked an idealized past, a world order or political civilization like that of classical Rome, an expansive and inclusive regime that would spread republican institutions across the continent.

Whatever negative associations empire may have had for Revolutionaries were purged by extirpating monarchical authority and breaking from Britain: the whole point of the resistance movement, after all, had been that the empire could be redeemed from ministerial (then parliamentary, finally royal) corruption so that Britons throughout its far reaches would be secure in their respective rights and participate generally in its benefits.[15] Patriot leaders could only contemplate the final break, and they did so very reluctantly, because they believed that the American remnant of the British empire was destined to fulfill this vision of peace, prosperity, and union. By the summer of 1776, when Jefferson drafted the Declaration, the most persuasive argument for independence was that the British "tyrant" had already "dissolve[d] the political bands" that constituted the empire by making war on America: his erstwhile subjects faced the stark choice of submitting to this political "slavery"—the antithesis of their definition of empire—or pursuing their own imperial destiny as one of the "powers of the earth." By vindicating their independence, American Revolutionaries would vindicate the imperial idea, the great legacy of antiquity and the great hope of progressive and enlightened peoples everywhere.[16]

Jefferson and his Revolutionary colleagues first invoked the law of nature and nations in order to define satisfactory terms of union within the empire. Only when rebuffed by a corrupt and tyrannical imperial administration did they declare independence and form a more limited American union. As Jefferson insisted in 1825, the Declaration was "the fundamental act of union of these States."[17] According to the text of the Declaration, this union claimed "the separate and equal station to which the Laws of Nature and of Nature's God entitle them."[18] The new nation was now entitled by the law of nations to negotiate new "political" (that is, diplomatic) ties with other European powers. Independence was clearly a means toward higher ends: far from leaving the American states in their natural, anarchic condition with respect to one another, it drew them into a new and unprecedented "union," a union that could in turn forge further alliances—or unions—across the Atlantic. Frustrated in their quest for imperial reform, American patriots became proponents of an independent federal union and a more liberal world order.

The language of the Declaration suggests that eighteenth-century Anglo-Americans did not make a clear distinction between domestic—or imperial—and foreign relations.[19] Patriot leaders understood their colonies to be "states," and they hoped to reform the imperial constitution through agreements that could be described as "treaties." Indeed, the argument against parliamentary sovereignty suggested that imperial connection could only be "federal," a relationship constituted by treaty.[20] Jefferson recalled that John Adams and other congressional radicals insisted that the American colonies had always been "independent" with respect "to the people or parliament of England," "that so far our

connection had been federal only & was now dissolved by the commencement of hostilities."[21]

For eighteenth-century Americans "empire" was a protean concept, a
bundle of emergent, potentially contradictory definitions. As a complex, extended polity, the British empire provided a template for American federalism, but it was also a kind of embryonic world order.[22] One
of the empire's leading weaknesses was the absence of authoritative definitions and common understandings that could have legitimized ministerial reform efforts. The shared language of British constitutionalism
did not promote but instead probably impeded the articulation of an
imperial constitutional order. Not surprisingly, leaders of the colonial
resistance movement turned in frustration toward natural law—the law
of nature and nations—in defense of their political rights and civil liberties. But American patriots did not see their efforts to codify a new constitutional order as a rejection of the imperial connection: quite the contrary, most of them continued to believe, until the bitter end, that the
negotiation of strategic and commercial "treaties" would lay the foundation of a more perfect and enduring Anglo-American union.[23]

If the extended polity of the British empire was an inchoate states-
system, the European balance of power was equally inchoate, particularly so in the extra-European world. Indeed, at the time of the American
Revolution, the law of nations was the law of European sovereigns: Europe was the world. In declaring their independence, Americans boldly
claimed membership in this international community, the "commonwealth" or "federal republic" of European sovereignties. They did not
seek to isolate themselves from Europe, nor were they eager to participate—without powerful allies and on radically unequal terms—in the
anarchic struggle of all against all that was supposed to be the natural
state of nations. Visionary republican Revolutionaries wanted to change
the world: by extending the boundaries of the European system, by en-
hancing the system's capacity for progressive improvement through the
practice of enlightened diplomacy, by perfecting a legal regime among
their own state-republics that would eliminate the causes and pretexts of
war.[24]

Thinking imperially, Revolutionary Americans had first thought of
themselves as Britons, with all the cultural baggage and national pride

that that identification entailed.[25] Independent Americans sloughed off some of the more extreme and impolitic manifestations of this British identity, including their militantly intolerant Protestantism. But the Americans' sense of their genius for liberty, of their success in preserving and improving on British models, sustained this almost racial sense of continuity and connection with British Whig tradition. Freed from metropolitan domination, independent Americans grasped and deployed the imperial idea in myriad concrete, idiosyncratic ways. Despite or, as Tocqueville suggested, because of their diverse local loyalties and proliferating forms of association, Americans took on increasingly distinctive and recognizable "national character."[26] This emergent national identity was not merely "creedal," or the lowest common denominator of rational calculators: it was simultaneously grounded in particular places—such as Jefferson's "country," Virginia—and imperial in its visionary aspirations.

KILLING THE KING

Jefferson's conception of republican empire grew out of his experiences as a leader of Virginia's revolution against British imperial rule. In seeking to vindicate his colony's corporate rights and to impose radical limits on royal authority, Jefferson assumed a boldly republican stance. Yet Jefferson's animus against George III, culminating in the passionate denunciations of the Declaration of Independence, was inspired by a powerful identification with an idealized British empire. The legacy of this imperial vision was apparent in Jefferson's conception of an American union in which his beloved Virginia would flourish.

Jefferson's challenges to royal authority before the Revolution provided the conceptual framework for his imperial vision. "Kings are the servants, not the proprietors of the people," he provocatively asserted in his *Summary View of the Rights of British America* (1774), thus deflating and reversing conventional formulations. Jefferson was determined to explode the "fictitious principle that all lands belong originally to the king," whose proprietorship thus defined his dominions and constituted his subjects as a people.[27] Elaborating the theory of expatriation that Virginian Richard Bland had sketched out a decade earlier, Jefferson imagined a more direct relation between the king and his people, unmediated by property relations and the degrading implication that George III "owned" his Virginian subjects. "America was conquered, and her settlements made and firmly established, at the expence of individuals, and not of the British public," Jefferson explained. "Their own blood was spilt in acquiring lands for their settlement, their own fortunes expended in making that settlement effectual. For themselves they fought, for themselves they conquered, and for themselves alone they have right to hold."[28] By identifying the king with one of the "peoples" over whom he ruled—"the British public"—Jefferson framed the issue in terms of the equal (property) rights of another, wholly distinct people, the Virginians, who had "submitt[ed] themselves to the same common sovereign." In Jefferson's imaginative reformulation the empire was constituted by the voluntary submission of its component communities to the authority of the king, "the central link connecting the several parts of the empire thus newly multiplied."[29]

The *Summary View* offered a rationale both for a radically diminished conception of royal authority and for denying Parliament, the legislature of the British people, any authority at all. For most commentators the conclusion was irresistible: Jefferson and his fellow radicals meant to make British America into an independent sovereignty and rival power. Yet there was a countertendency in Jefferson's Revolutionary writings, a quest for an enduring "union" that would sustain and expand the British empire. George III might be a "servant" of his people(s), but he played an absolutely crucial role as "the only mediatory power between the several states of the British empire."[30] This union of peoples, the fundamental meaning of "empire" for Jefferson, was a higher good, indeed the highest political good. "We are willing on our part," he would have had the Continental Congress say, "to sacrifice every thing which reason can ask to the restoration of that tranquility for which all must wish. On their part let them be ready to establish union on a generous plan. Let them name their terms, but let them be just."[31]

Jefferson's hatred of monarchy, the animating premise of his political thought throughout his subsequent career, was a function of increasingly exaggerated expectations and their inevitable frustration. The sense of personal betrayal in the Declaration of Independence seems extravagantly excessive in Jefferson's recital of George III's "long train of abuses," inviting as it did the editorial excisions of his soberer colleagues and the psychological speculations of his biographers.[32] Yet Jefferson's indictment of the king in the Declaration was a measure of the importance he attached to imperial union, not simply of guilty misgivings about assaulting patriarchal authority. This was much more than a case of disclaiming responsibility and projecting guilt in a psychodrama of national self-determination. George III's abuses carried enormous rhetorical weight for Jefferson because the constitutional controversies of the imperial crisis had eliminated every other "link" between British metropolis and the British-American provinces or "states." This was a union that Jefferson cherished, even as it was progressively ruptured, not only because he shared the Anglophilic tendencies of provincial elites but because empire—his idealized version of the old regime— provided the conceptual framework for his enlightened, cosmopolitan republicanism.[33]

George III was important to Jefferson because his sovereign authority, constitutionally limited in order to secure the rule of law and legitimately exercised only in service to his subjects, was the last remaining link of imperial union. In one of the passages of the original draft of the Declaration that was excised by Congress, Jefferson recurred to the mythical history of Anglo-America he had outlined in the *Summary View.* The settlement of the colonies had been "effected at the expense of our own blood & treasure, unassisted by the wealth or the strength of Great Britain"; the empire was the product of colonial initiatives: "In constituting indeed our several forms of government, we had adopted one common king, thereby laying a foundation for perpetual league & amity with them." Significantly, this union, made possible by the "mediatory power" of the king, was between distinct peoples, or "states." It had been destroyed because George III had proved incapable of rising above a partial, self-interested identification with one of his peoples at the expense of the others. Yet the ultimate blame for this unhappy state of affairs lay not with George himself but with the British people, those unfeeling "brethren" who in the final crisis encouraged their "chief magistrate" (he was no longer a "common king") to pillage and plunder the Americans, not to make peace with them and so perpetuate imperial union.[34]

Jefferson's antimonarchical turn was complete. Not only had the British monarchy proved incapable of preserving the complex and extended imperial polity, but it also worked to foment discord and enmity among peoples who were "natural" allies by virtue of ties of birth, culture, sentiment, and interest. Indeed the unnatural behavior of the British people was eloquent testimony to the pernicious effects of a corrupt monarchical regime in making friends into enemies. True union would only be possible if monarchy and aristocracy were extirpated: to endure and prosper, an empire had to be republican.

The important work of Jefferson's Declaration was to persuade Anglo-Americans that loyalty to the king could no longer sustain union between Britain and the American colonies. But if these "political bands" were "dissolve[d]," Jefferson believed that declaring independence forged new bands. No longer united through the mediation of the British monarchy, the American states were now "Free and Independent," with "full Power to levy War, conclude Peace, contract Alliances, establish Commerce, and to do all other Acts and Things which Independent States may of right do." Yet as the American states dissolved their ties with Britain and recognized each other's free and equal status, they proceeded to form a new and more enduring union: "We mutually pledge to each other our Lives, our Fortunes and our sacred Honor."[35]

Union, like the republican governments of its member states, was based on "the consent of the governed"; "the Laws of Nature and of Nature's God" entitled these states to a "separate and equal station," just as the Creator endowed all men with "unalienable Rights."[36] In both cases the recognition of equal rights guaranteed closer ties, more perfect unions of men and of republican states, than had been possible under British monarchy. The monarchical connection had not only fostered unnatural divisions between metropolitan Britons and provincial Anglo-Americans, but it had set colony against colony in a mutually destructive competition for relative advantage.

The British empire's radical flaw was the fundamental premise of inequality, manifest in the pretensions of the central government to exercise rule over distant provinces, in the unequal distribution of benefits in the imperial economy, and in the hierarchical order of monarchical society. The collapse of Britain's monarchical empire showed that such unequal pretensions could only be sustained by the exercise of coercive force that soon proved self-defeating: disunion was the result. By contrast, Jefferson's republican empire would be built on the more durable foundation of equal rights.

Jefferson's conception of union was reflected in the way the Declaration recognizes the claims of a plurality of distinct states and at the same time speaks for them in a single voice. It would be a mistake to conclude either that Jefferson and his colleagues were themselves confused about the sources of their own authority (for whom were they speaking?) or that they meant to sow confusion at home and abroad as a cover for their bold assumption of authority. For Jefferson, recognition of the master principle of equality enabled Americans to discover and promote unity in diversity both within and among their state-republics. The genius of a republican empire, its great source of power, was that the singular and the plural would thus define and support one another: securing the rights of the parts, citizens and states, was the threshold for recognizing the transcendent claims of the whole. What could signify this recognition more powerfully than the willingness of congressmen to pledge their "Lives . . . Fortunes and . . . sacred Honor" to one another?

PART AND WHOLE: VIRGINIA AND THE UNION

Jefferson's republican empire was predicated both on the rejection of monarchical rule and on constitutional guarantees of the kind of provincial autonomy and self-determination that Anglo-Americans had long enjoyed. Certainly, as his biographers have emphasized, Jefferson was a loyal Virginian, dedicated throughout his long life to the interests of his "country" and his class. But it was precisely because Jefferson was a localist, so prosperously and self-confidently situated on the imperial periphery, that he could envision a republican alternative: an empire without a dominant metropolitan center that would expand across the continent, securing the rights of its member states and spreading its benefits equally.[37]

Jefferson offered a blueprint for the new republican empire in his *Notes on the State of Virginia.* The "Old Dominion" may have once taken pride in its British connections, but the imperial crisis had revealed the ways in which proud Virginia was in fact subject to the commercial exploitation and despotic rule of a distant, "unfeeling" metropolis. Independent Virginia would not go its own way, however, despite its imperial dimensions ("This state is . . . one third larger than the islands of Great Britain and Ireland, which are reckoned at 88357 square miles") and the extraordinary prospects for future development so exhaustively cataloged throughout the *Notes*.[38] For Jefferson, Virginia's future and America's were inextricable, even indistinguishable.

The *Notes* constituted an imaginative effort to situate Virginia in a dynamic and expanding union. The first two queries tell contrasting stories of contracting territorial limits and expanding commerce and settlement. In the first query (on "Boundaries"), Jefferson recounted successive limitations on Virginia's vast domains, beginning with "the grant of Maryland to the Lord Baltimore" in 1632 and culminating (for the time being at least) with "the cession made by Virginia to Congress of all the lands to which they had title on the North side of the Ohio" in 1784. If Virginia diminishes in the first query, however, its prospective influence extends far beyond its contracted boundaries in the next query ("Rivers").[39] Indeed, Jefferson's horizon now extends across the continent: "The country watered by the Missisipi and its eastern branches, constitutes five-eighths of the United States, two of which five-eighths are occupied by the Ohio and its waters: the residuary streams which run into the Gulph of Mexico, the Atlantic, and the St. Laurence water, the remaining three-eighths."[40]

Even while Virginia was bounded within increasingly narrow limits, Virginians found themselves favorably situated to participate in the boundless opportunities afforded by the great system of inland waterways. During the colonial period boundary changes were imposed by the crown, as new colonies were created and international agreements negotiated. In theory, these changes violated the Virginia's territorial integrity: crown jurisdiction derived from—and therefore could not legitimately diminish—the corporate property rights of a community of expatriated Englishmen. But "our ancestors . . . who migrated hither, were laborers, not lawyers," Jefferson wrote in the *Summary View*, and just as the colonists submitted to crown management of public lands, they had tacitly accepted boundary limitations.[41]

At Jefferson's suggestion the state's first constitution (adopted in June

1776) insisted on Virginia's original territorial right even as it legitimized colonial boundary changes: "The territories contained within the Charters erecting the Colonies of Maryland, Pennsylvania, North and South Carolina, are hereby ceded, released, and forever confirmed to the People of those Colonies respectively, with all the rights of property, jurisdiction, and Government, and all other rights whatsoever which might at any time heretofore have been claimed by Virginia." This acknowledgment of the jurisdictional status quo would preempt boundary conflicts and facilitate union among the new American republics. Jefferson envisioned this process of progressive self-limitation continuing under the new republican dispensation. According to his draft constitution, the legislature would be empowered to lay off "one or more territories" west of the mountains as "new colonies . . . established on the same fundamental laws contained in this instrument, and shall be free and independant of this colony and of all the world." (As finally adopted by the convention, the constitution authorized the legislature to form "one or two" new states in the West but eliminated Jefferson's discussion of their future constitutional and political status.)[42]

Jefferson's conception of republican empire was encapsulated in his provision for "free and independant" new states in his draft constitution and in his subsequent Ordinance for Territorial Government, adopted by Congress in 1784, calling for the admission of new western states to the union "on an equal footing with the . . . original states."[43] His apparently paradoxical premise was that the recognition of the equal rights of political communities, and therefore of their complete independence of each other and of "all the world," was the necessary precondition for creating enduring, consensual bonds of union among them. State boundaries that were drawn to secure the rights and promote the real interests of republican citizens would preempt wars and facilitate peaceful exchanges. Empire thus was not simply the happy consequence of the natural affinity of republics; Jefferson also assumed that the boundaries which defined the effective limits of self-governing republics would be permeable, facilitating the proliferation of interdependent economic interests and social connections that would establish union on the most solid (and "natural") foundation.[44]

The *Notes on the State of Virginia* constituted both a promotional tract, celebrating the state's and the nation's prospects for economic development, and Jefferson's blueprint for completing the republican Revolution in his beloved Commonwealth. In explicating this reform program, scholars have appropriately focused attention on Jefferson's dissatisfaction with the Virginia constitution of 1776 and his frustrated efforts to effect a comprehensive revisal of the Commonwealth's laws (discussed at length in Queries XIII and XIV).[45] Jefferson thought that the ongoing process of making the state smaller was equally important to the progressive perfection of republican government in Virginia.[46] But small republics presupposed a republican context, a consensual union of "free and independant" states: making Virginia smaller only made sense to the patriotic Jefferson to the extent that it could freely exploit its advantageous situation in an ever larger, more perfect republican union. For Jefferson, contracting boundaries and boundless opportunity were inextricably, dialectically linked: this was his vision of republican empire.

Jefferson's vision reflected his faith in the beneficent, harmonizing, and civilizing effects of commerce that was widely shared by enlightened political economists of his day. The notion of reciprocally beneficial exchange was particularly attractive to colonists who chafed under a mercantilist regime that they believed enriched the metropolitan core at the expense of the provincial periphery.[47] Indeed, the growing conviction among alienated American patriots that the British empire was designed not to secure the rights of all Englishmen but rather to make invidious distinctions and render unequal benefits among them gave apparently trivial constitutional quarrels an ultimately Revolutionary urgency. For Jefferson and many other Revolutionaries, the specter of metropolitan domination and the "enslavement" of subject provinces inexorably led to the rejection of monarchical authority and therefore of the British connection. But it did not lead, as Jefferson's *Notes* eloquently attests, to the rejection of empire.

Jefferson celebrated the prospective operation of a liberal regime of free trade within the framework of a more perfect republican empire. This would be an empire without a center, or dominant metropolis. Dynamic and expansive, it would spread, diffuse, and equalize benefits through the vast system of inland waterways, improved and extended by the art of man, to its farthest reaches: this would be an empire without peripheries. American "nature" made this great project possible: indeed, Jefferson's imperial vision took on a reassuring concreteness and specificity in the inventories in the *Notes* of resources and developmental opportunities that stood in stark contrast to the unnaturalness and artificiality of the old imperial regime.

Jefferson's hostility to cities is well known, and frequently misunderstood.[48] His main concern was not to forestall commercial development but rather to preempt the (unnatural) concentrations of population, wealth, and power that would recapitulate the structural inequalities and inefficiencies of the monarchical empire. The most eloquent statement of Jefferson's urban vision is not to be found in his strictures in Query XIX ("Manufactures")—"the mobs of great cities add just so much to the support of pure government, as sores do to the strength of the human body"—but rather in Query III ("Sea-Ports"). Jefferson left this query blank: "Having no ports but our rivers and creeks, this Query has been answered under the preceding one" on "Rivers."[49] Of course, Jefferson knew that this assertion was literally not true: America would not exist without links to the larger world through its ports— and even Virginia had them. But what Jefferson had imaginatively abolished were great port cities that dominated the hinterland; in their place he projected a great system of inland commerce that rising cities, like the Chesapeake ports of Alexandria and Baltimore, would serve but not dominate.[50]

Jefferson turned westward when he imagined his republican empire, away from the domination of a corrupt British metropolis and the colonial seaports through which it exercised its dominion. His profound aversion to the old imperial regime and the degrading dependency and subordination that it supposedly entailed provided the animus for his assault on cities and celebration of agrarian virtue. When Jefferson railed against urban workers and mobs, he was conjuring up the pervasively corrupting effects of the monarchical empire on the American colonists generally: "Dependance begets subservience and venality, suffocates the germ of virtue, and prepares fit tools for the designs of ambition."[51] Like the opposition of slavery and freedom, the opposition of city vice and rural virtue was a compelling trope for provincial Americans: what fate could be more horrible than to be drawn into the metropolitan vortex?

The successful conclusion of the War for Independence did not banish the metropolitan threat. American staple producers remained vulnerable to the vagaries of foreign markets and credit; as a second-rate power the United States could do little to enforce its rights against Britain's maritime hegemony. Nor did the great western hinterland, the site of Jefferson's rising republican empire, offer refuge from metropolitan entanglements: Indian nations, "merciless Indian Savages" serving as the corrupt tools of European monarchical power, stubbornly resisted the westward spread of settlement; when the Indians were pushed back and American planters and farmers brought new lands under cultivation, their burgeoning production made the new nation even more dependent on foreign markets. More troubling still, many nominal republicans seemed all too prepared to accommodate to and prosper from the insidious forms of metropolitan power that threatened to subvert American independence and reverse the outcome of the Revolution.

FRIENDS AND ENEMIES

Jefferson's conception of republican empire was premised on his profound hostility to metropolitan domination. His images of urban corruption expressed persistent anxieties about provincial subordination and dependence: British influence penetrated far beyond the port cities that serviced the transatlantic trade. Yet it was also true that many city people demonstrated their independence and virtue in supporting the Revolution; during the 1790s manufacturers and workers in northern cities provided crucial support for the Jeffersonian opposition. Jefferson was not talking about real American cities in the *Notes*. Instead, he showed how the metropolis, operating through provincial proxies, could continue to exercise a pervasive, insidious influence on Americans even after independence.

Jefferson imaginatively sought to banish the metropolis from American soil when he concluded that we should "let our work-shops remain in Europe." A similar purifying impulse was apparent in his speculations on transatlantic commerce: "It might be better for us to abandon the ocean altogether, that being the element whereon we shall be principally exposed to jostle with other nations: to leave to others to bring what we shall want, and to carry what we can spare."[52] But, of course, Jefferson knew that such a complete separation from the trading world was impractical and undesirable.[53] The fantasy was that Americans, having withdrawn from the carrying trade, would (thanks to competition among the remaining carriers) be able to meet its former imperial masters on a plane of commercial equality, trading agricultural surpluses ("what we can spare") for manufactured goods ("what we shall want"). Paradoxically, the next best thing to complete withdrawal from the carrying trade was complete engagement, free trade: "Our interest will be to throw open the doors of commerce, and to knock off all its shackles, giving perfect freedom to all persons for the vent of whatever they may chuse to bring into our ports, and asking the same in theirs."[54] Equality here was conceived in terms of commercial reciprocity—the presence of American merchants in European ports would balance that of Europeans in America—and of a free competition in which Americans actively participated.[55]

Both of Jefferson's prescriptions—no carrying trade or free trade—were inspired by his determination to preserve the new republican empire from the pernicious effects of metropolitan domination. Indeed, Jefferson's vaunted agrarianism was an artifact of his devotion to a republican political economy, not its fundamental premise. It was only by means of internal commercial expansion through its great system of rivers that the American union could offer a viable alternative to the mercantilist regime of unequal benefits in a monarchical empire. Commercial expansion into the hinterland was the necessary precondition for the proliferation of Jefferson's freeholding farmers; similarly, Jefferson's apotheosis of the yeomanry ("I repeat it again, cultivators of the earth are the most virtuous and independant citizens") constituted his tribute, cast in the most self-consciously archaic, neoclassical, republican terms, to the dynamic, decentered, and progressive political economy of the postmercantilist age.[56]

Yet the distinction between symbolic representations and real people and places was never so clear in Jefferson's thought and practice as this analysis suggests. The binary oppositions—between aristocratic inequality and republican equality, city and country, slavery and freedom, vice and virtue—that enabled Jefferson to make sense out of the new nation's new relation to the old metropole suggested problematic and shifting identities, loyalties, and boundaries among Americans. In times of crisis Jefferson and his coadjutors could imagine that the revival of metropolitan influence and monarchical sentiment had led to the gangrenous corruption of a geographically defined portion of the union. Even more devastating was the awful possibility that Americans as a whole were insufficiently virtuous—that is, resistant to metropolitan influence—to preserve their independence. This possibility cast a darkening shadow over the Republican opposition to the High Federalist ascendancy of the late 1790s.

James Madison offered a particularly chilling image of the sociology and psychology of metropolitan corruption in an anonymous essay published in the Philadelphia *Aurora* in 1799. He showed how British trade could make Americans into foreigners. "Every shipment, every consignment, every commission," he wrote, "is a channel" through which British influence "flows." Madison depicted the very system of inland trade that Jefferson had suggested would release the American economy from the commercial domination of the old metropole as the medium of British penetration and corruption. In this hyperbolic formulation no American who participated in the market was safe from corrupting influences. Conceiving of market relations in terms of the unequal relations of debtors and creditors rather than of the exchange of reciprocal benefits among equals, Madison evoked an atavistic, anticommercial agrarianism. In effect, he acknowledged that a genuinely republican empire was a practical impossibility. If metropolitan power was ultimately irresistible, the Revolution had been pointless. The metropolitan center would yet again give rule to subject provinces on the periphery.[57]

High Federalists, aided and abetted by their British sponsors, clearly intended to remodel the government of the union along monarchical lines. As they demolished the constitutional forms of republican empire, embattled Jeffersonians despaired of the union, turning to their state governments to defend their liberties. Jefferson followed the logic of this descending spiral in his original draft of the Kentucky Resolutions (October 1798): unless the lengthening train of Federalist abuses, culminating in the Alien and Sedition Acts, was "arrested at the threshold," they would "necessarily drive these States into revolution and blood, and will furnish new calumnies against republican government, and new pretexts for those who wish it to be believed that man cannot be governed but by a rod of iron."[58] The virtuous remnant would be forced to reenact the American Revolution: in doing so, however, they would have to make war on their once-fellow Americans, recognizing the impossibility of sustaining a truly republican federal union. Of course, such an outcome would betray Jefferson's geopolitical vision in the *Notes*, a vision that linked Virginia's contracting boundaries and republican perfection with boundless opportunity in an ever expanding, ever more perfect "empire for liberty."

For Jeffersonians, the "spirit of 1776" evoked both the Revolutionaries' vaulting ambition to inaugurate a new world order and the desperate measures they had been driven to by the collapse of the old imperial order. To enjoin the rising generation to reenact the Revolution may have revived dedication to the regime's first principles, but it also constituted the implicit recognition that the Revolution had failed to change the world. Indeed, the more faithful later generations were to the Revolutionaries' original script, the more difficult it was for them to recapture the progressive, enlightened thrust of Revolutionary ideology. Resisting domination by a despotic central government became an end in itself, not what it had been for the young Jefferson, the means of redeeming and republicanizing an empire.

Endemic divisions over early national foreign and commercial policy encouraged Americans to see each other as foreigners. Characteristically, Jeffersonians took this tendency to ideological extremes; eager anticipation of the free trade millennium, when competition among foreign consumers would bid up the prices of American staples, threw the pernicious operations of monopolizing capitalists into stark relief. Old Republican John Taylor of Caroline thus identified the manufacturing interests of the North who impoverished southerners by manipulating tariff policy as an emergent "foreign" power. "Let the capitalists or factories stand for Britain," Taylor wrote in *Tyranny Unmasked* (1821), "and all the other occupations for the colonies, and very little difference between the two cases will appear."[59] If anything, Taylor suggested, American capitalists exercised a more tyrannical rule over agriculturalists than their foreign counterparts, who at least had to compete with one another.

When Jeffersonians found themselves on the defensive in the competition for relative advantage in the federal political arena, they characteristically invoked the specter of metropolitan domination that had inspired the Revolutionary fathers. Thinking in terms of the old empire—and taught by Jefferson to be vigilant against the constant and pervasive dangers of an aristocratic, monarchical revival—these "Old Republicans" lost sight of the new republican empire that inspired provincial Anglo-American Revolutionaries. As a result, the progressive strains of Enlightenment thought that had been integral to Jefferson's conception of the union were now increasingly turned against federal authority.[60]

A growing sense of sectional distinctiveness and grievance was fostered by appeals to liberal political economy and to the jurisprudence of liberal internationalism. Both of these strains of thought linked latter-day sectionalists with the progressive, antimercantilist, antistatist impulses of the American Revolution, the great touchstone of Jeffersonian Republican ideology. Yet these impulses were extricated from and ultimately directed against the Jeffersonian vision of republican empire. Obsessed with the dangers of an emergent American metropolis that would exercise despotic rule over subject provinces, these Republicans were able to sustain an imaginative identification with Revolutionary founders who had fought the same good fight. But the appeal to the principles of 1776 also led an influential cadre of latter-day Jeffersonians to question the very possibility of continuing union with Americans from other regions whose fundamental interests and values seemed increasingly alien.

Ever anxious about the reimposition of an older, centralized style of imperial rule, vigilant republicans increasingly cast their domestic opponents as "foreigners" who were conspiring to seize the federal government and foster the development of a dangerously powerful national metropolis. In other words, memories of the old (British monarchical) empire tended to have a corrosive, ultimately subversive effect on the new (American republican) empire. The existence of genuine threats from abroad or from European imperial powers on the American frontiers mitigated the tendency for American republicans to see the worst in their American foes. But when such threats subsided, a kind of ideological regress set in, as Americans imagined themselves in the embattled situation of the Revolutionary fathers, vindicating their liberties against a despotic imperial regime. The American Revolution thus simultaneously served as the unifying, universalizing, nation-making myth for subsequent generations of Americans and as a paradigm for a potentially divisive, increasingly sectionalized, nation-breaking politics. The Civil War constituted the ultimate regression: as they resisted the relentless encroachments of northern despotism, southern secessionists saw themselves as the true legatees of their Revolutionary fathers.[61]

The Revolutionaries' new republican empire finally failed because later generations of Americans could not, in moments of political and constitutional crisis, clearly distinguish it from the old monarchical empire that they had overthrown with independence. As the federal union verged toward collapse before the Civil War, the ideological legacy of the Revolution took on a deceptively reactionary cast. Southern secessionists looked backward, identifying themselves with the Revolutionary fathers as they sought to vindicate provincial liberties against metropolitan power. In doing so, they obscured from view the progressive, forward-looking dimensions of Jefferson's "empire for liberty."

Jefferson and his fellow patriots imagined that there was a world of difference between monarchical and republican rule, between an extended polity held in place by consolidated, coercive power and a consensual union of free republican states in a regime of reciprocal benefits and perpetual peace. This notion of a republican *imperium* enlisted the modernizing discourses of Enlightenment political economy, social theory, and jurisprudence to envision a postmonarchical future in which power would be domesticated, diffused, and decentered. The United States would be something new under the sun, a new political order that Europe, should it ever achieve sufficient enlightenment, might one day emulate. In sharp contrast to Old World regimes, the independence and prosperity of the new republican empire did not depend on the massive concentration of coercive force but rather on ties of affectionate union and harmonious interest.

NATION

Empire provided the conceptual framework for an emerging consciousness of American nationality. It did so by making the same fundamental issues that had driven provincial patriots to independence seem compelling to subsequent generations. Faced with continuing controversy over the conflicting claims of center and periphery in an expanding republican empire, Americans saw themselves reenacting the Revolution itself at every moment of crisis. Like the Revolutionary fathers, latter-day patriots understood (or imagined) that they confronted powerful domestic enemies who were prepared to sacrifice the common good for their own selfish advantage. Thus, even as the memory of the Revolution evoked images of transcendent brotherhood and union—the apotheosis of empire—it also taught young patriots to question the patriotism of their opponents and to mobilize against them.

Challenging the Federalists' identification of their administration with the "nation," Jefferson insisted that union was founded on Americans' subscription to "federal and republican principles," not on their submission to a powerful centralized state. Harking back to an idealized conception of the British empire, Jefferson's formulation also pointed forward to a notion of a people or nation, distinct from government and therefore the foundation of any government's legitimate authority. After a "reign of witches" in which Federalist "monocrats" attempted to construct a powerful central government on the ruins of civil liberties and states' rights, Jefferson's election constituted the belated fulfillment of the patriots' vision of an empire without a metropolis.[62] Yet that vision was no longer predicated, as it had been for Jefferson and fellow imperial reformers before independence, on the assumption of a transcendent British nationhood. Now he erected the superstructure of empire on the foundation of a radically distinct American national identity. Evoking the mythic Revolutionary citizen-soldier, Jefferson insisted in his First Inaugural Address that every American, "at the call of the law, would fly to the standard of the law, and would meet invasions of the public order as his own personal concern."[63]

Jefferson's "people" were "brethren of the same principle," bound together by their devotion to republicanism. His appeal to principle identified the patriots of 1800 with the Revolutionary Sons of Liberty who had sought to vindicate the "rights of Englishmen" against a corrupt ministry and Parliament. For this earlier generation of patriots, claims to rights constituted an assertion of an inclusive British identity, coterminous with the limits of empire. But the nationhood of independent Americans, disconnected from Britain, was no longer self-evident: the logic of Revolutionary republicanism led to the proliferation of self-constituted provincial "peoples" in an increasingly tenuous union. "Nationalists" in the Federalist administrations of the 1790s sought to counter these centrifugal tendencies by giving the expanding American empire a new metropolitan center. In resisting the Federalist juggernaut, Jefferson and his Republican allies insisted that they were speaking for a single united people whose existence as a people was not a function of adventitious constitutional arrangements. High-handed Federalists would destroy the union—making one people many—while Republican respect for "federal and republican principles" would preserve union. But when they conflated the "principles of 1798" with the "spirit of 1776," Republicans implicitly acknowledged that fealty to their platform did not make Americans into a single people. Recalling and revivifying the patriotic fervor of the Revolutionary fathers, Jefferson and his allies claimed to speak for a nation that preceded and transcended specific constitutional forms: they invoked the aspiration to equality and union-in-empire that had inspired provincial resistance to metropolitan tyranny before independence.

By emphasizing the historic struggle for liberty that bound successive generations of Americans, Republican patriots gave their idea of nationhood a genealogical and affective dimension that belied the universal, inclusive appeal of the enlightened abstractions they espoused. Republicans attributed their eroding position in the 1790s to insidious alien influences that penetrated the countryside through systems of commerce and credit. Their conception of a virtuous people under siege thus reflected a distinctly agrarian bias: the true patriots were freeholding farmers and planters with enduring attachments to the land; by contrast, the loyalties of merchants followed their ever changing interests: they had no country.[64] Emphasizing fundamental cleavages in American society, embattled oppositionists conjured up an inspiring vision of a truly homogeneous people, purged of "foreign influence" and united in dedication to republican principles. Just as the Revolutionaries had driven the tories into exile, the revolutionaries of 1800 would redeem the republic from corruption by enlightening the people to its true interests—to its existence as a people in command of its own destiny—so reducing their Federalist enemies to impotence. Then, a conciliatory Jefferson averred in his Inaugural, we can "let them stand undisturbed as monuments of the safety with which error of opinion may be tolerated where reason is left free to combat it."

The nation Jefferson imagined was united in principle, harmonious in its interdependent interests, homogeneous in character: an expansive family of families, cherishing the legacy of the Revolutionary fathers while looking forward to the spread of successive generations across an empty continent. The image of this particular people thus was imprinted on and shaped by the land it "possessed," "kindly separated by nature and a wide ocean from the exterminating havoc of one quarter of the globe; too high-minded to endure the degradations of the others; possessing a chosen country, with room enough for our descendants to the thousandth and thousandth generation."[65] Without the union imposed by a dominant metropolis or flowing from allegiance to a common sovereign, Jefferson's republican empire could only be said to exist, much less to grow and prosper, if Americans constituted a single nation.

Throughout the extended Revolutionary era, proponents of provincial and state rights always justified themselves by linking their particular interests with what they claimed were the true, enduring interests of the empire or union as a whole, the only proper object of popular patriotic feeling. When desperate Republicans broached extreme measures in resisting Federalist consolidationists in the 1790s—including nullification and disunion—their need to identify the part and the whole in a plausible way became increasingly compelling. With their own loyalties drawn into question, Republicans had to fashion a compelling vision of Americans as a nation. In doing so, they gave the abstraction or fiction of "popular sovereignty" a particularity and concreteness it had never had when provincial Americans imagined themselves Britons, or even when the peoples of the colony-states had mobilized to resist British tyranny or to constitute new governments.

The Republicans' "revolution of 1800" ensured that the national feeling they aroused and exploited would not, for the time being at least, be centered on the federal state. Repudiating the Federalists' version of a consolidated, "energetic" postimperial regime, ascendant Republicans promoted a radically diffuse and decentered national identity, constantly refreshed by electoral mobilizations that reenacted the Revolution for rising generations of patriots. Their thoroughly republicanized empire had become a nation when Americans, resisting the encroachments of a powerful central government, became conscious of themselves as a people.

CHAPTER 3

The Revolution of 1800

THOMAS JEFFERSON considered his election in 1800 a second "revolution," a peaceful reprise of the American War for Independence. In subsequent presidential elections the "federal and republican principles" that had triumphed in 1800 were repeatedly reaffirmed by "the voice of the nation." Only the U.S. Supreme Court, under the leadership of Jefferson's distant cousin John Marshall, failed to get the message. In defiance of the clearly expressed "will" of the nation, Jefferson told Judge Spencer Roane in 1819, "we find the judiciary on every occasion"—including the recent controversial decision in *McCulloch v. Maryland*—"still driving us into consolidation." The Sage of Monticello had written to congratulate Roane on the publication of his "Hampden" essays, a series of slashing attacks on the Marshall Court in Thomas Ritchie's Richmond *Enquirer.* Jefferson assured Roane that his pieces had hit the mark: "I subscribe to every tittle of them." Forcefully expressing the "principles" that had animated Jefferson's political life, "Hampden" evoked memories of earlier crises and triumphs, including what Jefferson for the first time called the "revolution of 1800."[1]

Jefferson's election had long since assumed mythic proportions, not only for the former president but for the great mass of Republicans who now dominated American politics. The catechism was certainly familiar to Roane, an ardent defender of the Old Republican orthodoxy who sat on Virginia's Supreme Court of Appeals.[2] "The revolution of 1800," Jefferson declaimed, "was as real a revolution in the principles of our government as that of 1776 was in its form; not effected indeed by the sword, as that, but by the rational and peaceable instrument of reform, the suffrage of the people. The nation declared its will by dismissing functionaries of one principle, and electing those of another, in the two branches, executive and legislature, submitted to their election. Over the judiciary department, the Constitution had deprived them of their control. That, therefore, has continued the reprobated system."[3] It was time for the younger generation to carry on the good fight, to recur to first principles as an aroused electorate had done in 1800. The struggle would be difficult, for the antirepublican consolidationists who were entrenched in the Court spoke for a widening array of powerful interests, including bankers, manufacturers, and—most ominously, as the Missouri crisis unfolded—opponents of slavery. But Jefferson and his fellow Republicans had overcome even more formidable obstacles during the dark days of the 1790s, when credulous Americans were "hoodwinked" by Federalists who stirred up a popular frenzy against France while exploiting popular reverence for General Washington, the father of his country.[4]

Jefferson and his fellow Republicans invoked the principles of the American Revolution as they mobilized opposition to the Federalist administration of John Adams. Under George Washington, Adams's predecessor, the United States had negotiated the controversial Jay Treaty with Britain (1795), alienating France and promoting party divisions in America. Republican leaders successfully exploited widespread enthusiasm for the French revolutionary cause—and gratitude for French aid in America's Revolution—as they fomented opposition to administration financial and foreign policies. But public opinion proved a fickle ally. Crude French efforts to influence the 1796 presidential election and subsequent depredations on American shipping provoked popular outrage against France, preparations for war between the sister republics, and an undeclared "Quasi-War" (1797–1800).[5]

War fever set the stage for the Alien and Sedition Acts of 1798.[6] This repressive (and imprudent) legislation extended the period of naturalization from five to fourteen years, gave the president the right to deport any alien (friend as well as enemy) without due process, and provided federal judicial remedies against "seditious" speech that jeopardized the administration's authority. Jefferson and his colleagues soon recognized that these challenges to civil liberties, separation of powers, and the federal-state balance could give their party viable campaign issues in 1800. Disentangling themselves from compromising ties to revolutionary France, the Republicans could now present themselves as the authentic legatees of a distinctively American republican and libertarian tradition. The presidential canvass of 1800 offered a final opportunity for American voters to redeem the Revolutionary experiment in republican government. The United States would "become again the patroness of peace, harmony & liberty," Governor James Monroe of Virginia told an English correspondent, and thus provide—as the French so clearly did not—"an illustrious example to an interested & beholding world, at an epoch the most solemn & awful that ever existed, of a people governing themselves in the practice of all these great & benevolent virtues."[7]

Republicans prevailed in 1800, Jefferson believed, because the Federalists overplayed their hand and disclosed their true colors, most conspicuously in the passage of repressive legislation designed to immobilize the Republican opposition. The Alien and Sedition Acts, new taxes, preparations for war, and other controversial measures constituted a wake-up call to apathetic voters who belatedly became aware that their very existence as a free, self-governing republican people was at risk. Americans became conscious of their national identity as the crisis deepened and the warnings of once scorned and neglected Republican leaders took on a prophetic cast. For years Republican oppositionists had insisted that Federalist "aristocrats" and "monocrats" had conspired to reverse the outcome of the American Revolution, reducing the people to abject submission and transforming the sovereign states into subject provinces. Such charges seemed increasingly plausible as Federalists prepared for war with France—a war in which the United States would serve as Britain's junior partner or "satellite"—particularly when the French signaled their willingness to negotiate.[8]

Jefferson's conception of American nationhood was crucially shaped by the crisis of the 1790s. If the meaning of the "revolution of 1800" depended on looking back to the Revolution of 1776, the reverse was also true. Distinguishing between revolutions in "form" and "principles" in the letter to Roane, Jefferson suggested that 1800 was not simply a reenactment of 1776 but, as he put it to Joseph Priestley in 1801, something "new under the sun."[9] The patriots of 1776 had declared and defended their independence, constituting a union of free states to succeed to the British empire in America. This union, given a more perfect form under the federal Constitution, provided the framework for American nationhood. But, as Jefferson insisted in his First Inaugural Address, the constitutional form could only be sustained if "fellow-citizens" would "unite with one heart and one mind," embracing the "federal and republican principles" that gave them their identity as Americans and, through them, gave life to the regime. With Jefferson's election in 1800, the inspiring vision of an independent people that he had set forth in the Declaration of Independence was fulfilled. In recognizing that they must govern themselves, Americans transcended party divisions to become a single, unified people, "brethren of the same principle."[10]

The crisis of the 1790s, seen by Republicans as a counter-Revolutionary assault on civil liberties and constitutional limitations, had roused the people from their slumbers, making them conscious of their national identity. This "revolution in principle" was definitive and irreversible, a legacy as crucial to Spencer Roane's generation as independence itself. Of course, the triumph of republicanism would not be as complete and final as Jefferson proclaimed in his Inaugural. New challenges to the nation's vital interests necessarily would take more subtle and insidious forms, less and less visible to a people busily engaged in its own pursuits. "Completely foiled by the universal spirit of the nation," the Federalists abandoned open advocacy of monarchical forms and donned "the pseudo-republican mask." So attired, Jefferson told Supreme Court Justice William Johnson in 1823, these latter-day "monocrats" would first pursue their other great goal, "consolidation," by "weaken[ing] the barriers of the State governments as coördinate powers."[11] Every generation would have to fight its own revolution, recognizing and resisting ever more sophisticated and insidious threats to republican self-government.

To preserve their liberties Americans must first know themselves as a people. Such knowledge did not come automatically in 1776, for even the most enthusiastic patriots, including Jefferson himself, could not then fully grasp what independence entailed.[12] It was only with the "revolution of 1800," Jefferson suggested to Roane, that inchoate patriotic feelings took on a self-conscious, principled form, with "heart" united to "mind." Once their national identity was thus secured, Americans could return to the questions of constitutional form that had absorbed the Revolutionary generation. The Republicans of 1798 had rallied in defense of a strictly construed federal Constitution in order to save the nation. But, as Jefferson repeatedly asserted, there was nothing sacred about constitutions as such: the people made constitutions to suit themselves; constitutions did not make the people. "Our republicanism [is] to be found . . . in the spirit of our people," Jefferson told Samuel Kercheval in 1816, "not in our Constitution certainly."[13] It was incumbent on constitutional reformers in every generation to refashion the constitution in accord with the "spirit" or genius of the people.

The "revolution of 1800" was a model for "rational and peaceable . . . reform."[14] Violence had been unavoidable in the break with Britain but should never again be necessary in the new republican empire. The success of the American experiment depended on the preservation and expansion of the federal union, not on reverence for specific constitutional forms. Americans would be able to sustain their union, restraining the authority of the central government within strict constitutional limits, as long as they remained conscious of themselves as Americans, as "brethren of the same principle." Not only must they resist foreign influence and entanglement, they must also resist the tendency to see their fellow Americans as foreigners. It was a tendency that Jefferson himself, as a veteran of the vicious party battles of the 1790s, could never completely overcome.

Jefferson's conception of a progressive and an expansive republican regime, a conception that harked back to an idealized British empire, was predicated on a precociously modern conception of American nationhood. As they were driven to the wall in the 1790s, Republicans were forced to ask themselves if their fellow Americans in fact constituted a single nation or people in any meaningful sense: as they did so, they contemplated the breakup of the union and the bankruptcy of their republican hopes. The sudden reversal of fortunes in 1800 seemed to realign empire and nation, justifying the extravagant and euphoric language of Jefferson's Inaugural Address.

The protracted political and constitutional crisis leading up to Jefferson's "revolution of 1800" and the end of Federalist rule in America produced a rich discourse on civil liberties and civil society. Jeffersonian printers and publicists argued persuasively that fetters on press freedom jeopardized free elections by insulating irresponsible elected officials from the scrutiny and censure of an enlightened public opinion. In the face of systematic political repression, these apostles of press freedom staked out an advanced libertarian position that drew on broad popular commitment to the "self-evident" principles of Jefferson's Declaration of Independence. They portrayed their struggle as nothing less than a reenactment of the American Revolution, a republican return to the regime's first principles. This became the Republican gospel when Jefferson ascended to the presidency in 1801, and so it passed on into American self-understanding.[15]

My purpose in this chapter is not to challenge this libertarian narrative or to join the great constitutional historian Leonard Levy in questioning the consistency and depth of Jefferson's commitment to the defense of civil liberties.[16] Instead, I show that Jefferson's libertarianism was inextricably connected to, and therefore contingent on, his definitions of citizenship and the collective body of citizens, the "people" or "nation." The vindication of individual rights depended on securing the jurisdictional autonomy of the state-republics that constituted the federal union. But Republicans combined the defense of states' rights and civil liberties with a conception of national history and identity that reconstituted autonomous parts—states and citizens—into a new whole. Jeffersonian nationalism celebrated the libertarian legacy of the Revolution, linking the "spirit of 1776" with the "principles of 1798." Subscription to these principles was the test of American identity, a test that Federalists who supported energetic federal government and curbs on state power would fail.

PARTY TO NATION

Jefferson's conception of American nationhood was profoundly shaped by his need to justify his defection from the Washington administration and to explain his role in the emerging opposition. While Jefferson and his Republican coadjutors identified themselves with—and as—the "American" people, they also had to fend off charges that they were "secret emissaries" of the French, or that they constituted a *faction . . . disposed to overturn the government"* and working to advance the global ambitions of "the *French Republic*."[17] Jeffersonian nationalism thus grew out of the party's compelling need to disclaim any foreign entanglements, open or covert. Republicans instead focused on the exceptionally propitious conditions for republican self-government in the New World and emphasized the importance of insulating the United States from foreign interference and contamination. "Foreign influence is the present and just object of public hue and cry," Jefferson reported to Thomas Pinckney in May 1797, "and, as often happens, the most guilty are foremost and loudest in the cry."[18] It was the Federalists who promoted a "political union" with Britain that would entangle the United States in European affairs and so subvert American independence.[19]

Republicans portrayed themselves as "true Americans" who would rise up to repel any invader. "We have no improper attachments to any foreign nation," Jefferson's friend George Nicholas protested; "if the time shall really come that they are attacked, by any foreign nation, we will give the lie to those who now slander us."[20] The Republicans were the authentic, uncorrupted voice of the people, not a "party" or faction; they opposed administration policy only with the greatest reluctance, as the intentions of Federalist "monocrats" to establish an aristocratic and a monarchical regime became unmistakable. Federalists were "foreigners" who would sacrifice the people's liberties for their own selfish advantage; "true Americans," like the patriots of 1776, would seek to preserve their republican self-government at all costs.

The problem for Jefferson and his followers was that the distinction between "republicans" and "monocrats" remained obscure to so many American voters throughout the 1790s. To the extent that Americans failed to recognize their own true enemies, Republicans might be mistaken for mere partisans, lusting for the loaves and fishes of office, their patriotism fatally compromised by their partiality for the French republic.

Jefferson's aversion to partisanship and his unwillingness to acknowledge his own role as a party leader are well known.[21] In his most famous pronouncement on the subject, in a letter from Paris in March 1789, Jefferson told Francis Hopkinson that he was neither a Federalist nor an Antifederalist: "If I could not go to heaven but with a party, I would not go there at all."[22] Because Jefferson was no partisan, he needed a more exalted justification for turning against the Washington administration, particularly while still serving in it as secretary of state. His solution, to charge Treasury Secretary Alexander Hamilton with "the purpose of subverting step by step the principles of the constitution" and remodeling it along English lines, vindicated his own loyalty to the new government, notwithstanding his failure to take a stand in the ratification controversy. Jefferson had criticized the unamended Constitution for lacking a bill of rights and for allowing the president to be reelected. As he told Washington in an extraordinary self-exculpatory letter in September 1792, "the sense of America has approved my objection and added the bill of rights, not the king and lords" that Hamilton had called for in the Constitutional Convention. A single, longer term "would have made a President more independant"—he could have said, less susceptible to Hamilton's pernicious influence—but "my country has thought otherwise, and I have acquiesced implicitly."[23]

The attack on Hamilton may have been intensely personal, but it served to deflect Jefferson's attention (if not Washington's) from questions of personal loyalty to the principles of the new regime as they were understood by the "people" who, through the process of ratification and amendment, had given it life. A series of conflicts over the implementation of Hamilton's financial plan, culminating in Jefferson's portentous capitulation on the pivotal question of the federal assumption of state debts in the Dinner Table Bargain of 1790 ("Of all the errors of my political life, this has occasioned me the deepest regret," he told Washington), convinced Jefferson that Hamilton was inimical not only to the Constitution but to the "country" as well. Jefferson's identification of Constitution and country evoked the Anglo-American Real Whig position, but it also pointed forward to a more expansive conception of American nationhood.[24]

If "parties here divided merely by a greediness for office, as in England," Jefferson told his loyal ally William Branch Giles in 1795, "to take a part with either would be unworthy of a reasonable or moral man." The conflict in America was not between competing, morally equivalent parties within the nation but rather between a corrupt faction—defined by its bias against republican self-government and, therefore, national independence—and patriotic defenders of the country as a whole. "Where the principle of difference is as substantial, and as strongly pronounced as between the republicans and monocrats of our country," Jefferson concluded, "I hold it as honorable to take a firm and decided part, and as immoral to pursue a middle line, as between the parties of honest men and rogues, into which every country is divided." The line of division between the parties was the boundary of American nationhood.[25]

Republicans suggested that the Federalists constituted an alien force in republican society, barely checked by constitutional forms. Through their suffrage the people exercised direct control over only one branch of the federal government, but their "representatives" were susceptible to Hamilton's corrupting machinations. The "shameless corruption of a portion of the Representatives to the first and second Congresses, and their implicit devotion to the treasury" was Jefferson's "one political topic" after he left the administration at the end of 1793 and retreated to Monticello.[26] Exposing the extent of Hamilton's pernicious influence became a Republican obsession. For party theoretician John Taylor of Caroline, the only hope for "recover[ing] the lost principles of a representative government, and sav[ing] the nation from being owned—bought—and sold" was "a constitutional expulsion of a stock-jobbing paper interest, in every shape, out of the national legislature."[27] According to Taylor's characteristic formulation, the "nation" itself was present in Congress, but representatives could be "bought—and sold," alienating the nation from itself and thus making its government "foreign."

Talk about conspiracy and corruption had a familiar ring to Revolutionary Americans.[28] What Federalists found outrageous was the suggestion that the same malign forces that had destroyed the British empire were now at work in America and that the constitutional machinery of the federal republic could no longer secure the people's liberties. In Taylor's influential polemics the federal government was depicted instead as the site of ongoing conflict between two nations: on one side, the Hamiltonian "paper junto" promoted foreign, specifically British, interests; on the other, Jeffersonians sought to arouse a dangerously apathetic American people to the counter-Revolutionary threat.[29] It was a contest for the political souls—and national identity—of the people's putative representatives: "I consider the future character of our republic as in the air," as Jefferson told Aaron Burr in June 1797.[30] The language Republican polemicists employed evoked British oppositionists of an earlier day—Hamilton was the second coming of Robert Walpole, the epitome of ministerial corruption—but its purpose was to rekindle the "spirit of 1776," to remind Americans that the purpose of their Revolution was to vindicate their claims to nationhood.[31]

It was an article of faith with Republicans that, as Jefferson wrote James Sullivan of Massachusetts, "the great body of our native citizens are unquestionably of the republican sentiment." Jefferson conceded that "foreign education, and foreign connections of interest, have produced some exceptions in every part of the Union, north and south, and perhaps other circumstances in your quarter, better known to you, may have thrown into the scale of exceptions a greater number of the rich."[32] The boundary between genuine patriots and "the foreign and false citizens" whose loyalties lay with Britain proved fluid and problematic.[33] British influence, flowing through channels of exchange and credit, reached far into the countryside. The root of all evil, as Taylor showed, was the control that capitalists exercised over widening circles of dependents. Hamilton's national bank gave these grasping "aristocrats" an institutional base at the nexus of the national economy. "Without a pretence of claim upon the community," Taylor charged, the bank "has found means to occupy the station precisely, which Great-Britain was striving to fill." Americans could win a conventional war, where the enemy could be clearly defined: "She defended her property against open violence, to be cheated of it by private fraud. . . . America has defeated a nation, but is subdued by a corporation."[34]

The "false citizens" who held bank stock might not be immediately recognizable as foreigners. But their acquisitiveness, their aristocratic pretensions and ambitions, would draw them inexorably into the vortex of British capital. Taylor explained how this might happen—perhaps it had already happened?—in his *Enquiry into the Principles and Tendency of Certain Public Measures* (1794): "If a number of the members of Congress are stockholders, or bank directors, then an illegitimate interest is operating on the national legislature—then the bank hath seduced away from their natural and constitutional allegiance, the representatives of the states—and then, even foreigners—our late most malignant and inveterate enemy—have obtained an influence on our national councils, so far as they have obtained bank stock. The English who could not conquer us, may buy us."[35] For Republican true believers the subsequent controversy over John Jay's "English Treaty" in 1794 and 1795 made Taylor's analysis seem chillingly prophetic. The challenge for Jefferson and his allies was to explain how popular indignation against the treaty's supposedly degrading terms could so quickly give way to acceptance. It became increasingly, distressingly clear that the "people" themselves, and not just their representatives in Congress, were vulnerable to foreign influence.

Madison attributed a crucial role to bankers in precipitating the remarkable turn in public opinion. As he told Jefferson in April 1796, when the antitreaty majority in the House was evaporating before his eyes: "The Banks have been powerfully felt in the progress of the petitions in the Cities for the Treaty. Scarce a merch[an]t. or Trader but what depends on discounts, and at this moment there is a general pinch for money." Signers of protreaty petitions were not free agents: "A Bank Director soliciting subscriptions is like a Highwayman with a pistol demanding the purse." The virtuous republican citizen was thus alienated from his true nature, submitting to the superior force of the "Highwayman."[36] These bankers were agents of a foreign power, acting in concert with *"British capitalists"* to promote a treaty that would put the nation in the same dependent position as their hapless creditors.[37]

In seeking to explain how so many Americans could have been coerced or "hoodwinked" into support of what Jefferson called the "Anglican monarchical aristocratical party," Republicans developed a political sociology for the new nation premised on the primacy of market relations.[38] These accounts sought to define the irreducible core of American nationhood, suggesting how speculators, merchants, and even farmers could be turned against their own country. Madison offered the most elaborate analysis in his essay in the *Aurora* in January 1799. One obvious source of "British influence" was the "fifty or sixty thousand native subjects of the British Empire" who lived in the United States, many of whom were wealthy and influential. But "the great flood-gate" was *"British Commerce."* British merchants and "Angliciz[ed]" Americans trading on British capital constituted a powerful British fifth column in America. "Every shipment, every consignment, every commission," Madison wrote, "is a channel" through which British influence "flows. . . . Our Sea-port towns are the reservoirs into which it is collected. From these, issue a thousand streams to the inland towns, and country stores. . . . Thus it is, that our country is penetrated to its remotest corners with a foreign poison vitiating the American sentiment, recolonizing the American character, and duping us into the politics of a foreign nation."[39] Madison struck a variety of resonant Republican themes in this passage, including anxieties about the corrupting influence of trade and credit and the loyalties of merchants.[40] This "Anglicizing" influence was remarkable for both its pervasiveness and its insidiously secret operation, vitiating the body politic from within like a "poison" and thus "duping" a credulous people. Appearances could be deceiving: "a very respectable proportion" of the native-born Britons were true Americans, "not only in allegiance, but in *principles* and *attachment*"; meanwhile, large numbers of Americans had been seduced by British connections, and many more were at risk.

British influence also jeopardized American virtue through the Federalist press. Information and opinion flowed through the same channels that spread British commerce and credit across the countryside. "The inland papers . . . copy from the city papers," Madison explained, and "the city papers are supported by advertisements . . . furnished by merchants and traders. In this manner British influence steals into our newspapers, and circulates under their passport."[41] Now the few Republican printers who, like William Duane of the *Aurora,* still held out against this insidious British influence faced a more direct challenge from an administration determined to throttle what it self-servingly considered "seditious" speech.

Madison and his Republican colleagues offered a bleak vision of a corruptible people, everywhere yielding to the pervasive seductions of British influence. The Federalists' repressive legislation merely made explicit the new nation's servile subjection to its old colonial masters. Under such circumstances it was a challenge for increasingly desperate Republicans to sustain their faith in the wisdom and virtue of a sovereign people capable of governing itself. The emphasis on influence implied alien forces at work, but it also underscored the vulnerability of their credulous and corruptible countrymen. The rhetorical solution was to depict the American republic as a nation under siege and to define partisan opponents as "foreigners." This logic worked both ways of course: Federalists considered Republicans dupes of the French and sought, in the Alien Acts, to neutralize the danger of foreign connections. But the emergent Republican conception of American nationhood was not simply the mirror image of official patriotism. In seeking to explain and overcome their present political impotence, Republicans imagined a truly independent American regime, disentangled from the European balance of power in which it functioned as a "contemptible satellite" of Britain, a "subaltern dependant power."[42] They imagined a republican millennium when civil liberties would be fully secured and when freedom, not force, would be the bond of union.

Controversy over the character of the American regime was embedded within a broader debate over who was qualified to be an American. In the Alien Acts, Federalists sought to counter "Jacobin" influence by setting stricter standards for citizenship and enabling the president to remove aliens more easily. In response, Republicans defined their opponents as "foreigners" who were subject to the influence and direction of Britain, leader of the counterrevolutionary coalition against republican France. The Republicans' conception of nationhood triumphed with Jefferson's election in the "revolution of 1800." Thereafter, libertarianism and nationalism in the United States were inextricably linked, defining and qualifying one another.[43]

Republicans believed that a free press would constitute an enlightened and irresistible public opinion, dedicated to upholding self-evident federal and republican principles: freedom would generate publicity, the best guarantee of freedom. The challenge for Republicans was to explain why so many American voters remained unenlightened, impervious to their appeals. In his *Aurora* essay Madison approached a radically skeptical position on the very possibility of a free press, showing how—even in the absence of official persecution—British commerce and credit shaped the thinking of "American" merchants, advertisers, and editors. An uncorrupted public opinion, the only foundation for a durable republican government and therefore for the free exercise of civil liberties, depended on purging the new nation of dangerous foreign influences.

As the Republicans' circumstances became more desperate, their definition of what was "foreign" became more expansive, and the boundaries of nationhood contracted.

Over the next two years, a revolution in public opinion vindicated the Republicans' faith in the wisdom of the people. Jefferson's Inaugural Address of March 1801 is the mirror image of Madison's bleak analysis of the vulnerability of popular sentiment to alien influence. Justly celebrated as a landmark in the libertarian tradition, the Inaugural Address calls for political as well as religious toleration. Where Madison had seen a pervasive and insidious network of dangerous influences, a veritable Britain-in-America, Jefferson now saw only a few relics from the past, "monuments" to discredited monarchical and antirepublican principles, totally lacking influence and fit only for the mockery and derision of a virtuous people.

The transformation of Madisonian pessimism into Jeffersonian optimism constituted a crucial epoch in American political history. The underlying logic of their positions was the same. Madison's despairing image of a nation besieged, juxtaposing a virtuous American people to the pernicious effects of corrupting foreign influence, was developed over the previous decade in Antifederalist and Republican polemics against Federalist rule; the Republican conception of nationhood inspired the Republican revival of 1800–1801 and was triumphantly reaffirmed by Jefferson in his First Inaugural Address. Jefferson promised a new era of freedom and conciliation in his Inaugural, but he excluded his most inveterate opponents—unrepentant and unreconstructed enemies of free government—from the new dispensation. Fealty to Republican party principles, "attachment to union and representative government," would be the definitive test of national loyalty.

STATES' RIGHTS AND CIVIL LIBERTIES

During the controversy over the ratification of the federal Constitution, Antifederalists agitated for explicit constitutional guarantees of fundamental rights. James Madison, the "father of the Constitution," sought to placate these critics by pushing the first federal Congress to endorse the amendments that became known as the Bill of Rights. The First Amendment prohibited Congress from making any law "respecting an establishment of religion" or otherwise interfering with its "free exercise" or from "abridging the freedom of speech, or of the press, or the right of the people peaceably to assemble, and to petition the Government for a redress of grievances."[44] Given the distribution of authority in the American federal system, Madison thought it highly unlikely that Congress would ever have occasion to interfere with the liberties secured by the amendments, or that such "parchment barriers" could be efficacious if it did.[45] But Jefferson recognized the heuristic value of articulating fundamental rights that would enable "subordinate governments" to mobilize an aroused public if the federal government should ever encroach on the reserved rights of the states or the people.[46] Passage of the Alien and Sedition Acts made the wisdom of Jefferson's counsel clear to Madison: the Federalists' apparent contempt for the First Amendment signaled an assault on republican government itself. Thwarted in Congress, muzzled in their efforts to appeal to the sovereign people by the Federalists' repressive legislation, the Republicans now followed Jefferson's script, turning in desperation to the "subordinate [state] governments" to vindicate the Constitution.

When Republicans invoked the "principles of 1776," the most obvious reference was to the natural rights of individuals set forth in the second paragraph of the Declaration of Independence; but when they talked about "republics," the reference was to states with corporate integrity and moral personality. The first law of nature was self-preservation: for a state this might well entail the sacrifice of an individual's civil rights, or indeed, as in the case of slaves in Jefferson's Virginia, of the rights of a whole class of persons. By the same logic, the preservation of the federal union could require sacrifices of individual or state rights, as Jefferson clearly thought when he imposed an embargo on American shipping (1807–9), or when he periodically imagined launching a surgical strike against a "gangrenous" member of the union such as Massachusetts or Connecticut.[47] The salience of natural law teaching was clearly a matter of perspective, and this too was clear to Jefferson: if the "liberties" of all men are "the gift of God" and "justice cannot sleep for ever," the slave owners of Virginia could only "tremble" at the prospect of servile insurrection and "a revolution of the wheel of fortune."[48]

Jefferson was not a libertarian absolutist. Instead, he conceived of civil liberties within the context of a complex republican regime of distinct and ascending levels or spheres of governmental authority.[49] According to the "true theory of our Constitution," he told Gideon Granger, "states are independent as to everything within themselves, and united as to everything respecting foreign nations."[50] Jefferson was a federalist who, in characteristically optimistic moments, looked forward and outward for ever more perfect and inclusive unions of individuals, wards, counties, states, and nations. Such unions were predicated on equality and consent, not the authoritative command of superior authority. Therefore, at times when would-be despots sought to consolidate power at the expense of "subordinate governments"—as for instance in the crisis of 1797–1801—unions tended to dissolve into their constituent parts. Only by doing so, or by threatening to do so, could states (or citizens) reaffirm the fundamental principles of equality and consent that distinguished republics from coercive, despotic regimes.

The Jeffersonian defense of civil liberties, or "republican principles," was thus shaped by—and contained within—an equally powerful commitment to "federal principles." The turn to states' rights in the 1798 Kentucky Resolutions (originally drafted by Jefferson) and Virginia Resolutions (drafted by Madison) was not merely opportunistic. These resolutions charged the Federalist Congress with "unconstitutional" violations of First Amendment rights of individuals, but they also argued that the Alien and Sedition Acts encroached on the reserved rights of the states. By "forced constructions" of the Constitution, wrote Madison in the Virginia Resolutions, the Federalists would "consolidate the states by degree into one sovereignty" and so "transform the present republican system of the United States, into an absolute, or at best a mixed monarchy."[51] To prevent this unhappy outcome, Jefferson told a correspondent, the people must sustain the federal balance, that "beautiful equilibrium on which our Constitution is founded."[52] Jefferson's friend John Page offered a good gloss on Republican constitutional doctrine in a campaign pamphlet: the federal Constitution "is the *Instrument* by which the people of the several *confederated states of America* meant to preserve to their respective states their *Independence,* and to secure to themselves and their posterity the *BLESSINGS of LIBERTY.*"[53]

The rights of states and the rights of individuals, the "federal and re-

publican principles" of Jefferson's Inaugural Address, were thus integrally linked in Republican constitutionalism. These principles constituted
bulwarks against monarchical tendencies to consolidate power and exercise despotic authority over subject provinces and people. "Our state
governments," explained Madison, "by dividing the power with the Federal Government, and forming so many bodies of observation on it,
must always be a powerful barrier against dangerous encroachments."[54]
Republicans insisted that the American union was predicated on "sincere affection," harmonious interests, and a scrupulous regard for constitutional limitations. In the words of Jeffersonian George Nicholas,
the union "can be supported only by the constitution, and . . . that constitution cannot long be preserved, unless it is considered as sacred."
Recognizing that assaults on the Constitution would lead to the collapse
of the union, patriotic Republicans resisted the unwarranted expansion
of the federal government's authority.[55]

Jefferson and his political friends combined a vigorous assertion of
individual and state rights with a conception of American national identity that vindicated their own patriotism and called into question their
opponents'. The universalism of rights claims thus emerged in counterpoint with increasingly exclusive definitions of American nationhood.
When Nicholas referred to "the welfare, independence and liberty of
our country," the reference was clearly to the United States, not to Virginia: the whole, not the part, was the primary locus of imaginative
identification.[56] Yet this whole was now bounded by new tests of principle and patriotism: to be a "true American" was to uphold a strictly construed Constitution that sustained the federal balance and thereby secured the rights of Virginia and the other states.

The apparently paradoxical logic of the Republican doctrine was that
the constitutional guarantee of states' rights would promote national patriotism. With republican self-government fully secured in the states,
liberty-loving Americans could freely express their shared principles, interdependent interests, and mutual affections. This expansive conception of consent and its consequences was predicated on the autonomy
and equal rights of the parts—individuals or states—that constituted
new wholes. Freedom made true consent possible, and free people, acting in accord with their sociable natures, would form ever more perfect

unions. The Republican party was the practical embodiment and highest expression of this associational impulse, combining the affectionate feelings of political friends with devotion to the fundamental principles of the American Revolution. Indeed, as Jefferson would later assert, "the republicans are the *nation*."[57]

The Republican dilemma in the dark days of the Federalist ascendancy was that Americans were not fully conscious of this incipient national identity and therefore failed to rally behind the party's candidates in sufficient numbers to drive their enemies from office. Fundamental misgivings about public opinion thus shaped the Republicans' response to the Alien and Sedition Acts. The political education of a dangerously deluded and self-alienated citizenry was now more imperative than ever. Yet, as John Taylor complained to Jefferson, too many voters betrayed an apparent "insensibility to the effects both of tyranny and despotism, exhibiting in the background, sordid avarice and skulking fear," leading him to despair of the "national character."[58] Republican patriots held fast to the principles that defined the new nation. But they recognized that the truth was not always transparent, even in the realm of constitutional interpretation. "Now a days," St. George Tucker conceded, "there is no text so explicit, as not to be susceptible of different interpretations."[59] Republicans might be truth tellers, but the people were not listening.

Republican principles would only triumph if the party's leaders could overcome the Francophobic "phrenzy" of the Quasi-War.[60] It was at this critical moment that the Adams administration sought to suppress the few remaining opposition printers. "If these papers fall," Jefferson warned as the sedition bill moved through Congress, "republicanism will be entirely brow-beaten."[61] But the Federalists' repressive measures backfired, as Jefferson soon recognized. By March 1799 he could tell a correspondent that "the spirit of 1776 is not dead." The American people "have been the dupes of artful manoeuvres, and made for a moment to be willing instruments in forging chains for themselves. But time and truth have dissipated the delusion, and opened their eyes." Driven to the brink of despair, Republicans found a winning issue in their struggle for civil liberties. The means and ends of republicanism became fused in Republican rhetoric: free speech was the essential means to educate

Americans that their precious liberties—including free speech—were at risk. In rousing Americans from their slumbering condition, Republicans could overcome their own sense of alienation.[62] They were "true Americans," giving the nation a voice as it belatedly came to its senses.[63]

"THE SPIRIT OF 1776"

St. George Tucker offered a characteristic panegyric to press freedom, "*that* FREEDOM, capacious as the human mind, the image of its Creator; filling all space; present every where; viewing all things; penetrating the recesses of the human heart; unfolding the motives of human actions; estimating all things according to their true standard." Freedom of the press was nothing less than the "great *Progenitor* and only stable *Bulwark*" of "our *constitution*." In Tucker's account the struggle for civil liberties defined the essential meaning of the American Revolution, providing a quasi-mythical paradigm for the Republicans' struggle against Federalist repression. In the Revolutionary crisis "the stern resolution[s] of those who preferred death to slavery were communicated from Massachusetts to Georgia, with electrical rapidity by the *press*," Tucker explained; "the bond of union among the states from *thence* received its stamp." A free press had made the Revolutionaries invincible against British tyranny: "Destroy *that freedom,* and you proclaim to your respective constituents, that it is time to seperate."[64]

Republicans developed an interpretation of the history of the American Revolution that celebrated the irresistible power and authority of an enlightened public opinion. "The present period," Jefferson wrote in 1798, "is the most eventful ever known since that of 1775, and will decide whether the principles established by that contest are to prevail, or give way to those they subverted."[65] The Revolution was defined in terms of the "principles" that inspired patriots in 1775 or the "spirit" they manifested in declaring their independence in 1776. In these years patriotic Americans had vindicated their liberties against the overwhelming force of a tyrannous central government that monopolized power and subverted the colonies' constitutions. "The generous spirit of 1776 must not slumber, nor loiter in silent confidence," a writer in the *Aurora* exhorted in March 1799; "it will be useless in the end to have broken the chains of the British tyrant, if we were tamely to suffer the fetters that appear ready forged for us by a domestic faction."[66]

The "Whigs" of 1798 faced long odds against latter-day "Tories" who had seized the central government and now sought to draw the new nation into a counter-Revolutionary crusade against French—and American—republicanism.[67] For Republican patriots the Virginia and Kentucky Resolutions reenacted the Revolution itself, reaffirming republican and federal principles against the monarchical tendencies of the Federalist administration. Initially cool responses from other states demonstrated the pervasiveness of British influence and the servility and insensibility of so many "Americans." Invoking the legacy of their Revolutionary predecessors, Republican editors risked martyrdom in defense of free speech and civil liberties; so too, in questioning the constitutionality of the Alien and Sedition Acts, the legislatures of Virginia and Kentucky invoked the rights of their self-governing state-republics against the encroachments of a "foreign" federal jurisdiction, thus risking their own continuing independence. In 1798, as in 1775 and 1776, principle was juxtaposed to power: Republicans called on the people to rise up against a government that had forfeited legitimacy by its egregious violations of the Constitution.

The analogy between the Revolution and resistance to Federalism in the late 1790s was an inspiring (and comforting) one to embattled Republicans. It enabled Jefferson and his political friends to explain why the patriotic Americans who constituted the "nation" or "people" should find themselves in the minority, on the defensive, and deprived of an effective voice in the federal government. Throughout the Revolution, and particularly during the dark days when "sunshine patriots" ran for cover, the British had enjoyed wide (if not deep) support from corrupt, timid, and ignorant Americans. The boundary of American nationhood thus ran along this ideological fault line, between those who embraced republican principles and those who advocated a return to monarchy. To Federalists who were the targets of Republican polemics, Jeffersonian talk about "aristocrats" and "monocrats" seemed overheated and hysterical, without any plausible foundation in fact—a judgment shared by most scholars. But the power of Republican rhetoric was in its mythic historiography, in forging a link between 1776 and 1798 that offered a clear and compelling definition of American national identity.[68] It was hardly surprising that crypto-monarchists had not avowed their enmity to republicanism: the Republican analysis of "foreign influence" sought to illuminate and expose their misrepresentations and covert operations. Yet if the enemies of republicanism were often hard to identify, Republicans knew themselves to be authentic patriots. Furthermore, by articulating the principles of republicanism—by translating this self-knowledge into unequivocal public commitments—Republicans could throw down the gauntlet to their opponents, forcing them to disclose their true loyalties.

Federalists were manifestly hostile to the principles that Jefferson and his colleagues claimed constituted the defining test of American patriotism. The Adams administration's apparent contempt for the legacy of the Revolution, its encroachments on state sovereignty and civil liberties, demonstrated the power and pervasiveness of "foreign" influence. Britain's "*hatred and fear* of the *republican example* of our governments" were reflected in the Federalists' repressive legislation.[69] Just as Britain's corrupt and tottering regime, fearful for its own future existence, struggled to reverse the republican tide in Europe, the "British Party" in America sought to reduce a proud, self-governing people to a state of cringing subservience and submission.

Republican oppositionists sought to inspire their followers, and themselves, by portraying their struggle in epochal terms, as the last desperate stand for free government in the world. It was this global, ideologically charged perspective that enabled Republicans to depict their Federalist enemies as "foreigners." The great contest of principle, pitting republicanism against despotism, offered a powerful cosmopolitan sanction to localist opposition to central governmental authority. Harking back to the imperial crisis, doctrinaire republicans were prepared to see any distant central government, even one that was located in America, as "foreign": the British "placemen" who, with their venal and corrupt American followers, had constituted imperial government in America were obviously alien; a "standing army" was by definition an alien force, subject to the will of despotic authority and designed "to keep in awe the free citizens of our republican government."[70]

The federal government might not be by definition "foreign"—indeed, had the Constitution been strictly construed, the government's federal and republican credentials would have been unassailable—but it was, to Republicans, all too obviously vulnerable to penetration and capture by "foreign influences." This is precisely what happened to the British empire on the eve of the American Revolution: recognizing the growing discrepancy between imperial administration and the constitutional principles that legitimized British rule in America, American patriots had suddenly discovered, as Jefferson wrote in the Declaration, that they were a distinct people entitled to a "separate and equal station ... among the powers of the earth"—and that the British, their erstwhile countrymen, were now foreigners, constituting "another" people.[71]

Yet the Republicans' ultimate success in linking their resistance to the Federalists' repressive legislation of 1798 to "the spirit of 1776" depended on circumstances beyond their control. The Federalists could hold Anglophobia in check as long as France represented the most imminent threat to American interests, honor, and independence, and while they could plausibly claim that "French emissaries were swarming over the whole territory of the United States." The "duty of self-preservation" then justified military mobilization, high taxes, even the suspension of civil liberties.[72] Republican leaders could hardly challenge this premise while French assaults on American shipping mounted or in the wake of the XYZ affair, when the French Directory contemptuously rebuffed an American peace initiative. To the contrary, they insisted that if Congress should finally declare war, they would rally to the cause. "Much as I abhor war, and view it as the greatest scourge of mankind, and anxiously as I wish to keep out of the broils of Europe," Jefferson assured Elbridge Gerry on the eve of Gerry's ill-fated mission to France as one of the XYZ negotiators, "I would yet go with my brethren into these, rather than separate from them."[73]

It was only when the French signaled their willingness to reopen diplomatic negotiations and the war scare subsided that the Republicans gained a new lease on political life. Once begun, this turnaround revived Jefferson's faith in the possibility of popular enlightenment and republican self-government. The Republican cause was aided immeasurably by growing divisions among Federalist ranks. With President Adams apparently determined to avoid war, continuing efforts by belligerent High Federalists to raise taxes, mobilize the provisional army, and enforce repressive legislation only added fuel to Republican fires.

Analogies between 1776 and 1798 seemed increasingly powerful, enabling Republicans to claim the patriotic high ground and portray themselves as the true exponents of Americanism. Federalists, subject to foreign influences and looking backward to the monarchical and aristocratic principles of the past, offered negative definitions of this new national identity.

REVOLUTION OF 1800

Jefferson's inauguration as president in March 1801 marked the cresting of a "mighty wave of public opinion" that had swept over the United States in the previous three years.[74] In May 1798, when "all the passions are boiling over," few Americans had remained immune to war fever. But Jefferson predicted that new taxes would have a "sedative" effect, soon cooling the people's "ardor."[75] "Because the patients are essentially republicans," he assured John Taylor, "this disease of the imagination will pass over." To finance the war, the administration would have to raise taxes, and "excessive taxation . . . will carry reason and reflection to every man's door."[76] In the southern states, Jefferson reported to Elbridge Gerry in 1799, "the alien and sedition acts have already operated . . . as powerful sedatives of the X.Y.Z. inflammation."[77] By 1800 the public appeared to be regaining their senses. As the possibility of war with France dimmed, resistance to high taxes spread, and Federalists were increasingly hard-pressed to justify encroachments on civil liberties.

These changes in public sentiment were certainly gratifying to Jefferson and his fellow Republicans. But how could they be sure that the people would not be duped in the future? And how could Jefferson pretend that Americans had spoken with a clear and decisive voice when so many of them still voted for the Federalists in 1800? Republicans now enjoyed solid majorities over the Federalists in the House (69 to 36) and Senate (18 to 14), but the margin of victory in the Electoral College was not impressive: Jefferson and Aaron Burr had received 73 votes each, while the Federalists, Adams and Pinckney, polled 65 and 64 votes respectively. The outcome might easily have been different had Burr not so expertly managed the state assembly elections in New York, or if Hamilton and his High Federalist supporters had not turned against

Adams. The Republican vote, it should also be emphasized, was decisively inflated by the three-fifths clause of the Constitution.

Republican analyses of the vagaries of public opinion in the 1790s provided an arsenal of explanations for any apparent discrepancies between the "people" and actual voters: having argued for so long that they truly represented the "essentially republican" people even when the people voted for Federalist enemies of republican government, Republicans would have little trouble hearing the vox populi in the 1800 returns. Furthermore, as firm believers in progressive popular enlightenment, Jefferson and his supporters could look forward to constantly expanding electoral support.

Yet Jefferson had another, more compelling reason to believe he now enjoyed the unanimous support of all true Americans. In the original organization of the Electoral College, votes for president and vice president were not distinguished: the recipient of the greatest number of votes was named president, and the runner-up (Jefferson himself in 1796) served as vice president.[78] With Jefferson and Burr deadlocked at 73 votes each, the election was referred to the House of Representatives that had been elected in 1798 and was still dominated by Federalists. The opportunity to bargain for concessions, or even to elevate a compliant and unscrupulous Burr over Jefferson, was hard for Federalists to resist. The result was an electoral impasse—and constitutional crisis—that lasted through thirty-six ballots over nearly a week (February 11–17). The revolution of 1800 was only complete when the Federalists, recognizing the futility of resisting the people's mandate, finally and gracelessly capitulated.

Jefferson had good reason to believe that his supporters would not allow the Federalists to steal the election.[79] Republican governors Thomas McKean of Pennsylvania and James Monroe of Virginia had both put their states in a state of military preparedness should Jefferson's enemies attempt to seize the government. Throughout the period of Federalist repression, Jefferson and Madison had sought to restrain impetuous Republicans: as public opinion gradually progressed, it was crucial for oppositionists not to forfeit the ideological high ground by violating the Constitution or threatening to leave the union.[80] But now, when desperate Federalists, facing the imminent loss of power and the prospect of political disgrace, abandoned any pretense of respect for constitutional forms, good Republicans must be ready to act. "In the event of an usurpation," Jefferson told McKean shortly after his inauguration, "I was decidedly with those who were determined not to permit it." Not permitting it meant, if necessary, resorting to force.[81]

Public opinion would be well prepared for this patriotic appeal to first principles. Federalist usurpers at last stood revealed before their countrymen—including the credulous and misguided voters who had elected them—for what they had always been: enemies of their country, foreigners in principle and in practice. The impasse over the presidential election in Congress provided a climactic chapter in the Republican narrative of the republic's redemption. The fiction of a sovereign people proclaiming their will was brought into dramatic focus by the Federalists' fumbling efforts to block Jefferson's path to the presidency. Republicans now could juxtapose "the will of faction" to "the will of the people," unanimous in support of the Virginian.[82] The Federalist House, elected in 1798 when Americans were caught up in the delirium of the Quasi-War, "is not the Representative of the people at this time."[83] The people would not be denied: the "unanimous and firm decision of the people throughout the U.S. in favour of Mr. Jefferson will be irresistible."[84]

For Republican editors public opinion and popular sovereignty were synonymous. The press now played the same crucial role it had in the Revolution. "With the solicitudes of millions centering on the deliberations of their representatives," the editor of the *National Intelligencer* solemnly intoned, "it becomes the sacred duty of the press to make that people, whose rights are involved, the despositary of the earnest and most correct information."[85] Through the press the nation became conscious of itself in the election crisis, one of "the most solemn eras which have existed in the annals of our country." "Accounts received from individuals at a distance" combined with "the feelings of citizens on the spot" to produce an extraordinary sense of simultaneous presence, an awareness of national identity.[86]

In retrospect, Jefferson came to see the crisis as a virtual plebiscite, a moment of national reaffirmation and reconstitution. "There was no idea of force, nor any occasion for it," he told Joseph Priestley in late

March. Had the election failed, and the constitutional "clock . . . run down," the sovereign people would have soon set it in motion once again; "a convention, invited by the republican members of Congress, with the virtual President and Vice-President, would have been on the ground in eight weeks, would have repaired the Constitution where it was defective, and wound it up again." For Jefferson this exercise of popular sovereignty would have been the ultimate act of "self-preservation," the vindication of American independence and nationhood. Americans might divide into parties over men and measures, but they acted as one in reaffirming republican principles, in their "implicit obedience" to the will of the people.[87]

Throughout the crisis of the 1790s, Republicans identified the American nation with the union of states and its constitutional charter. For Jefferson and his followers, the "revolution of 1800" reinforced this identity, recapitulating the birth of the nation in 1776 and the constitution of a more perfect union in 1787. "The storm through which we have passed, has been tremendous indeed," Jefferson wrote soon after his inauguration, and "the tough sides of our Argosy have been thoroughly tried." These epochal moments in the new nation's history demonstrated the strength and stability of a regime founded on the federal and republican principles that Jefferson reaffirmed in his Inaugural Address. "We shall put" the American argosy "on her republican tack," Jefferson promised, "and she will now show by the beauty of her motion the skill of her builders."[88]

Jefferson believed he made his greatest contributions to his country by articulating the widely shared principles, grounded in nature and self-evident to the common understanding, on which its republican government was founded. There were times, of course, when the people lost sight of these landmarks, times when they were carried away by "delusion" or "contagion" and "hoodwinked from their principles." But at moments of crisis, when national independence, state sovereignty, and civil liberties were at risk, the people saw clearly, demonstrating once again "that a free government is of all others the most energetic."[89] The people had rallied to Jefferson's, and their own, cause in the election crisis, just as they had done in 1776: across the country Republicans were poised to intervene if Federalists attempted to seize power. More significantly, Jefferson learned from correspondence and news reports that rank-and-file Federalists were ready to join their former partisan adversaries in resisting challenges to public order.[90] By threatening to tamper with the people's will, Federalist diehards thus transformed Jefferson's narrow majority in the Electoral College into resounding unanimity—and a powerful affirmation of national identity.

Republicans had emerged victorious in the 1800 elections because a significant proportion of former Federalists, "real republicans, and honest men under virtuous motives," had returned to the fold. "The suspension of the public mind" during the presidential election crisis of February, "the anxiety and alarm lest there should be no election, and anarchy ensue," produced "a wonderful effect . . . on the mass of federalists who had not before come over." Jefferson thus intended to be conciliatory in his Inaugural in order to consolidate support among the Federalist rank and file. But he would "never turn an inch out of my way to reconcile . . . the leaders of the late faction, whom I abandon as incurables."[91] As this passage suggests, Jefferson believed that the "mass of Federalists" had already been severed from their quondam leaders: "The recovery bids fair to be complete, and to obliterate entirely the line of party division which had been so strongly drawn."[92]

Jefferson's Inaugural Address is one of the great texts in the American libertarian tradition, a blast against "political intolerance" and persecution: "Error of opinion may be tolerated where reason is left free to combat it." But its statement that "we are all republicans, we are all federalists" did not mean that Jefferson welcomed the competition of parties dedicated to conflicting principles.[93] Instead, Americans must be conscious of themselves "as brethren of the same principle"; we must "unite with one heart and one mind." Indeed, the revolution in public opinion was so far advanced, its unanimity so assured, that Jefferson could boldly reappropriate the very term "federalist" from his former foes, now defining "federal principles" in terms of "our attachment to [a] union" of sovereign states. Toleration of "error" thus was predicated on a broad popular commitment to fundamental principles that left the "desperadoes of the quondam faction in and out of Congress" virtually impotent.[94] There might be a few unreconstructed Federalists "who would wish to dissolve this Union or to change its republican form," but they represented no threat to the health of the renovated body politic: "Let them stand undisturbed as monuments of the safety with which error of opinion may be tolerated."[95]

Jefferson could not have been clearer on the limits of free speech and civil liberties generally. The Inaugural Address was first and foremost an affirmation of American national identity, predicated on shared principles and bonds of affection and interest. Error of opinion only could be tolerated when public opinion was sufficiently enlightened, when the nation was fully conscious of itself, when "desperadoes" stood exposed as foreigners and enemies of their country. Jefferson now proclaimed a total victory in this great struggle of principle, offering amnesty to former opponents who saw the light. But should "delusion" and "phrenzy" spread once again, he would be prepared for war. The first law of nature was self-preservation, and a nation must always be ready to vindicate its rights against domestic as well as foreign enemies.

"STRONGEST GOVERNMENT ON EARTH"

The Jeffersonian conception of American nationhood was predicated on the identification of Anglophile Federalists as foreigners. During the 1790s Republicans showed themselves to be authentic American patriots by resisting the seductions of "foreign influence" and defending the libertarian legacy of the Revolution. The revolution of 1800 translated the embattled Republican remnant into electoral majorities and then, in the final spasm of Federalist reaction, into virtual unanimity. When Federalists threatened to obstruct the people's will by denying Jefferson the presidency, Americans were jolted into national self-consciousness. Threatened with the loss of their precious liberties, Americans reenacted their republican Revolution and reaffirmed their independence. Most remarkably in Jefferson's estimation, this return to first principles had not been accompanied by civil disorder and a resort to arms. Instead, the threat of Federalist resistance evaporated before the "irresistible" force of enlightened and outraged public opinion. In the sudden glare of publicity, the perfidy of the Federalists stood revealed, resulting in a great "revolution of opinion." The bloodless rout of the Federalists enabled an exultant Jefferson to claim that the United States possessed the "strongest Government on earth."

Jefferson offered a stirring vision of the republican millennium in his Inaugural Address. With foreign influence suppressed and the people united "with one heart and one mind" in dedication to republican principles, Americans could exercise the liberties secured to them in the Bill of Rights to the fullest extent. Yet Republican patriots could not afford to be complacent: the greatest danger was that the United States would be drawn once again into foreign entanglements, thus giving rise to the kinds of domestic divisions that had nearly destroyed the union in the 1790s. "To avoid, if possible, wasting the energies of our people in war and destruction," Jefferson promised Thomas Paine, "we shall avoid implicating ourselves with the powers of Europe, even in support of principles which we mean to pursue." Isolated from foreign connections and influences, Americans "can enforce those principles, as to ourselves, by peaceable means."[96]

The fulfillment of the libertarian promise of the American Revolution depended on suppressing partisan and sectional divisions and maintaining a clear boundary between Old World and New World. But because these conditions could not be met, the republican millennium was postponed. In the meantime, the Republicans forged an account of the nation's history and destiny that justified violation of the very liberties they celebrated. Republicans preached their gospel of liberty, equality, and union to all mankind. At the same time, however, they invoked these universal principles to define the boundaries of American nationhood—boundaries that could alienate and exclude native-born Americans. If, as Jefferson claimed, "the republicans are the *nation*," their partisan opponents were potentially dangerous internal enemies. Unrepentant and unreconstructed Federalists had spurned Jefferson's conciliatory offer in the Inaugural Address, rejecting the republican principles that made Americans into a great and powerful people. Wherever they had been born, however plausible their professions, these "monocrats" and "aristocrats" were false patriots, worse than foreigners.

CHAPTER 4

Federal Union

❧

IN HIS RETIREMENT YEARS Jefferson sought to extricate himself
from the political controversies of the day. Pleading ill health, he told
James Donaldson in February 1820 that he was "obliged to withdraw my
attention from every thing beyond the walls of my chamber, and particularly from politics."[1] The impulse to retreat from public affairs may
have reflected growing discomfort with the causes advocated by Donaldson, a protectionist, and other latter-day "Jeffersonians." Jefferson
had always found conflict distasteful, even when leading—or inspiring—the crusade against the "monocrats" and "aristocrats" who had
held sway during the Federalist ascendancy in the 1790s. Surely the great
battle had been won, and the enemies of republican government had
been routed. Jefferson did not want to hear that his political heirs were
deeply divided on fundamental questions—the tariff, banks, internal
improvements, foreign policy—much less would he be willing to take a
part in their unseemly squabbling.

Yet one issue did draw Jefferson out, even as he proclaimed his withdrawal from politics. In February 1819, in the waning days of the second
session of the Fifteenth Congress, Representative James Tallmadge, Jr.,
of New York proposed an amendment to a bill providing for Missouri's
admission to the union that would have banned slavery in the new
state.[2] Though Jefferson could have followed the unfolding controversy
in the Richmond *Enquirer*—the only newspaper he subscribed to at this
time—he remained silent on the slavery restriction question until December. By then its ominous implications had become all too clear. "I
am so completely withdrawn from all attention to public matters," he

wrote his old friend Hugh Nelson in March, "that nothing less could [have] arouse[d] me than the definition of a geographical line, which on an abstract principle is to become the line of separation of these States, and to render desperate the hope that man can ever enjoy the two blessings of peace and self-government."[3] Jefferson characterized the controversy as "a fire-bell in the night" that had forced him out of his domestic repose, thus confessing to his own failure to grasp its significance—as he slept through its early phases—and his belated recognition that everything he had struggled to achieve in his political career was suddenly at risk.[4]

Jefferson's aversion to conflict is apparent in the conciliatory and concessive tone that characterizes most of his correspondence.[5] But his letters on Missouri betray no equivocation, no willingness to palliate differences, no concession that the restrictionists might be acting in good faith, no consciousness that his northern friends might share their scruples. Jefferson first broached the Missouri issue with John Adams in a letter of 10 December 1819, responding to Adams's of 23 November. Adams had predicted that the coming session of Congress would produce "thunder and Lightning" on various fronts—including the Spanish treaty ceding Florida (but affirming Spanish dominion over Texas), the manufacturers' campaign for protection, "the plague of Banks," and the question of slavery in Missouri, all complicated by "the bustle of Caucuses for the approaching" presidential election.[6] Barely pausing to salute his old friend, Jefferson impatiently discounted the importance of every issue Adams had raised except for Missouri. "These are occurences which like waves in a storm will pass under the ship," he wrote. "But the Missouri question is a breaker on which we lose the Missouri country by revolt, and what more, God only knows."

For Jefferson, who characteristically invoked nautical imagery in times of acute stress, "breakers" conjured fundamental threats to the ship of state, a more profound crisis than the American Revolution itself.[7] "From the battle of Bunker's hill," before Jefferson had written the Declaration of Independence, "to the treaty of Paris we never had so ominous a question."[8] In effect, Jefferson suggested, the restrictionists had reversed the course of American history, making a mockery and jest of his own life's work and returning the United States to that critical period when independence and union remained visionary projections. The "sons" had betrayed the Revolutionary "fathers," Jefferson explained to John Holmes, a former representative from the Maine District of Massachusetts who had supported Missouri's admission in order to promote the district's statehood ambitions—and in defiance of his constituents' pronounced antislavery sentiments. "I regret that I am now to die in the belief, that the useless sacrifice of themselves by the generation of 1776, to acquire self-government and happiness to their country, is to be thrown away by the unwise and unworthy passions of their sons."[9]

Complicated negotiations in Congress culminated in the compromise measures of March 1820, authorizing both free Maine and slaveholding Missouri to draft state constitutions and banning slavery in the remainder of the Louisiana Purchase territory north of 36°30′ (Missouri's southern boundary). Congressional controversy flared again in November, however, after Missouri submitted a constitution that prohibited the immigration of free blacks and mulattoes into the new state. The tenuous compromise was saved only when Henry Clay devised a new formula, adopted by Congress on 3 March 1821, requiring Missourians to agree that the offensive provision would not be construed in a way that violated the claims of any U.S. citizen to "Privileges and Immunities" in the new state under Article IV, Section 2 of the federal Constitution.

On 22 January 1821, while restrictionists still struggled to block Missouri's admission, Jefferson wrote again to Adams. For conspiracy-minded observers like Jefferson, this second phase of the Missouri controversy was in some ways more ominous than the first: restrictionists would stop at nothing in their campaign to obliterate states' rights and destroy the union. "Our anxieties in this quarter," he reported, "are all concentrated in the question[,] What does the Holy alliance, in and out of Congress, mean to do with us on the Missouri question?"[10] Identifying the anti-Missouri forces with the Holy Alliance, the league of reactionary sovereigns who sought to enforce an antirepublican, counterrevolutionary settlement in Europe, was no mere rhetorical flourish. For Jefferson, the restrictionists' pretended solicitude for the welfare of the slaves was as transparently fraudulent as the cause of "legitimacy" in Europe: the Missouri controversy "is not a moral question," he had written Lafayette in December, "but one merely of power."[11]

Jefferson shared the prevailing view in his "quarter" that "the Missouri question is a mere party trick," a desperate ploy by Federalists to foster and exploit sectional divisions over slavery to resurrect their moribund and disgraced party.[12] But Jefferson moved quickly beyond politics to what he considered the heart of the issue. "The real question, as seen in the states afflicted with this unfortunate population, is[,] Are our slaves to be presented with freedom and a dagger?" The same power that Congress assumed to dictate statehood terms to Missourians would be invoked to free the slaves. Because southerners would never submit to this degradation, the union would be dissolved—perhaps, in every essential sense, it already was—and a struggle for power ("another Peloponnesian war to settle the ascendancy between them") inevitably would ensue. "Or," Jefferson asked his old friend, "is this the tocsin of merely a servile war?" Jefferson again imagined his own death, hoping that he and Adams would not live to witness the carnage: "Surely they will parley awhile, and give us time to get out of the way."[13]

Jefferson's stand on Missouri has proved an embarrassment for his modern admirers, an occasion for righteous moralizing by his critics, and a confusing combination of the two for everyone else. John Chester Miller strikes a characteristic note, concluding that "the Missouri dispute seemed to mark the strange death of Jeffersonian liberalism."[14] In no respect was this fall from grace more conspicuous than on the issue of slavery restriction. For it was Jefferson himself, in his draft of the Territorial Government Ordinance of 1784, who proposed to ban slavery from the new western states.[15]

My goal in this chapter is neither to exonerate Jefferson nor to explain away his stand on Missouri. Instead, I show that the agonies Jefferson suffered over efforts to block the admission of the new state of Missouri reflected tensions in his conception of the Americans' new republican empire. These tensions grew out of his understanding of, and commitment to, the principle of equality, the foundational principle of his "empire for liberty." Jefferson did not retreat from a commitment to civil liberties or embrace a notion of states' rights in order to defend the interests of southern slaveholders. From the very beginning of his political life, Jefferson recognized the central importance of the autonomy, integrity, and equality of republics as corporate entities—as well as of the republican institutions that alone could guarantee the equal rights of self-governing individuals within the new states. The 1784 ordinance was a bill of rights for new western states, and its lasting significance was to establish new state equality—incorporated in the Northwest Ordinance of 13 July 1787—as the fundamental principle of an expanding federal republic.

Beginning with the Missouri controversy and moving backward, I explain how Jefferson's conception of a powerful and perpetual union was a casualty of its own logic, as well as of the more familiar sectional division over slavery extension. The survival and prosperity of Jefferson's republican empire depended on disentangling and distinguishing America from Europe, freedom-loving republicans from vicious and corrupt sovereigns and subjects. Before 1819 Jefferson had every reason to think that the great experiment in federalism would be a success, and that the frontier against Europe and European influences would become progressively more secure. The events of 1819–21 challenged this complacency in fundamental ways. Jefferson was increasingly hard-pressed to define the difference between foreigners and fellow Americans—and increasingly conscious of the "geographical line" that separated Americans from each other.

LINES OF DISTINCTION

"The idea of a geographical line once suggested will brood in the minds of all those who prefer the gratification of their ungovernable passions to the peace and union of their country," Jefferson wrote Massachusetts congressman Mark Langdon Hill in April 1820.[16] This "idea" was that fundamental differences of interest—and principle—divided Americans, making them foreigners to each other. No longer restrained by bonds of union, the disunited states would find themselves in a state of war, governed only by their "passions." Jefferson, the prophet of intractable sectional divisions, thus looked forward to the American Civil War. What he saw was an image of Europe, the negation of everything the new nation stood for, and "treason against the hopes of the world."

Jefferson's dilemma was that he was not simply a witness to these terrifying developments but a participant in them. No one had a more portentous sense of what was at risk: nothing less than the success of the great experiment in republican government that Jefferson's Declaration had helped launch in 1776. Yet no one felt more keenly the sense of sectional grievance, the "renewing irritations" that "kindle[d] such mutual and mortal hatred" and unleashed such "angry passions." Jefferson could plumb the depth of such feelings because he shared them; he knew that the union he cherished was in jeopardy because he could not stop himself from imagining its destruction. It is hardly surprising that Jefferson, torn between the need to preserve the Revolutionary fathers' great achievement and the irresistible impulse to demolish it, should speak of "suicide"—or that he should displace this death wish, or murderous impulse, onto others: the rising generation, with its "unwise and unworthy passions," or the dangerous demagogues beyond the "geographical line," who "have ever had in view [the union's] . . . separation."[17]

For Jefferson, liberty and union were inextricable: the destruction of one necessarily entailed the destruction of the other. It was only by sustaining the federal republic that the essential distinction between Europe and America could be sustained. This was the fundamental "geographical line" the American Revolutionaries had established between Old World and New World: the line Jefferson had extended to the West through the Louisiana Purchase and that Madison had recently vindicated in the War of 1812, the second war for American independence. In the wake of the Spanish Empire's collapse, this was the "meridian of partition through the ocean which separates the two hemispheres."[18] But as the line between North and South appeared so suddenly, and in such heightened contrast, that other line dimmed to the point of disappearing.

The connection between the Missouri crisis and Jefferson's conception of the global significance of the American Revolution became clear during the interval between the two phases of the crisis, in the summer and fall of 1820. Jefferson could then confidently reaffirm that "the principles of society" in Europe and America "are radically different."[19] The escalating pattern of sectional grievance might be irreversible, but Jefferson now imagined that destructive passions would be spent in the process of its demolition: the "traitors" would then come to their senses, recognizing that their real interests, rightly understood, depended on founding a new and more durable union.

Northern leaders might think that they had established "a line of separation" between slavery and freedom in the West, Jefferson wrote South Carolina congressman Charles Pinckney in September, but they would discover a "very different" line if they did not abandon their campaign against southern institutions and the union disintegrated: "As manufacturing and navigating States, they will have quarrelled with their bread and butter." Yet if the northerners' rational calculations of interest provoked sober second thoughts, the impulse to reunion would reflect their better natures. "After a little trial they will think better" of separation, Jefferson confidently predicted, "and return to the embraces of their natural and best friends."[20]

Jefferson imagined this happy reconciliation of the sectional crisis—the counterpoint to the themes of death and destruction that dominate his earlier and subsequent correspondence on Missouri—in more extravagant, and revealing, language when in October he wrote to Richard Rush, the American minister at the Court of St. James's in London and son of Jefferson's old, now deceased friend Benjamin Rush. Should the "schism be pushed to separation, it will be for a short term only," he told Rush; "two or three years' trial will bring them back, like quarrelling lovers to renewed embraces, and increased affections."[21] The emphasis on affective and affectionate ties, on a sentimentalized conception of bonds of union—joined by God, and which no man (or foreign power) dare put asunder—spoke to the fundamental premise of Jeffersonian social and political theory. Liberty and equality of the contracting parties, whether individuals or states (in this case, the new state of Missouri), were the essential preconditions of true and lasting union. Only by securing this equality—defined as the absence of any external coercion or control—could lasting commitments and obligations be voluntarily undertaken and the passions that fostered social harmony be given full scope.

Yet Jefferson could not sustain this optimistic gloss on the Missouri question in the face of renewed congressional controversy (over the new state's constitution), his irrepressible animus against his Yankee tormentors, and his anxieties about emancipation and servile insurrection. Jefferson's misgivings were already apparent in the letter to Rush, as he speculated on what the controversy might look like from the European perspective. Even if "the experiment of separation" should result in a stronger union, the immediate effect would be to reinforce the contempt of the European powers for republican government: "Were we to break to pieces, it would damp the hopes and the efforts of the good, and give triumph to those of the bad through the whole enslaved world. As members, therefore, of the universal society of mankind, and standing in high and responsible relation with them, it is our sacred duty to suppress passion among ourselves, and not to blast the confidence we have inspired of proof that a government of reason is better than one of force."[22] Jefferson could not pretend that the passions of his countrymen were any different from the passions that moved the despots and destroyers of Europe. He could only hope that Americans would return to their senses, and to first principles, once the damage had been done. In the meantime, the new nation's example would no longer inspire the "whole enslaved world": the crucial line of distinction between New World and Old—the premise of Jefferson's statecraft and the practical test of his political philosophy—had ceased to exist.

Jefferson's cosmopolitan perspective reinforced his sense of the significance of union and the agony he experienced in imagining its demise. From this perspective the union was an integral whole, just as the Americans constituted a single people. To acknowledge fundamental differences among Americans—differences that would make a durable union impossible—was to acknowledge that Americans were no different than Europeans. This was another way of saying that republican governments, and the republican "character" they presumably fostered in the people at large, could not preserve peace and harmony in America: the states could guarantee neither their own existence as republics nor the integrity of the American people as an all-embracing union of liberty-loving republicans.

Jefferson was convinced that securing the sovereignty and equality of the respective states—for him, the central issue of the Missouri controversy—was the essential condition for guaranteeing republican government and promoting a durable union. Disunion could only be attributed to the restrictionists' contemptuous disregard for that essential condition and to the political ambitions that lurked beneath their self-righteous "Jeremiads on the miseries of slavery."[23] Thus far, Jefferson's formulation of the problem echoed arguments of antirestrictionists in Congress and the press who projected the entire responsibility for the crisis onto their partisan opponents beyond the "geographical line." Yet if Jefferson had convinced himself of his and his region's blamelessness, he had—from the cosmopolitan perspective that made the American Revolution meaningful for him as an epochal event in world history—proved far too much. For if the restrictionists were such obdurate opponents of state equality, and if this was the fundamental premise of the federal system, then it was hard to envision any future circumstances in which union with them would be possible.

When the restrictionists cynically exploited "the virtuous feelings" of northerners who opposed slavery, they linked "a marked principle, moral and political, with a geographical line," and that line, "once conceived, I feared would never more be obliterated from the mind."[24] The projection of a line that threatened to reduce the southern states to a subordinate, minority status under a "consolidated" federal regime unleashed Jefferson's boundless hatred for his northern enemies. Such hatred, he knew, had embroiled Europe in a never-ending sequence of bloody wars, and the very existence of such feelings constituted a definitive refutation of his gospel of love in affectionate union. In imagining northerners as foreigners, he obliterated the line between Europe and America and so became complicit in the very "treason against the hopes of the world" with which he charged the rising generation.[25]

UNION AND DISUNION

Jefferson's idealized conception of the American union prepared the way for his radical disillusionment during the Missouri crisis. Jefferson was convinced that the axioms of European political science did not apply in America. From the European perspective the size of the American republic was its greatest liability. As the new nation projected its authority across the continent, republican institutions would have to be jettisoned in favor of the despotic forms that enabled the great European kingdoms to rule far-flung subject populations; otherwise, the proliferation of new states would strain the bonds of union to an early breaking point, and an American system of disunited sovereignties would soon be indistinguishable from its European prototype. But Jefferson turned this familiar logic inside out, insisting that the states' republican constitutions and their equal standing under the federal compact would secure perpetual peace. "Contrary to the principle of Montesquieu," he told an old European friend in 1817, "it will be seen that the larger the extent of country, the more firm its republican structure, if founded, not on conquest, but in principles of compact and equality."[26] State "equality," the formal capacity to engage in the compact, was the essential condition for creating a true union; as long as the federal government upheld that fundamental principle, the union would endure.[27]

Jefferson's thinking about the nature of the federal union could be as confusing to his contemporaries as it has been to subsequent commentators. "Union," the affectionate embrace of like-minded individuals or states, was in his more extravagant formulations indistinguishable from "disunion," the protean condition of equals who, in their uncoerced and independent condition, were alone capable of such affectionate engagements. This conflation of union and disunion, whole and parts, was most conspicuous in Jefferson's most confident and optimistic moments, as, for instance, when he looked toward the emergence of "a great, free and independent empire" on the Pacific coast. Let republican institutions be planted there, he wrote John Jacob Astor in 1813, and it hardly mattered that—at this point—there would be no formal, constitutional connection with the Atlantic states, for it would inevitably follow that "liberty and self-government" would spread "from that as well as this side" until "their complete establishment over the whole." The crucial thing was to keep the English, with their "habitual hostility to every degree of freedom," from interfering with Astor's settlement on the Columbia River.[28]

Jefferson's casual attitude toward union among American republicans was thus counterpointed to his anxieties about European interference. Europeans—English in the Northwest or French in the Mississippi Valley—could alone Europeanize American politics, exporting their balance of power (or, rather, terror) to their imperial outposts on the American continent and enlisting credulous Americans in their unholy alliances. A letter to John Breckinridge in August 1803—written after the successful negotiation of terms with Napoleon for the purchase of Louisiana but before Senate ratification of the purchase treaty—best illuminates Jefferson's paradoxical thinking. Responding to Federalist predictions that the overextended union would collapse, with disastrous consequences, Jefferson insisted that there was no reason for the "Atlantic States" to "dread" the separation of the "nations" on the "western waters": "The future inhabitants of the Atlantic and Mississippi States will be our sons. We leave them in distinct but bordering establishments. We think we see their happiness in their union, and we wish it. Events may prove it otherwise; and if they see their interest in separation, why should we take side with our Atlantic rather than our Mississippi descendants?"[29] Jefferson could be sanguine about the prospects of disunion because it would not bring into existence new nations that would be "hostile" to each other, as were England and France. Indeed, it was only because "the French nation" had been so suddenly, even miraculously, dislodged from New Orleans that Jefferson could assume this disinterested, benevolent posture about the political future of the West.[30] Whether or not westerners chose to remain in the union, they would not be foreigners: they would be our "descendants," bound to us—and to each other—by "relations of blood [and] affection." Their "happiness" was in a profound, almost genealogical, sense our happiness: recognizing this, their eastern fathers and brethren would never attempt to preserve a political connection by force of arms.[31] In any event, the American nation would survive and prosper.

Jefferson's theory of union rested on the same premises and was in a fundamental sense indistinguishable from his notions of intergenerational equity.[32] The development of Jefferson's political philosophy and his plans for educating Virginia's youth were closely linked. Spending on education constituted the grand and significant exception to Jefferson's minimal state, for this was precisely the kind of public investment that would foster the welfare of the rising generation without wasting its future prospects.[33] Jefferson's most elaborate discussion of the character of the federal union emerged out of his proposals for a three-tiered school system in Virginia and the implications he drew from these proposals for reforming the state's constitution. His projected "ward republics," as he explained to Joseph Cabell and Samuel Kercheval in 1816, would provide simultaneously for the schooling of young people and the political education of their fathers through active participation. Not surprisingly, these letters are the canonical texts for theorists who celebrate Jefferson as a "strong democrat." Yet they also, and not coincidentally, constitute his most systematic effort to divide and subdivide authority, and they did so in ways that called into question the very possibility of government itself.

For Jefferson, the necessary condition of an active citizenry was equality, defined as noninterference and the absence of coercion by other citizens situated at the same level in the ascending hierarchy of authorities or by any "higher" authority that should seek to exceed its strictly delegated powers.[34] Jefferson's most schematic elaboration of his "gradation of authorities" can be found in his letter to Kercheval of 12 July 1816.

> We should thus marshal our government into, 1, the general federal republic, for all concerns foreign and federal; 2, that of the State, for what relates to our own citizens exclusively; 3, the county republics, for the duties and concerns of the county; and 4, the ward republics, for the small, and yet numerous and interesting concerns of the neighborhood; and in government, as well as in every other business in life, it is by division and subdivision of duties alone, that all matters, great and small, can be managed to perfection. And the whole is cemented by giving to every citizen, personally, a part in the administration of the public affairs.[35]

He might have added, as he did in his earlier letter to Cabell, that his system finally "ends in the administration of every man's farm by himself," thus constituting a comprehensive theory linking individual rights to a federal constitutional design.[36]

The notion of layered authorities was hardly original with Jefferson and can be traced through Madisonian federal theory to classical antecedents.[37] Every successive level of association is called a "republic," suggesting that, according to its respective purposes, each government at every level is complete and self-sufficient, fully equal to and independent of other governments at the same level. "Equality" is the operative term, and for Jefferson that term was naturally equated with sovereignty. Thus, just as Jefferson's conception of ascending layers made possible the conflation or confusion of individual rights with the rights of corporate associations, so too notions of independent sovereign authority could move down through these layers. Under such downward pressure, driven by competition for relative advantage and anxious solicitude for endangered rights, the republican empire threatened to explode: "republicanism" would give way to "liberalism."

In the course of discussing and defending the three-fifths clause in one of his letters to Kercheval—four years before the "knell of the Union" aroused him from his slumbers—Jefferson showed how easy it would be to take that imaginative leap into the abyss. In Connecticut only "freemen" who met a property qualification and were "admitted by a vote of the freemen of the town" could exercise the full rights of citizenship. Nonetheless, Connecticut's representation in the House of Representatives was computed according to its entire population. "So, slaves with us [in Virginia] have no powers as citizens," Jefferson explained; "yet, in representation in the General Government, they count in the proportion of three to five." Others might well complain about this manifest inequity, but the agreement on representation was a sacred compact, a pillar of the existing union, and Jefferson would not tamper with it. Nor would he question the wisdom of Connecticut's suffrage exclusions. "In truth," he concluded, "the condition of different descriptions of inhabitants in any country is a matter of municipal arrangement, of which no foreign country has a right to take notice."[38]

Here was the hallowed principle of noninterference, the hallmark of liberal internationalism and the only effectual guarantee of peaceful relations among independent states.[39] Here too, casually and reflexively, Jefferson could speak of his "country" (Virginia) and of the "foreign" countries that together constituted the "General Government." It was no accident that when Jefferson identified a specific "foreign country," it should be Connecticut, one of the last bastions of Federalist strength and a place where English influence was still palpable, if—he then thought—no longer to be feared.

DESTROYING NEW ENGLAND

The identification of slavery restrictionists with the Holy Alliance came easily to Jefferson. As the Republicans strengthened their hold on the national government after the "revolution of 1800," Jefferson saw his Federalist opponents as sectionalists who sought to destroy the union and forge an alliance with their secret British sponsors. During the last days of the War of 1812, New England Federalists gathered at Hartford to consider the possibility of separation or a separate peace with Britain. Though they finally backed away from these extreme measures, the Hartford Federalists stood condemned as traitors when the administration's diplomatic efforts brought the war to a sudden and welcome conclusion.[40] Jefferson exulted in his opponents' disgrace but worried about their future moves. In the event of another war, desperate Federalists would not hesitate to seek foreign support. And the defeat of Napoleon meant that a Holy Alliance of European legitimists could now direct its united energies against republican America.

During the Missouri debates antirestrictionist Republicans repeatedly invoked the Hartford Convention in order to link restriction with Federalism, and both with traitorous designs against the union. Given continuing anxieties about the new nation's security and misgivings about European intentions, the equations of the Congress of Vienna and the "Congress" at Hartford or of the Holy Alliance in Europe and the campaign against slavery in Missouri did not seem as far-fetched then as they do now. For Jefferson it was not simply a question of plausible, rhetorically effective parallels but rather of a dangerous new alignment of antirepublican forces.[41] The "geographical line" that the restrictionists imposed on the new nation inevitably would dissolve the union and so enable the "Hartford nation" to enter into alliance with like-minded Europeans.

Jefferson conducted his war against the Federalists on two fronts. The vindication of American independence and recognition of its equal standing in the family of nations meant that foreign powers would no longer presume to interfere in its domestic politics. (For Jefferson, this principle was equally crucial in his indictments of restrictionists in the Missouri crisis and of the interference of the Holy Alliance in the domestic affairs of other European states.)[42] Meanwhile, the triumph of Republicans at the polls would complete the Federalists' isolation, demonstrating conclusively the futility of further foreign efforts to "anarchise us."[43] One-party rule was the sine qua non of union and the best guarantee against foreign interference.

Jefferson's attitudes toward New England revolved around calculations of the relative strength of the Federalists there and the prospects for recruiting moderates into the Republican ranks. At moments of political crisis—when New Englanders resisted the ill-fated Embargo, or failed to rally enthusiastically to the American cause during the War of 1812, or presumed to interfere in the domestic affairs of Missouri in the controversy over slavery restriction—Jefferson was hard-pressed to sustain the conventional and comforting distinction between malignant leaders and their deluded followers. He had emphasized this distinction between leaders and followers in his Inaugural Address, when he urged that those "among us who would wish to dissolve this Union or to change its republican form" be left to "stand undisturbed as monuments of the safety with which error of opinion may be tolerated where reason is left free to combat it."[44] Following Jefferson's script, the Republicans routed "error of opinion" in every quarter of the union and demolished the Federalists as a viable national party. But the destruction of the "Essex Federalists" was not yet complete when the outbreak of war with Britain gave them a new lease on life.[45] As a result, Jefferson began to imagine a more sanguinary, less principled sort of "combat" against his old Federalist foes.

Jefferson's ruminations about the fate of New England during the War of 1812 prefigured his response to the Missouri crisis. In both cases advocates of dangerously unrepublican principles held sway within a specific geographical region; having lost their national base of support, these unreconstructed "monarchists" exploited sectionalist grievances in order to prepare the way for disunion and foreign alliances. Yet, despite these apparent parallels, Jefferson's response to the earlier crisis was profoundly different. In 1813 and 1814 he welcomed a war with the New England Federalists that he knew the loyal Republican states would easily win. The subsequent restoration of the union, purified of the last vestiges of monarchical corruption, would redeem the promise of the American Revolution.

In September 1813 Jefferson outlined the steps that could lead to a war between the states and then to a predictably happy outcome. War undoubtedly could be averted and Federalists be driven from power by less violent means, if the people of Massachusetts were given the opportunity to "declare themselves members of the Union, and obedient to its determinations": "Put this question solemnly to their people, and their answer cannot be doubtful." The "people," by whom Jefferson meant that half of the electorate generally inclined to support Republican candidates, would be decisively augmented by the "dispassionate part" of "the federal moiety": moderate Federalists would recognize that the state's "vital interests" depended on preserving the union. They understood that Massachusetts could not even feed itself without importing foodstuffs and that exclusion from American ports would make them "look to Europe for the deficiency."[46] Yet, after exhaustively rehearsing all the sound reasons that would deter the large majority in Massachusetts from defecting, Jefferson concluded that the High Federalist leadership would nonetheless "brave all these obstacles" and break from the union.

Federalist leaders were "monarchists in principle, bearing deadly hatred to their republican fellow-citizens, impatient under the ascendency of republican principles, devoted in their attachment to England, and preferring to be placed under her despotism, if they cannot hold the helm of government here." Such men deserved to be destroyed, and Jefferson reveled in the prospect: a temporary Europeanization of American politics would lead to the union's ultimate purification—the elimination of all European influences. "Much of the population" would abandon Massachusetts in the event of war, and the inevitable result would be "an early and humiliating return to the Union."[47]

Jefferson's imaginative scenario enabled him to remove the good republicans of Massachusetts out of harm's way and so enact a ritual humiliation on the remaining "army of officers." (Jefferson had envisaged a similar, if less violent humiliation in his Inaugural Address, when he cast his foes as "monuments," or objects of popular mockery and contempt.) The practical effect of this exercise was to draw a "geographical line" between the traitors who stayed and the good republicans who moved on to friendlier climes. Jefferson was eager to draw such a line at this time both because its extent was so limited (he persisted in the belief that the "Essex Federalists" would succeed only in Massachusetts and that the other New England states would remain loyal) and because it justified the projection of his own "deadly hatred" against his "fellow-citizens." Jefferson made Federalists foreigners and gave them a country of their own (Massachusetts), so that he could imagine making war on them—and so persuade himself that he was not violating the republican gospel of peace and affectionate union.[48]

When Jefferson visualized the possible sequence of events in his imaginary war against Massachusetts, as he did in a letter to William Short in late November 1814, he recalled the good republicans of the state from their exile and accorded them a key role in the hostilities. One possibility was civil war: "If their administration determines to join the enemy, their force will be annihilated by equality of division among themselves"; "their own people will put down these factionists as soon as they see the real object of the opposition." Should desperate Federalists finally "call in the English army, the republicans [would call in] ours." Here was the opportunity Jefferson—and as he saw it, his countrymen generally—had been so long awaiting, for the result of Massachusetts's defection and an open alliance with Britain "will only be a transfer of the scene of war from Canada to Massachusetts; and we can get ten men to go to Massachusetts for one who will go to Canada."[49] In other words, the "defection of Massachusetts" would strengthen the American war effort: the rupture of the union would bring its real enemies out into the open, enabling good republicans in Massachusetts and its sister states to rally to the cause.

That Jefferson could so confidently assert that the secession of Massachusetts would be a boon to the American war effort is a good measure of his hatred for his Federalist enemies. Jefferson had always insisted that a strong union was the crucial barrier to foreign interference and counterrevolution. But now, in the midst of war, he could contemplate a rupture of the union that would give the British a significant strategic advantage. Jefferson thought that the "danger" here was more apparent than real, however, for the differences that had led to war with Britain were ultimately negotiable.[50] When the British recognized the futility of attempting to enforce their will on an aroused and united people, now purged of its former secret enemies, they would withdraw beyond the line that distinguished "the American hemisphere," with "its separate system of interests," from the European balance of power.[51] But the "Essex Federalists" would not respond to such rational calculations: they could only "return" to Europe as individuals in another diaspora of tory exiles. As long as they held sway in Massachusetts, the Federalists represented a cancerous and potentially fatal growth on the American body politic. The ultimate design of these monarchists, Jefferson explained to John Melish in January 1813, was to establish their "favorite government [in Massachusetts], from whence the other States may gangrene by degrees."[52] The frustrating history of the Republicans' efforts to extend their influence in the region—and thereby strengthen the union— demonstrated conclusively that further negotiations with such enemies were pointless. Radical surgery was the only solution.

Jefferson's response to the prospect of Massachusetts's secession reflected his overriding concern with preserving the distinction between Europe and America. "The meridian of the mid-Atlantic should be the line of demarkation between war and peace," Jefferson wrote early in 1812, shortly before the beginning of hostilities with Britain that were supposed to vindicate that line.[53] The presence of a monarchist fragment in Massachusetts was a dangerous anomaly in the American system that demanded a preemptive response. But Jefferson could still confidently assume—as he could not in the Missouri crisis—that the threat could be localized and therefore easily removed. In striking contrast to his contemporaneous bromides about harmonious, voluntary, and affectionate union among republicans, Jefferson's prescriptions for dealing with the separatist threat in New England relied on mobilizing the "extended republic"'s coercive capabilities. As he wrote in March 1814, "I see our safety in the extent of our confederacy, and in the probability that in the proportion of that the sound parts will always be sufficient to crush local poisons."[54]

Jefferson's hatred of New England was the deep-seated source of the "geographical line" that shattered the tranquillity of his old age. For Jefferson, New England had always been the "anti-republican portion of our country."[55] Before the Missouri controversy, however, he remained confident that the cancer would eventually, and without much "difficulty," be localized and destroyed. This confidence allowed him to link unrepublican principles with a particular state or region, and so draw a line between "sound" and "unsound" parts of the federal union. The line would be obliterated as soon as the Republican party achieved its long-delayed triumph in these last bastions of Federalist strength—or when the "overwhelming force" of the union destroyed its "anti-republican" enemies on the battlefield.

The unexpected success of American negotiators at Ghent made military measures against Massachusetts unnecessary. But in Jefferson's mind the devastation of his old foes was nonetheless complete: it was as if they actually had broken from the union and then been reduced to submission. In March 1815 he sketched out the terms of reunion to Henry Dearborn, the Massachusetts Republican who had been his secretary of war. "Oh, Massachusetts!" he declaimed, "how have I lamented the degradation of your apostasy! Massachusetts, with whom I went with pride in 1776, whose vote was my vote on every public question, and whose principles were then the standard of whatever was free or fearless." Yet it was not too late to "return to the bosom and to the principles of her brethren," for "should the State once more buckle on her republican harness, we shall receive her again as a sister." The triumph of Republicans at the polls would constitute an "act of repentance," making it once again possible to distinguish the state from its corrupt leaders. The state's "wanderings," culminating in the abortive Hartford Convention, could then be reckoned "among the crimes only of the parricide party, which would have basely sold what their fathers so bravely won from the same enemy."[56]

The "crimes" of the Federalists were now cast in the same generational terms Jefferson would invoke during the Missouri controversy. The "venal traitors" who had led Massachusetts to the brink of disunion were parricides intent on destroying the Revolutionary fathers and squandering their legacy of liberty. Jefferson's conception of union thus reached back to 1776, when the fathers had marched forth under the same "standard," while looking forward to a time when the sons would renounce and suppress their unnatural, parricidal impulses by purging the last vestiges of Federalism. As Jefferson's insistently familial language reveals, this union was based as much on affection as on principle: a renewed commitment "to the principles of her brethren" would draw this wayward "sister," naturally and irresistibly, back to the "bosom" of her republican family.[57]

Having thus imagined the demise of the Federalists and Massachusetts's restoration to the union, Jefferson could view the political landscape over the next few years in increasingly confident, even complacent terms. This complacency, the sleepfulness so suddenly and traumatically disrupted by the "fire-bell in the night," was a key ingredient in Jefferson's response to the Missouri crisis. And when Jefferson awoke from his slumbers, the magnitude of the threat to liberty and union was immediately apparent. For Jefferson had already drawn a "geographical line" around New England (or Massachusetts) that "coincide[d] with a marked principle."[58]

New England's Federalist leaders, he was certain, had made no secret of their hostility to republican principles—and to the union—during the protracted political and diplomatic crisis that culminated in the War of 1812. That such men should ever return to popular favor, as they did under the pretext of promoting slavery restriction, was either a measure of the people's extreme credulity or of their own "anti-republican" tendencies—it hardly mattered which. What Jefferson most feared was precisely this link between party leaders and followers, "officers" and "soldiers": this was the relationship that made Massachusetts a "foreign" country during the war, and that would make the self-professed "free" states such a formidable danger to republican liberty during the Missouri controversy.

Dedicated as he was to preserving the fundamental distinction between New World and Old, Jefferson externalized all threats to the union: Federalists who challenged administration policy were either dupes of the English or worse, homegrown "foreigners" unresponsive to the claims of prudence, principle, or fellow feeling. Again, it hardly mattered which. Either temporarily, in the case of the war crisis, or permanently, in the case of Missouri, the geographical lines Jefferson projected distinguished "Europe-in-America" from the healthy, still republican, and authentically American portions of the union. If the line could be obliterated, as Jefferson so confidently predicted in his meditations on the fate of Massachusetts, the Revolution would be secure against "the unwise and unworthy passions" of parricidal sons. But the line between slavery and freedom, "once conceived," could "never be obliterated from the mind." When this happened, Americans would become foreigners to each other; America would become Europe.

Jefferson's rehearsal of the main themes of the Missouri controversy in his earlier responses to antiwar and separatist sentiment in New England strongly suggests that his profound hostility to the restriction of slavery was not simply the product of reactionary hysteria or of an exaggerated solicitude for class or regional interests. To the contrary, Jefferson was stunned by the congressional controversy over Missouri statehood because it seemed to fulfill so completely and disastrously the nightmarish script for disunion and counterrevolution that he had glimpsed—and dismissed—in earlier dark moments. That the future of the institution of slavery was at issue is what makes the Missouri debates so compelling to historians. But for Jefferson something much more momentous was at stake: the legacy of the American Revolution, and of his whole political career.

Before their recent humiliation the Federalists of Massachusetts had conspired to destroy the union, thus drawing the new nation into the vortex of European politics and making America over in Europe's image. Now, incredibly, the new state of Missouri—anxious to join and strengthen the union, not to withdraw from or demolish it—was rebuffed at the threshold. Missouri's rejection would mark the death knell of Jefferson's republican empire, the expanding union of self-governing republican states that guaranteed peace and prosperity to the New World. The patriotic republicans—and Republican loyalists—who settled the vast frontiers of the Louisiana Purchase would be cast beyond the restrictionists' pale. Here, at a time when his old Federalists foes were supposed to be suffering in "silent but unresisting anguish" as the Republicans established their "decided ascendency" across the union, Jefferson could only look on in horror as neo-Federalist restrictionists seized control of Congress and threatened to destroy his cherished union.[59]

EMPIRE OF LIBERTY

If the Hartford Convention revealed the disloyalty and antirepublican principles of New England separatists during the War of 1812, the great American victory at New Orleans in January 1815 demonstrated the patriotic fervor of western citizens. "The people of Louisiana are sincerely attached to the Union," Jefferson exclaimed, as he contrasted their patriotism with Massachusetts's "apostasy."[60] Unlike their Yankee counterparts the Louisianans could not claim republican liberty as their birthright: they had only begun to enjoy the full benefits of self-government with their admission to the union in 1811. Yet, with the timely assistance of the other western states, they had successfully defended New Orleans—and the entire Mississippi Valley—from British invasion. The Battle of New Orleans "proved the fidelity of the Orleanese"; it also proved that the city "can be defended both by land and water," and "that the western country will fly to its relief."[61] The British would have received a much warmer welcome and enjoyed far greater success had they landed in Boston.

For Jefferson, Andrew Jackson's victory at New Orleans, though it had no effect on the already concluded negotiations at Ghent, was a particularly gratifying vindication of the union's durability in a time of great crisis. Separatist sentiment in Massachusetts showed how native-born "foreigners" like the Essex Federalists could jeopardize the union by extending their gangrenous influence throughout the federal body. The timely reaction of the healthy parts of the union, those farthest removed from the source of corruption, constituted the only effective antidote. Jefferson would be inclined to think in such schematic terms after a political lifetime of combating Federalist heresies in New England and recruiting allies to the Republican cause in the new western states. As he looked west, the prospects for an expanding, progressively more populous, prosperous, and powerful union seemed virtually unlimited. Meanwhile, eastern apostates and parricides appeared all too eager to squander their fathers' priceless legacy by demolishing the union and so returning to the dark ages of despotic government and never-ending war.

Yet, however accurately such comparisons and juxtapositions hinted at underlying tendencies and ultimate prospects, Jefferson understood that they represented at best only an imperfect sketch of the federal republic's present circumstances. After all, the great majority of New Englanders (once they came to their senses) were good republicans, dedicated to the preservation of the union. Nor was Jefferson under any illusions about the motives and character of the adventurers and speculators who flocked west, where unsettled conditions and the settlers' ignorance and credulity gave such scope to their selfish ambitions. Jeffer-

son's exultant response to the American triumph at New Orleans reflected his consciousness of these ambiguities, and his sense of relief is apparent. The British invasion was only the latest—and, Jefferson imagined, the last—of a series of crises that had tested western loyalties to the
union. Having demonstrated such extraordinary "fidelity," westerners
could claim as a matter of right, once their numbers were sufficient, the
full benefits of self-governing statehood and admission to the union.

That Missourians should be drawn toward the union by voluntary
"attraction" instead of coercive "impulse" was not a foregone conclusion
when American settlers first flowed into the region.[62] It was instead,
Jefferson could argue as he reviewed the history of the region over two
decades, the result of his own diplomatic triumph in securing Louisiana
to the union (1803), the responsiveness of his and subsequent administrations to settlers' legitimate grievances and demands, timely action
against Aaron Burr and his alleged coconspirators (1806–7), and, above
all, the remarkable success of the Republican party in inculcating "federal and republican principles" in a widely dispersed and rapidly growing
electorate.

Jefferson emphasized the importance of party mobilization for the
security of the union in a letter to Republican editor William Duane in
March 1811. "During the *bellum omnium in omnia* of Europe," the
"union of all [this country's] . . . friends" was absolutely essential in order "to resist its enemies within and without. If we schismatize on either
men or measures, if we do not act in phalanx, as when we rescued it
from the satellites of monarchism [in the election of 1800], I will not say
our *party,* [for] the term is false and degrading, but our *nation* will be
undone. For the republicans are the *nation.*"[63] Beginning in Jefferson's
second term, the deepening diplomatic crisis with Britain over neutral
rights, the ultimately successful resistance to a commercial embargo
(particularly in New England) that was supposed to offer a peaceful alternative to war, and ominous portents of divisions in Republican ranks
all served to exacerbate anxieties about the future of the union and
therefore to reinforce the identification of "nation" and "party." But if
the union was once again at risk, as it had been in the crisis of
1798–1800, Jefferson and his followers could take comfort from the collapse of Burr's Conspiracy, one of the few successes of his second term.

The union had proved strongest where, by all conventional accounts, it should have been most vulnerable.

The conflation of "union," "nation," and Republican party was reflexive for Jefferson, and characteristically self-serving. Yet it was as much the result of what Jefferson heard from constituents as it was a projection of personal and party ambitions. In late 1806 and early 1807 Jefferson was inundated with adulatory addresses from every part of the union urging him to stand for a third term. Loyal Republicans extolled Jefferson's "pacific system of policy, so congenial with our hearts, and with the great principles of our representative government."[64] "Your solicitude to preserve the enjoyments of peace to our country, amidst the storms which agitate the world," as a committee of New Yorkers told Jefferson, "demands the approbation of every virtuous patriot."[65] Many feared that if Jefferson retired, a succession crisis would unleash the "hydra of *apostasy*," as "the enemies of our principles" began "sowing the seeds of disunion amongst us."[66] "Foreign enemies and *domestic Traitors*" like Burr—who was not yet in custody—were naturally linked;[67] it was imperative that Jefferson remain in office so that, in the words of the Maryland legislature, "the same wisdom which has guided and protected us thus far may be able to annihilate the demon of conspiracy[,] the offspring of desperate and abandoned men who backed by foreign aid expect to benefit and aggrandize themselves from the destruction of that Constitution which has exalted us to our now elevated station."[68]

It was Aaron Burr's preparations for his descent down the Mississippi, with the supposed intention of launching an unauthorized private war against Spanish Mexico, and perhaps of seizing New Orleans in order to seduce the western states from the union, that gave these addresses such an urgent quality.[69] Burr's offers of cheap land, Spanish treasure, and the end of the federal government's territorial regime in Orleans (Louisiana) and adjacent territories constituted the first great test of the loyalties of western territories and states since the Louisiana Purchase. Westerners rushed to reassure Jefferson that "no real or visionary prospect of advantage will ever induce us to sever that bond of union which is our only security against domestic violence and foreign invasion."[70]

Westerners could demonstrate their loyalty in 1806–7 simply by not responding to Burr's seductive appeals: there was as yet no need to take up arms. Indeed, the genius of the American system, "where every citizen is a soldier, and every soldier a citizen," was to preserve peace until the time when "life, liberty and independence" were truly threatened. The resources of the union would be correspondingly enhanced, as would the patriotic determination of a grateful and growing population to repel all "those who may unjustly assail us."[71] The federal republic would become powerful, even unconquerable, if its leaders recognized and honored the distinction between war and peace. Of course, this was a distinction never recognized by despotic regimes, with their standing armies, their predatory policies toward their own subjects, and their aggressive designs against one another.[72] Jefferson's pacific system insulated the new nation from the "throes & convulsions which afflict the European world": "Behold[ing] the effusion of human blood, which flows from the wounds of slaves, to satiate the unbounded thirst for power & ambition, obliges us still more to approbate those measures of policy which have averted from us similar horrors & calamities."[73]

Jefferson recognized that the preservation of the union depended on common principles and common interests—the themes repeatedly struck in the public addresses he received during the Burr crisis—and not on the exercise of force, even against those who were temporarily led astray. On 27 November 1806 Jefferson issued a proclamation warning against any unauthorized "military expedition or enterprise against the dominions of Spain" and "enjoining all faithful citizens who have been led without due knowledge or consideration to participate in the said unlawful enterprises to withdraw from the same without delay."[74] Jefferson conducted his campaign against Burr by mobilizing public opinion, not a military force, and by urging local and federal authorities along the conspirator's route to initiate appropriate legal measures.[75] Then he could only wait, "looking with anxiety to see what exertions the Western country will make."[76]

For Jefferson, this test of western loyalties was a great plebiscite, a massive election campaign in which westerners determined their own political future. The collapse of the Burr Conspiracy was one of Jefferson's most gratifying moments, even if—thanks to Chief Justice John

Marshall—its leaders did not receive the punishment he thought they so richly deserved.[77] Burr's failure offered the "most remarkable . . . proof" of the "innate strength of our government." "Apprised . . . that there were traitors among them," an aroused citizenry "crushed by their own strength what would have produced the march of armies and civil war in any other country."[78] "On the whole," Jefferson told William C. C. Claiborne, the territorial governor at New Orleans, "this squall, by showing with what ease our government suppresses movements which in other countries requires armies, has greatly increased its strength by increasing the public confidence in it."[79] The American system's great "strength," its exceptional character, was grounded in the people's confidence in a "mild and efficient Government" that would not send armies into the field at the slightest provocation and, equally importantly, in the government's confidence in the people.[80]

The survival and strength of the federal republic depended on reciprocal trust and the recognition of an identity of interests between republican citizens and their elected leaders. But Jefferson never assumed such trust or imagined that all Americans would always recognize their own best interests. Burr's supposedly imperial ambitions thus constituted a critical test of Jefferson's "pacific system," of whether the government was capable of pursuing measures that would build trust and confidence. Far from remaining inert, as some critics supposed, the administration actively sought to shape public opinion, encouraging and exploiting expressions of support from all quarters of the union. Appeals to Jefferson to stand for a third term reinforced and reflected his own sense of the perilous conjunction of European war, insurrection on the western frontiers, and schism in the Republican party. To conceive of the crisis in these terms—to recognize these connections—was the necessary precondition for its resolution. Seen as yet another crisis of the union, the Burr Conspiracy provoked the sentiments of loyalty and national identity that constituted the union's only durable foundation. "The fidelity of the western country was not to be shaken," Jefferson exulted, and the union emerged from its crisis with renewed vigor.[81]

Though some leading Burrites may have been Republican—including Senator John Smith of Ohio and an embarrassingly large contingent from Kentucky, where Federalists took the lead in exposing and resisting

Burr's plans—Jefferson could only interpret the conspiracy's collapse as a triumph for the administration party.[82] He was convinced that Federalists expected the union to fall apart, sooner or later, whether or not they actively supported Burr; they "chuckle" at the notion "that the people of the US are qualified for self government."[83] And after Burr was apprehended, Jefferson complained to his congressional lieutenant, William Branch Giles, the Federalists happily made "Burr's cause their own, mortified only that he did not separate the Union or overturn the government, and proving, that had he had a little dawn of success, they would have joined him to introduce his object, their favorite monarchy, as they would any other enemy, foreign or domestic, who could rid them of this hateful republic for any other government."[84] For Jefferson, Burr was a sort of honorary Federalist (as he had most certainly been an opportunistic Republican) who shared and acted on their notorious contempt for the "federal and republican principles." Burr "has meant to place himself on the throne of Montezuma," Jefferson shuddered, "and extend his empire to the Alleghany," thus destroying the federal union, the only effective barrier to the Europeanization of American politics.[85]

Jefferson's conception of union depended on the common principles and harmonious interests of republican citizens across the continent. Westerners' loyalty during the Burr crisis vindicated this conception; Jefferson was also gratified by the swift action of local authorities. "The promptitude and energy displayed by your State," Jefferson wrote Governor Edward Tiffin of Ohio, "has been as honorable to itself as salutary to its sister States." Though conventional wisdom called for a powerful federal presence along the frontier, the collapse of the conspiracy confirmed Jefferson's faith in a radically decentralized federal regime. Here was "a happy illustration," he told Tiffin, "of the importance of preserving to the State authorities all that vigor which the Constitution foresaw would be necessary, not only for their own safety, but for that of the whole."[86]

In Jefferson's scheme the "energy" and enterprise that guaranteed national security came from below, from the determination of patriotic citizens to defend their own liberties and those of their countrymen.[87] The apparently paradoxical effect of eschewing a strong central government and respecting the autonomy and agency of the state governments was to increase the total amount of force that could be raised when the union was truly threatened. The genius of the American system, as Jefferson envisioned it, was that the firm foundation of popular patriotism made the federal constitutional superstructure of limited, checked, and balanced powers a potentially great, ultimately irresistible force in a war-torn world. Respect for constitutional limitations was the best guarantee that the nation's "resources"—and the confidence of the people—would not be squandered "on dangers which have never happened."[88] When war finally did come, and the people were persuaded of the justice of their cause, American victory was assured.

From the beginning of his administration in 1801, Jefferson celebrated the new nation's increasing population, prosperity, and power. "We contemplate this rapid growth," he assured Congress in his first annual message, "not with a view to the injuries it may enable us to do others in some future day, but to the settlement of the extensive country still remaining vacant within our limits [and] to the multiplication of men susceptible of happiness, educated in the love of order, habituated to self-government, and valuing its blessings above all price."[89] Of course, these were just the sort of liberty-loving republicans to resent and resist "injuries" inflicted by others, and the implicit warning to the new nation's imperial neighbors—including the Spanish in Louisiana—was clear. "We feel ourselves strong, and daily growing stronger," Jefferson wrote William Short in October 1801. "The day is within my time as well as yours, when we may say by what laws other nations [in this case, the British particularly] shall treat us on the sea. And we will say it."[90]

Jefferson's prospectus for America's future power betrayed misgivings about the character of westerners—what if they were not properly "educated" and "habituated" to the virtues of "self-government"?—and the vulnerability of the union before it came into the fullness of its latent powers.[91] According to Jefferson, political adventurers such as Burr hoped to exploit this vulnerability, seducing westerners before their republican principles and loyalty to the union were irrevocably fixed. But Burr miscalculated, and Jefferson was gratified by the proof this failure offered that his "pacific system" already operated effectively across the western frontiers, even among the "Orleanese Creoles."[92] Combined with the timely interposition of local constitutional authorities, the political mobilization of Republican loyalists against Burr demonstrated—at least to Jefferson's satisfaction—that westerners were prepared to meet any military challenge. Predictions of future strength thus gave way to the conviction that the union was already strong enough.

Jefferson's confidence was reflected in the aggressive posture his administration assumed in the deepening conflict with the European belligerents over violations of American neutral rights. In a letter to Kentuckian James Brown in late 1808, Jefferson suggested that Burr's failure had demonstrated not only the futility of separatist assaults on the union but how little need there was to "fear foreign invasion." Educated in federal and republican principles, Jefferson's countrymen transformed what the followers of Montesquieu considered the new nation's greatest liability—its size—into its greatest asset. As long as Americans resisted the seductive appeals of "foreign adventurers, and native malcontents," as long as they upheld and perfected a federal union that expressed and cultivated their better political natures, the line of separation between Europe and America would remain impregnable. "For myself," Jefferson told Brown, even in the "most flattering periods" of Burr's Conspiracy, "I never entertained one moment's fear. My long and intimate knowledge of my countrymen, satisfied and satisfies me, that let there ever be occasion to display the banners of the law, and the world will see how few and pitiful are those who shall array themselves in opposition."[93]

When Jefferson looked westward, he saw no limits to the "federative principle."[94] But such limits would become painfully clear as the unreconstructed "monarchists" of New England sought to subvert Jefferson's commercial diplomacy and then "Mr. Madison's War." If expansion to the west vindicated Jefferson's conception of union, the treason of eastern "parricides" threatened to destroy it. A union that would not embrace Missouri was not the same union that Jefferson and the Revolutionary fathers had established with the Declaration of Independence in 1776.

FIRST PRINCIPLES, LAST RITES

The Declaration of Independence is the classic statement of Jefferson's Revolutionary principles. The "self-evident" "truths" set forth in the second paragraph justified the colonists in severing all links with a British sovereign who had "evince[d] a design to reduce them under absolute Despotism." "All men are created equal," wrote Jefferson, and "they are endowed by their Creator with certain unalienable Rights, that among these are Life, Liberty and the pursuit of Happiness." Instituted in order "to secure these rights," governments derived "their just powers from the consent of the governed." Equality was the ultimate rationale for independence, dissolving all connections with the old imperial regime. For Jefferson, it was also the fundamental premise of a new federal republican system. George III's manifest design was to establish "an absolute Tyranny over these States"; by destroying the colonies as political communities, he would deprive the colonists of their liberty and property. To vindicate their rights as individuals, Americans would have to rally to the defense of their states, and those states in turn would have to forge an effective federal union. At each stage in this process, the consent of equals—individuals or states—was predicated on the absence of coercion or prior connection: disunion was the necessary precondition of union.[95]

Jefferson's federal design in the Declaration is most fully elaborated in passages (deleted by his congressional colleagues) that set forth his idealized version of the imperial relationship. "We might have been a free & a great people together," Jefferson wrote, "but a communication of grandeur & of freedom it seems is below . . . [the] dignity" of "these unfeeling [British] brethren." In Jefferson's imaginative account of colonial history, the first settlers in America had already established their independence through exercising the fundamental right of expatriation: "These [settlements] were effected at the expence of our own blood & treasure, unassisted by the wealth or the strength of Great Britain."[96] This original independence should have been the foundation for lasting union (a formulation many of Jefferson's colleagues probably found bafflingly paradoxical). "In constituting indeed our several forms of government," he explained, "we had adopted one common king, thereby laying a foundation for perpetual league & amity with them." In other words, a federal (treaty) relationship securing the equal rights of every member of the great imperial family would have been the constitutional foundation for "a free and a great" Anglo-American nation. But instead of offering peace, as family feelings naturally enjoined, the British chose to make war against the colonies, so giving "the last stab to agonizing affection."[97]

Nearly fifty years later, in 1821, when—in the midst of the Missouri crisis—Jefferson drafted his *Autobiography*, he was still disgusted with his "pusillanimous" colleagues for excising these passages, as well as the clause "reprobating the enslaving the inhabitants of Africa." Determined to set the record straight, Jefferson now offered his own version of the Declaration alongside the version adopted by Congress. Far from agreeing with most subsequent commentators that the excisions improved the text, eliminating potentially embarrassing and certainly confusing passages that would have alienated readers and listeners at home and abroad, Jefferson remained convinced that his message had been mutilated.[98] It was the motivations of the excisers, not his own, that demanded a closer look, for "the sentiments of men are known not only by what they receive, but what they reject also."[99] Jefferson, for his part, would stand by the "sentiments" his colleagues had denounced in 1776: they, not he, were the ones concerned with rhetorical effects. And the principles he had articulated in 1776 were of much more than historical interest in 1821: fidelity to those principles alone could preserve the union and vindicate American independence.

Jefferson's colleagues had revised his text for the same reason so many of them had dragged their feet on the question of independence itself. "The pusillanimous idea that we had friends in England worth keeping terms with, still haunted the minds of many," Jefferson recalled. "For this reason, those passages which conveyed censures on the people of England were struck out, lest they should give them offence." Jefferson presumably risked "offence" by postulating a familial relationship, even an identity, between the British and American people: the violation of these natural ties was the most hideous possible crime. Unwilling to recognize the hideousness of this crime, Jefferson's cautious colleagues revealed the limits of their own commitment to independence, a lingering sense of connection that ultimately would give rise to a monarchical party determined to reestablish British authority in the new nation on the most humiliatingly unequal terms. In retrospect, Jefferson may have imagined that his draft of the Declaration had drawn a "line of demarcation" between patriotic advocates of American principles and the reactionary avatars of the European old regime. But the blurring of that line by the mutilation of his text had left the door ajar for lukewarm friends and secret enemies to call themselves Revolutionaries—and then to subvert independence from within.

Jefferson's account of Congress's deliberations in 1776 thus constituted a kind of preface to the "history of the parties" he hoped some good Republican would undertake (in refutation of the Federalist version offered by John Marshall's *Life of Washington*) and that was told in the *Anas,* the three volumes of documents and commentaries on Jefferson's term as secretary of state that he collected in 1818.[100] But more was at stake in the *Autobiography* than getting the history of the Declaration right—or setting the stage for a proper understanding of the 1790s—and this was most conspicuously apparent in Jefferson's comments on the excision of his blistering attack on George III for "wag[ing] cruel war against human nature itself" by enslaving Africans and then resisting all colonial efforts to stop the slave trade. The question remained compelling in 1821: why had Jefferson's colleagues forfeited the opportunity to stake out the moral high ground? Why would they hesitate to dissociate themselves from this nefarious traffic in human beings or to lay responsibility for this "piratical warfare" at the feet of the supposedly "CHRISTIAN king of Great Britain?"[101]

Jefferson offered two related explanations for the failure of fellow congressmen to follow his lead on slavery, beyond the "pusillanimous" unwillingness of moderates who secretly hoped for reconciliation with the British. One was economic interest: "The clause . . . reprobating the enslaving the inhabitants of Africa, was struck out in complaisance to South Carolina and Georgia, who had never attempted to restrain the importation of slaves, and who on the contrary still wished to continue it." The other explanation was more complex and problematic, but much more relevant to the situation of American politics in 1821: the bad conscience of congressmen from the northern states. "Our northern brethren also I believe felt a little tender under those censures," wrote Jefferson, "for tho' their people have very few slaves themselves yet they had been pretty considerable carriers of them to others."[102] Northerners had an interest in the slave trade which they—unlike the Carolinians and Georgians—were unwilling to disclose; by 1821 this dissembling had evolved into self-righteous, hypocritical denial. (It was an article of faith for Jefferson and like-minded Old Republicans that northern prosperity continued to depend on slave-based plantation agriculture after the abolition of the slave trade in 1808.) Astonishingly (to Jefferson), northern restrictionists now had the gall to turn his moral indictment of George III back on Jefferson and his fellow planters—the long-suffering victims of a "piratical warfare" that had enriched no one more than the northerners themselves.

Jefferson's tortuous logic—either in 1776 or in 1821—hardly seems compelling to us today.[103] Yet Jefferson did establish, to his own satisfaction at least, that he had taken the most advanced possible position on slavery in 1776: he was prepared to identify the cause of American freedom with the "most sacred rights of life & liberty" of enslaved Africans.[104] But cautious congressional colleagues held back because they were not fully committed to a final break with Britain. Now, in the Missouri crisis, restrictionists feigned a solicitude for the slaves that could only be attributed to their determination to reverse the outcome of the American Revolution. Heedless of the "blessings of peace and self-government" that union alone could preserve, restrictionists raised the slavery extension issue as a "party trick" in order to gain power.[105] Yet, as any sincere opponent of slavery should know, emancipation was "more likely to be effected by union than by scission."[106] Restrictionist rhetoric notwithstanding, the real enemies of freedom in 1821, as in 1776, were those who resisted American independence and subverted the affectionate, harmonious union of citizens and states that was its only guarantee.

The passionate, blood-soaked language of rage and betrayal that Jefferson's colleagues excised from the Declaration—and that he restored in his *Autobiography* in 1821—was the same language that spilled out, seemingly beyond authorial control, in his despairing response to the Missouri crisis. Just as George III had administered "the last stab to agonizing affection" by waging war on the colonies, the American people—driven to distraction by the restrictionists—were now committing a hideous act of "suicide on themselves, and of treason against the hopes of the world."[107] In both cases family bonds were violated by "unfeeling brethren." Jefferson repeatedly recognized this perfect, awful symmetry: as he wrote William Short in April 1820, for the present generation "this treason against human hope, will signalize their epoch in future history, as the counterpart of the medal of their predecessors," the Revolutionary fathers.[108]

The powerful feelings manifest at these two crucial epochs may provide important clues to Jefferson's psychology. But we should respect his sense of the principles involved in both crises. Jefferson certainly did not believe that his resort to such highly charged language was prompted by propagandistic impulses to arouse and manipulate the anger of others (in the Declaration) or by a therapeutic impulse to give vent to the morbid sentiments of a disappointed and deluded old man (in his letters on the Missouri crisis). To invoke his own language against such reductive psychologizing, Jefferson might insist that reason and sentiment, the "Head and the Heart," were always in dialogue with one another, and nowhere more momentously than in the construction and preservation of the American union.

Jefferson was a constitutionalist, a man of reason ever vigilant against abuses of power, and a sentimental nationalist who believed in the natural harmony and affectionate union of all freedom-loving people. It was the duty of the head, with its "science," to guarantee the equality and integrity—the self-possession and self-preservation—of every free man and every free state. But "morals were too essential to the happiness of man to be risked on the incertain combinations of the head. She laid their foundation therefore in sentiment, not in science." Reason could devise a constitutional order that was the essential precondition of a union that it was itself impotent to achieve. The American Revolution was the greatest testimonial to the power of the heart, Jefferson explained to Maria Cosway in his letter of October 1786: "If our country, when pressed with wrongs at the point of the bayonet, had been governed by it's heads instead of it's hearts, where should we have been now?" The answer was: dead, "hanging on a gallows as high as Haman's."[109]

Union was meaningless without equality, an equality that made consent possible and gave rise to fellow feeling and affectionate attachment. Yet by the same logic, equality could not be sustained and its promise would not be fulfilled without union.

Jefferson was sorry to be in Philadelphia in the summer of 1776, for the real work of nation making was being done back in Virginia and its sister states, where new republican governments were being constituted. On his return to Virginia, Jefferson would more than compensate for having missed the chance of drafting the new state constitution (which he soon came to see as radically defective) by his herculean efforts as a republican lawmaker, law reformer, and executive.[110] And in 1784, during another brief tenure as a Virginia delegate to Congress before leaving for Paris, Jefferson took the leading role in drafting the first ordinance for the government of the union's western territory.

The rhetorical contrast between the 1784 ordinance and the emotionally charged Declaration could not be greater. Yet for Jefferson they were clearly complementary expressions of his conception of the American union—first from the heart, and then from the head. For it was crucial in 1784, as massive settlement of the West was already beginning, to lay down the fundamental principles that would govern relations between new states and old. The challenge was to create the conditions for union that the British had so conspicuously failed to secure for their erstwhile countrymen in America. The expansion and perfection of the union—and of American nationhood—depended on fostering republican government on the western frontier, on not recapitulating the tragic errors of the British by establishing a despotic, colonial regime.[111]

Jefferson's anticolonial vision rested on two integrally related premises. First, once a new western state (defined according to boundaries prescribed by the ordinance) crossed a minimal population threshold (20,000 free inhabitants), it should proceed to draft its own constitution, subject only to the proviso "that their respective governments shall be in republican forms, and shall admit no person to be a citizen, who holds any hereditary title." Then "whensoever any of the said states shall have, of free inhabitants, as many as shall then be in any one the least numerous of the thirteen original states, such state shall be admitted by it's delegates into the Congress of the United States, on an equal footing with the said original states," given the assent of the requisite number of existing states under the Articles of Confederation.[112] Significantly, in Jefferson's scheme a "state" existed as a self-constituted political community before it claimed admission. There would be no confusion then— as there was in the case of Missouri—about Congress's role in state constitution writing or in determining a state's "republican" character. For as Jefferson clearly intended in 1784, a state could only be a republic if it constituted itself, without outside interference, and if it was received into the union "on an equal footing."[113]

When Jefferson was in Paris, his ordinance was subjected to successive revisions and ultimately was superseded altogether by the Northwest Ordinance of 13 July 1787. Jefferson was troubled by the changes—most notably the redefinition of new state boundaries and provisions for a more elaborate scheme of "temporary" territorial government under congressional authority—but could take comfort in the fact that his successors had reaffirmed his fundamental principle, that new states be admitted "on an equal footing with the original States."[114] New state equality was essential to an expanding, harmonious union, just as the equality of the original states was the fundamental premise of the union Jefferson and his fellow Revolutionaries had established in 1776. This was the principle the restrictionists attacked in the Missouri crisis. In doing so, they rendered the federal Constitution a dead letter; they also revealed—and provoked—the hostile feelings that made affectionate union impossible and so betrayed the promise of Jefferson's Declaration of Independence.

The controversy over the admission of Missouri as a slave state constituted a crisis for the federal union. Few contemporaries personalized this crisis as much as Jefferson; most hoped that a spirit of compromise would preserve and sustain the union. Where Jefferson harked back to 1776, and so identified union with Independence, the compromisers of 1820–21 invoked the inspiring example of the federal Convention of 1787 and the "bundle of compromises" that had then enabled James Madison and his fellow founders to form a more perfect union.[115] In retrospect, with the devastation of the Civil War in view, we are inclined to honor Madison's union (inadequate as it may have been in the final crisis) and to lay the blame for its destruction at the feet of Jeffersonian states' rights advocates whose "union" proved to be no union at all.

The uncompromising, self-righteous, and dangerously doctrinaire Jefferson forms a striking contrast to the moderate, conciliatory, and statesmanlike Madison who devoted so much energy in his waning days to the preservation of his union.[116] Thus, even as Madison disowned the states' rights doctrines that he and his fellow Republicans had flirted with in 1798, Thomas Ritchie and the nullifiers of Virginia and South Carolina claimed Jefferson as their patron saint. After all, as Jefferson had written in his original version of the Kentucky Resolutions in October 1798, "where powers are assumed which have not been delegated [by the federal Constitution], a nullification of the act is the rightful remedy."[117] The genealogy of secession—from 1861 back to 1798, and then to 1776—seems straightforward enough; it was a genealogy that Jefferson's words and deeds authorized, and that Madison, defending the legacy of 1787, resisted to his dying day.[118]

Much can be said for this juxtaposition of Madison and Jefferson. But the story of Jefferson's Missouri crisis—not to mention the lifelong collaboration of these devoted friends—suggests that the juxtaposition obscures as much as it illuminates. Most revealing is the contrast between Jefferson's despairing, self-dramatizing, and ultimately tragic perspective on Missouri and the (characteristically American) note of optimistic self-righteousness struck by the southern states'-rightsers and proto-nationalists who invoked the authority of his principles.[119] Jefferson and Madison shared a common sense of foreboding about the future of the union, even as their legacies were deployed by opposing camps in the ideological crossfire that led to the Civil War. Or, it may be more accurately said that Jefferson, more deeply pessimistic than his friend, believed that the union had already been rent by the restrictionists' "geographical line," probably irrevocably. It was not an outcome he could view with equanimity. For Jefferson, the Missouri crisis marked the fundamental failure of the Revolution itself; far from welcoming the opportunity to put the states' rights "principles of 1798" into practice, Jefferson considered the fatal necessity of doing so a kind of death. To return to the first principles of 1776 was not to start afresh, an opportunity to invent the world anew; in sounding the "knell of the Union," in committing this "treason against the hopes of the world," the protagonists in the Missouri crisis had enacted the last rites for the great American experiment in federalism and republicanism. The obverse of the "medal" that had been struck to honor Jefferson and his fellow Revolutionaries was now being inscribed to the everlasting dishonor of their parricide sons.

A suddenly disillusioned old man, Jefferson may have indulged himself in a solipsistic fantasy of death and destruction. Yet in glimpsing the horrors of civil war, Jefferson was much more than a prophet of doom. Jefferson's despair in 1820 and 1821 illuminates the promise of 1776, the vision of a republican empire founded on enlightened principles that inspired many Americans with patriotic fervor. It also raised to the fore fundamental dilemmas of American republicanism that his countrymen would not face and could not resolve. The Missouri crisis juxtaposed the claims of state equality, self-constitution, and noninterference, the foundational premises of Jeffersonian federalism—and liberal internationalism—against restrictionist assertions that regimes founded on slavery could not be republican because they were not based on the free consent of their peoples.[120] In effect, the natural rights language of Jefferson's Declaration was turned against the equally natural rights of states to assert their equality and independence and so join in affectionate union.

These were and are America's dilemmas, not just Jefferson's. How can we reconcile the claims of individuals with the claims of states? How can guarantees of liberty and equality be made to serve, as Jefferson believed they must, as the threshold of harmonious union and true nationhood? How can we promote the sense of community, the dedication to common principles, the national identity, that would make claims of rights liberating and empowering? I offer these questions with trepidation, in a not quite hopeful spirit, for they were questions that drove a despairing Jefferson to imagine his own death and the destruction of his cherished union, thus "rendering desperate the experiment which was to decide ultimately whether man is capable of self-government."[121]

CHAPTER 5

"To Declare Them a Free and Independant People"

✿

THOMAS JEFFERSON, a lifelong enemy of tyranny and despotism, had no doubt that the institution of racial slavery in his beloved Commonwealth of Virginia was a crime against humanity. "I tremble for my country when I reflect that God is just," he wrote in Query XVIII of his *Notes on the State of Virginia.* Jefferson was convinced that God's "justice cannot sleep for ever: that considering numbers, nature and natural means only, a revolution of the wheel of fortune, an exchange of situation, is among possible events: that it may become probable by supernatural interference! The Almighty has no attribute which can take side with us in such a contest." White Virginians must work toward their slaves' "total emancipation," for their freedom was sure to come, whether "with the consent" or by the "extirpation" of their masters.[1]

This strikingly apocalyptic passage seems to erupt from the page, invoking a conception of divinity—a just, if not wrathful, God—nowhere else to be found in Jefferson's writings: no abolitionist could have framed the moral dilemma in such compelling terms. For modern readers, however, Jefferson's antislavery credentials are seriously compromised by the racist sentiments elaborated elsewhere in the *Notes.* In Query XIV Jefferson offered the "opinion" and betrayed the "suspicion" that blacks "are inferior to the whites in the endowments both of body and mind."[2] Offered in the properly philosophic spirit to Jefferson's enlightened European readers, these observations were tentative and circumspect: in subsequent correspondence he expressed his fervent "wish" that these speculations were mistaken.[3] But the testimony on the evil of slavery and the imperative of emancipation was unqualified and absolute, thus presumably expressing a deeper level of conviction. In this testimony we can find a principled and passionate Jefferson who earns our respect—all the more so, perhaps, because he was unable to transcend the prejudices of his day (in his case, masquerading as science).[4]

The common ground for Jefferson's ideas about both race and slavery is his understanding of American and African national identities. Jefferson could not offer a conclusive judgment on the mental and physical capabilities of his slaves; but he did know, with as much certainty as his own experience and observation could authorize, that African-American slaves constituted a distinct nation. The crimes against slaves therefore had to be understood in national terms; the captivity, transportation, and amalgamation of different African peoples made enslaved Afro-Virginians into a single people subject to the despotic sway of masters who treated individual slaves as their private property. Under "such circumstances," Jefferson wrote in Query XVIII, "the man must be a prodigy who can retain his manners and morals undepraved." There certainly were benevolent masters (Jefferson undoubtedly imagined himself to be one) who did not abuse their slaves, but all free Virginians shared in the collective responsibility, as members of a self-governing people, for the enslavement of the African people. The moral responsibility of those who, like Jefferson, took an active role in affairs of the Commonwealth was thus much greater than that of the individual slaveholder: "With what execration should the statesman be loaded, who permitting one half the citizens thus to trample on the rights of the other, transforms those into despots, and these into enemies, destroys the morals of the one part, and the amor patriae of the other."[5]

Jefferson invoked the language of the "law of nature and *nations*" in his efforts to articulate the claims of African (or Afro-Virginian) as well as American (or Virginian) nationhood.[6] "Nation" in this conventional usage did not yet have the powerfully affective, quasi-familial connotations that it would take on for romantic nationalists in subsequent decades. Yet the jurisprudence that had developed over many centuries among European sovereigns provided the conceptual framework for republican Revolutionaries who sought to justify their assault on monarchical authority. "Nation" proved to be a protean concept in this Age of Revolution, capable of taking on new meanings both for proponents of popular self-government and for those who sought to make sense of its antithesis: the institution of slavery.

Virginia slaves were a people without a country, a captive nation, forcibly restrained from vindicating their rights against their white oppressors. This half of the population could have no "amor patriae," "for if a slave can have a country in this world, it must be any other in preference to that in which he is born to live and labour for another."[7] The blacks and whites of Virginia were two distinct nations whose natural relationship was one of war, and the only arbiter between nations at war was a "just God."[8] Slavery was certainly a great evil, but it did at least postpone the day of reckoning, in the meantime enabling white Virginians to secure their own lives and liberties. "Justice is in one scale," Jefferson told former congressman John Holmes during the Missouri crisis, "and self-preservation [is] in the other."[9] According to the great natural law treatises, "self-preservation" was the first law of nature; should slavery be destroyed, the dogs of war would be unleashed, and "justice" would be done.[10]

Africans in Virginia were a captive nation, restrained from violent retaliation by the organized power of the state. Defining slavery as a state of war, Jefferson could only conceive of its abolition in terms of a peace that would secure the independence and integrity of two distinct nations, each with its own "country." For those who did not understand the problem of slavery in national terms, it might seem sufficient to emancipate the slaves, transform them into citizens, and so incorporate them into the larger community. Jefferson himself posed this alternative scenario. "It will probably be asked, Why not retain and incorporate the blacks into the state, and thus save the expence of supplying, by importation of white settlers, the vacancies they will leave?" Surely such a solution made sense in the case of individual slaves: whatever defects might be imputed to the black race in general, Virginian slaves clearly were sufficiently skillful to take the place of a European-style peasantry. But Jefferson insisted that such a rational accommodation was impossible: whites and blacks would continue to see each other in racial or national terms; indeed, awareness of national distinctions would become much more acute—and dangerous—as the institution of slavery ceased to define and secure them. The end of slavery would inaugurate the state of war that the institution had held in suspense, making whites more conscious of, and prone to act on, their "deep rooted prejudices" and giving blacks a radically empowering sense of their own history—"ten thousand recollections . . . of the injuries they have sustained"—that slavery had suppressed. If history was not enough to provoke violence, the reciprocal awareness of racial difference that it promoted would inevitably give rise to "new provocations," so "divid[ing] us into parties, and produc[ing] convulsions which will probably never end but in the extermination of the one or the other race."[11]

Jefferson's solution to the slavery problem proceeded from this diagnosis. The captive nation must be liberated, "colonized" in some new country that they could claim as their own, and thus be declared and recognized as "a free and independant people." National consciousness—a people's sense of acting (and being acted on) in history—was only the threshold of true national identity. For enslaved Africans, loosening the chains of bondage would revive collective memories of captivity and displacement, of being a people without a country. But if they could not return to their homeland (and this would be impossible without the assistance of their former masters), blacks could only hope to achieve nationhood by destroying the whites and making Virginia their own country.

Jefferson did not expect slaves or former slaves to emerge triumphant in this genocidal struggle—however "just" his God might be. But this only compounded his moral dilemma, for the African nation that had been unjustly captured and enslaved would then be exterminated by their former masters. Jefferson therefore concluded that the only humane and prudent policy was expatriation—from a country that blacks could not claim as their own without violence—and colonization in a new land. Only then could blacks secure true independence—the recognition of other peoples—and fulfill their national destiny. Only then would white Virginians have the opportunity to redeem themselves from their crimes against black Africa: instead of making war on their former slaves—the inevitable, tragic outcome of emancipation without colonization—white Virginia could "extend to them our alliance and protection, till they shall have acquired strength." At this glorious moment, to borrow the language of the American Declaration of Independence, the black nation would achieve its apotheosis, "assum[ing] among the powers of the earth the separate and equal station to which the Laws of Nature and of Nature's God entitle them."[12]

Jefferson first developed his colonization scheme in connection with the post-Revolutionary revisal of the Virginia laws. He never submitted the proposal to the assembly, believing, as he recalled in his *Autobiography* (1821), "that the public mind would not yet bear the proposition, nor will it bear it even at this day," forty years later. Given the slow, indeed imperceptible, progress of public opinion, it is extraordinary that Jefferson could continue to promote colonization until his dying day. But "nothing is more certainly written in the book of fate than that these people are to be free," he wrote in 1821; "nor is it less certain that the two races, equally free, cannot live in the same government. Nature, habit, opinion has drawn indelible lines of distinction between them."[13] Three years later, in a letter to Jared Sparks, Jefferson asserted yet again that "our physical and moral characters . . . , our happiness and safety" depended on providing "an asylum to which we can, by degrees, send the whole of that population from among us, and establish them under our patronage and protection, as a separate, free and independent people, in some country and climate friendly to human life and happiness."[14]

INDEPENDENCE AND NATIONAL IDENTITY

In Jefferson's mind the moral imperative of colonization, the certainty that it must one day come to pass, was inextricably connected with his conception of the meaning of American independence itself. The ultimate independence of the black nation would replicate and complete American independence. Both nations were the product of British despotism.

The juxtaposition of slavery and freedom was a central motif in American patriot rhetoric in the years of the imperial crisis. That slave owners like Jefferson could imagine that British efforts to rationalize imperial reform—and raise a relatively trivial amount of tax revenue— would reduce them to the condition of their own human chattel has al-

ways seemed hyperbolic. But I would suggest a somewhat different relationship between anxieties about enslavement, familiar to Real Whigs
all over the Anglophone world, and Jefferson's understanding of the institution. To sensitive provincials in Anglo-America, British imperial
policy signaled the ministry's determination to treat the Americans as a
distinct and subject people, lacking the rights that defined Britons as a
uniquely free people.[15]

American Revolutionaries understood enslavement in collective, not
individual, terms. Further, the threat of slavery was not a distant
prospect discernible only to paranoid provincials but rather an increasingly compelling depiction of the present relationship between the
British and American peoples. The crux of the problem was apparent in
Sir William Blackstone's formulation of the imperial connection is his
Commentaries: the colonies were "distinct, though dependent dominions."[16] Few Anglo-Americans aspired to either distinctness or its inevitable correlative, dependence. And it was anxiety about the implications of this sort of dependence, the inability of a powerless people to
determine its own destiny, that made slavery such a powerful trope in
resistance rhetoric.

Only with the greatest reluctance did patriot leaders begin to think
of themselves and their countrymen as a distinct "people": provincial aspirations ran quite the other way, toward assimilation in an inclusive
greater British identity.[17] But if the Americans were to be treated as a
distinct people, provincial patriots insisted, then they must be secured
in their rights as transplanted Britons by formal and explicit constitutional guarantees—that is, by the kind of "union" that was constituted
by treaties between independent states under the law of nations.[18] Anything less would leave the American people in a state of impotent subjection to their imperial masters.

According to the paradoxical logic of the Revolutionary movement,
independence from Britain became the functional substitute for identification with Britain; assuming a "separate & equal standing . . . among
the powers of the earth" would enable Americans to secure the glorious
legacy of liberty and law that they had once supposed to be the
birthright of British people everywhere. The new national identity of
the Americans was an unintended consequence of the protracted crisis

of the imperial constitution, a consciousness of distinctiveness imposed on reluctant provincials by the force of British arms. It was within the context of this process of national self-definition, the creation of two peoples—British and American—in the place of one British people, that Jefferson began to think of African slaves as a captive nation. Independence for America made the national liberation of enslaved Africans a moral imperative.

Jefferson's efforts to conceptualize both American and African nationality are apparent in his *Summary View of the Rights of British America,* drafted in 1774 as instructions for Virginia's delegates to the First Continental Congress. Although not officially endorsed by the House of Burgesses, the *Summary View* was widely circulated, attracting much favorable notice and—in ministerial circles—considerable notoriety.[19] In this pamphlet Jefferson elaborated the peculiar conception of monarchical authority that would frame the subsequent indictment of George III in the Declaration of Independence. The king, claimed Jefferson, was "the chief officer of the people," "the only mediatory power between the several states of the British empire."[20]

It was only through the royal connection, as peculiarly defined by Jefferson, that Britons and Americans constituted one united people. It was the king's "important post," Jefferson told George III, to hold "the balance of a great, if a well poised empire." This meant that he must not allow the British Parliament to legislate for America, for "every society must at all times possess within itself the sovereign powers of legislation." Only by the fullest recognition of the rights of a "free people" would it be possible to preserve "that harmony which alone can continue both to Great Britain and America the reciprocal advantages of their connection. It is neither our wish, nor our interest, to separate from her. We are willing, on our part, to sacrifice every thing which reason can ask to the restoration of that tranquility for which all must wish." "Union" thus took on a double meaning for Jefferson, connoting both identity with the British people through submission "to the same common sovereign" and the equality of distinct political societies—or peoples— within the empire, to be established on "a generous plan."[21]

In order to justify the claim that Americans constituted a "free people," Jefferson rewrote colonial history: it was this history that provided the paradigm for his conception of black nationhood. He began with the premise that the original colonists, like "their Saxon ancestors" who had emigrated to Britain, were "free inhabitants of the British dominions in Europe" who "possessed a right which nature has given to all men, of departing from the country in which chance, not choice, has placed them, of going in quest of new habitations, and of there establishing new societies, under such laws and regulations as to them shall seem most likely to promote public happiness."[22] Jefferson's version of the Saxon myth, stipulating a primal national identity and a latent claim to independence for all migrating peoples, offered a narrative account of how the Americans could now find themselves on the threshold of independence, claiming equality in the empire as a question of right, not royal favor. This invented history also threw the forced migration of enslaved Africans to the New World into stark relief: indeed, the captivity of the blacks constituted the reverse image of Jefferson's right of expatriation, and an ominous portent of what the American people could expect for themselves should the British ministry's conception of the imperial relationship—and its interpretation of American colonial history—prevail.

Jefferson claimed in the *Summary View* that "the abolition of domestic slavery is the great object of desire in those colonies, where it was unhappily introduced in their infant state." This extraordinary assertion is hard for modern readers to take seriously: it was only in the last few years that the House of Burgesses had attempted to regulate the importation of slaves, and few if any would have acknowledged the intention Jefferson imputed to its members of wanting to abolish the institution. Yet, just as ministerial tyranny jolted Virginians into belated consciousness of their own history, one of those tyrannical acts—the Privy Council's veto of the colony's act to impose a small duty on slave imports—enabled Jefferson suddenly to see the situation of Virginia's slaves in a broad historical and geopolitical context. Before these slaves could be freed, "it is necessary to exclude all further importations from Africa," explained Jefferson, "yet our repeated attempts to effect this by prohibitions, and by imposing duties which might amount to a prohibition, have been hitherto defeated by his majesty's negative."[23]

White Virginians became aware of a ministerial plot to reduce them to slavery at the precise moment when they sought to prepare the way for the "enfranchisement" of their slaves. It was now appallingly clear that George III preferred "the immediate advantages of a few African corsairs to the lasting interests of the American states, and to the rights of human nature, deeply wounded by this infamous practice."[24] The king had already committed far greater crimes against the enslaved Africans, but his failure to consult "the lasting interests" of the colonies portended a similar fate for them. White Virginians and enslaved Africans thus constituted distinct nations, defined respectively by the state of war in which the estranged colonists found themselves with their king and by the debased condition in which they found their slaves, innocent victims of the British slave traders' war against human nature.

Jefferson's *Summary View* thus depicted the colonial era as a history of three peoples—British, American, and African—whose distinct identities only began to come into focus during the imperial crisis. What remained unclear were the implications of these national distinctions for the institution of domestic slavery itself. Jefferson's discourse emphasized the common experience of Africans and Americans, once and future victims of British belligerence. But if British traders had enslaved innocent Africans, Americans compounded the crime (however unwillingly) by holding them in continuing captivity. Thus, through no fault of their own, Americans found themselves in a state of war with their slaves. Jefferson's conception of enslaved Africans as a captive nation whose very existence as a nation implied perpetual war against their American masters was, not coincidentally, most fully elaborated when the Americans finally declared their own independence, asserting their national distinction from Britain.

Jefferson's original draft of the Declaration of Independence featured his most eloquent statement on the injustices committed against the black nation. By promoting the slave trade, George III "has waged cruel war against human nature itself, violating it's most sacred rights of life & liberty in the persons of a distant people who never offended him, captivating & carrying them into slavery in another hemisphere, or to incur miserable death in their transportation thither." The Africans, victims of the king's "piratical warfare," stood as proxies for the whole hu-

man race, stripped of their national identity and therefore of the freedom to make their own history. "Determined to keep open a market
where MEN should be bought & sold, [George III] has prostituted his
negative for suppressing every legislative attempt to prohibit or to restrain this execrable commerce." In the interest of this unnatural trade,
he has preempted every effort to liberate the nation that he and his
predecessors had reduced to captivity. The only hope for enslaved
Africans was a war of self-liberation against their American masters: "He
is now exciting those very people to rise in arms among us, and to purchase that liberty of which *he* has deprived them, by murdering the people upon whom *he* also obtruded them; thus paying off former crimes
committed against the *liberties* of one people, with crimes which he
urges them to commit against the *lives* of another."[25]

Critical commentators agree that the passages on slavery and the
slave trade in Jefferson's original draft of the Declaration were extravagantly and embarrassingly excessive. The idea that George III was somehow responsible for American slavery—and the implication that the
Americans, whose prosperity was based on slave labor, were not responsible—was not likely to command the respect of a "candid world."[26] Yet,
if the critics had a much surer sense of how prospective readers would
respond, Jefferson's rhetoric accurately registered his own complicated
sense of the dilemmas that independence would both resolve and pre-
cipitate. For Jefferson was not only declaring a state of war between the
British and American nations, he was also acknowledging the nationhood of enslaved Africans and the legitimacy of their claims to independence.

The passage on slavery that was eliminated by Jefferson's congressional editors was the culminating charge in a series of charges establishing that George III, having long since withdrawn his "protection" and
"declaring us out of his allegiance," was making war on a people who
had until this moment mistakenly thought of themselves as his subjects.
Significantly, the "allegiance & protection" formulation was also edited
out of the Declaration's final draft. For Jefferson, as for other students of
the law of nations, the abrogation of the protection covenant constituted the crucial pivot between domestic and international politics: king
and people now confronted each other as hostile powers in a state of

war. This invocation of the state of war was designed to introduce and illuminate the specific instances of George's barbaric belligerence that followed: military and naval assaults that "destroyed the lives of our people"; the resort to "foreign mercenaries"; his stirring up of "merciless Indian savages" on the frontiers and "treasonable insurrections in our fellow-subjects." But Congress's elimination of the "allegiance & protection" clause meant that the particular point of Jefferson's catalog of transgressions, culminating in the indictment of George for his role in the slave trade, was lost. Instead, these horrors were simply assimilated to the "long train of abuses & usurpations" previously set forth, no longer functioning as evidence for Jefferson's crucial claim, that the British king was waging war against his American colonies.[27]

Jefferson's conception of the slaves as a captive nation was brought into sharp focus by Lord Dunmore's proclamation of 7 November 1775 offering freedom to Virginian slaves who would help him suppress the American rebellion.[28] The escaping royal governor's desperate ploy had little immediate impact, beyond encouraging a rash of runaways. But sensitive patriots like Jefferson could not now escape the realization that their own struggle to define themselves as a people necessarily implicated the fate of enslaved Africans as a people. Dunmore's emancipation proclamation showed that the same arbitrary and despotic power that had established the institution of slavery could destroy it. In Jefferson's formulation the very *"lives"* of his countrymen, the self-preservation of Virginians as a people, depended on depriving enslaved Africans of their *"liberties."* Slavery thus stood exposed as an unnatural and illegitimate form of despotic rule, an armed peace that would give rise to violent conflict if the balance of forces should ever permit.

Jefferson's black nation thus emerged in counterpoint to his conception of a distinct and independent American people, defined in opposition to the British people. In Revolutionary retrospect, the history of the Americans, a free people who exercised their natural right of expatriation to found new societies in the New World, was starkly juxtaposed to the captivity of the Africans, forcibly removed to a strange land they could never possess as their own. But war threatened to be the great equalizer: by exercising preponderant power, the British would destroy American independence and reduce a free people to slavery; at the same time, they offered an unholy alliance to enslaved Africans, promising to annihilate their white masters and liberate them from captivity.

In the moral accounting of Jefferson's draft of the Declaration, the greatest crimes had been committed against the slaves, and the British sovereign was responsible for them: if a "just God" determined the fate of nations, as Jefferson later wrote in his *Notes on Virginia,* the slaves' liberation was inevitable. Yet it was not clear how justice could be done to them without jeopardizing the just claims of the American people to a "separate and equal station" among the family of nations. Jefferson recognized that the vital interests of Americans and Africans were fundamentally opposed: they were two distinct peoples whose natural relation, institutionalized and contained by slavery, was a state of war, a latent condition made manifest by the destruction of the imperial old regime and the prospect of successful servile insurrection. In seeking to achieve their own independence, the slaves would serve as the unwitting tools of their British allies, slaughtering their former masters and claiming the "country" of Virginia as their own.

The apparent clarity of Jefferson's indictment of George III, the projection (and denial) of moral responsibility, gave way in the actual circumstances of revolutionary war to a much more complex and ambiguous scenario. The American cause may have been morally and strategically compromised by slavery, but the struggle for black freedom was equally compromised by the malign intentions of its British sponsors to enslave the Americans. Jefferson's congressional editors may have been as troubled by the moral impasse suggested by this passage, the irreconcilable conflict of two distinct and naturally inimical peoples for control of a single country, as by the moralistic indictment of George III. For if Jefferson declared the independence of the Americans as a people, he also conjured up another people, held captive in America, whose claims to a "separate and equal station" were equally compelling.[29]

NATION AND RACE

Scholars have offered a wide array of intellectual and personal sources for Jefferson's ideas about racial difference.[30] My suggestion here is that Jefferson's conception of race proceeded from his recognition of distinct national identities—African, British, and American—during the extended Revolutionary crisis. Real Whig rhetoric of enslavement combined with the real world experience of sustaining racial order through the institution of slavery enabled Jefferson to see slaves collectively, as a people defined by the "unremitting despotism" of another people, their Virginian masters.

Before the imperial crisis Jefferson and his countrymen had had little reason to think of themselves and their human property in such generalized terms. "Nursed and educated in the daily habit of seeing the [slaves'] degraded condition," Jefferson recalled in 1814, few colonial Virginians "doubted but that they were as legitimate subjects of property as their horses and cattle. The quiet and monotonous course of colonial life has been disturbed by no alarm, and little reflection on the value of liberty." But when Virginians began to reflect, becoming conscious that their own rights were vulnerable, the debased, rights-less condition of the slaves suddenly became conspicuous—at least it did so for Jefferson and other progressive patriots. They could only conclude that the slaves' "degradation" was not natural but "was very much the work of themselves & their fathers." Aroused from their monotonous, unreflecting condition, Revolutionary Virginians became conscious of themselves and their slaves as distinct peoples.[31] Embracing the universalizing tendencies of Enlightenment thought, and particularly the teachings of law of nations writers on national self-determination, Jefferson could envision the day when blacks as well as whites would gain equality and independence as a separate people.

The terms "race," "nation," and "people" were not yet clearly distinguished before the era of the American Revolution. "Race" was understood to mean "tribe, nation, or people, regarded as of common stock"; only in the late eighteenth century (the first reference is from 1774) did a more familiar, modern notion of race begin to emerge: "one of the great divisions of mankind, having certain physical peculiarities in common." Meanwhile, the definition of "nation," originally referring simply to a "distinct race or people," also began to take on its modern meaning; a nation was "usually organized as a separate political state and occupying a definite territory."[32]

The American Revolutionary crisis precipitated a process of conceptual definition. As the American people broke away from, and defined themselves against, the British people, their nation became self-consciously political. "We might have been a free & a great people together," Jefferson wrote in his draft of the Declaration, but George's tyranny forced the colonists "to dissolve the political bands" that had constituted Anglo-American union. The social contract ideas of the Declaration's second paragraph, the claim that governments derive "their just powers from the consent of the governed," offered a theoretical rationale and mythic historical pedigree for this political definition of American nationhood. The exigencies of political and military mobilization further muted the traditional emphasis on race or ethnicity (derivation from a "common stock") in defining the new nation: in America, consent would supersede descent—at least in theory.[33]

Similarly, Jefferson's thinking about race began with the image of a powerless people or captive nation, the inverse image of the Americans' consensual community. The African nation did not govern itself, nor did it occupy "a definite territory" that it could claim as its own, but these national defects were not the inevitable consequence of a "natural," racial inferiority. On the contrary, enslavement and expatriation had deprived Africans of their natural rights, even as captivity defined their national identity. Provision for and recognition of the equality and independence of the black nation remained a moral imperative for Jefferson throughout his career. For national self-determination was the threshold and precondition of the moral life that distinguished humans from brute creation; it followed that the ultimate moral responsibility of one people toward another was to acknowledge and respect its independence as a people.[34] A "just God" therefore would punish the Virginians for their failure to emancipate their slaves and "declare them a free and independent people."

Jefferson's generalizing about racial characteristics, most provocatively conspicuous in the *Notes on Virginia,* may have set the pattern for modern American racism. But Jefferson's main concern in the *Notes* was to define and secure national identities; having conceptualized masters and slaves as two nations in a state of war, his proposal for African expatriation and colonization constituted a peace plan, the only way the two nations could recognize each other's equality and independence. But

Jefferson's project proved deeply problematic. The invidious distinctions he invoked in Query XIV reflect the conceptual and practical difficulties he faced in defining two distinct, and necessarily antagonistic, national identities in a single country.

The British invaded and nearly destroyed Virginia in the months immediately preceding Jefferson's retirement as war governor (in June 1781), when he began drafting the *Notes*. With British encouragement thousands of Virginia slaves, including some thirty from Jefferson's Elkhill plantation, escaped to freedom, some to fight against their former masters.[35] Jefferson's conception of a triangular conflict, with the captive black nation throwing off the shackles of bondage in order to serve as British auxiliaries, now seemed prophetic: under conditions of armed conflict, "liberty" for the slaves could only mean "death" for their erstwhile masters. Jefferson's sense that the vital interests of the two nations were fundamentally and irreconcilably opposed proceeded from his construction of national identities in the imperial crisis and was confirmed by the experience of revolutionary war. That war also, inevitably, gave rise to the inimical feelings, the "deep rooted prejudices," that Jefferson himself so fully expressed in the *Notes*.

Yet Jefferson was not simply blaming the innocent victim here or demonizing the "other." His developing conception of the American (or Virginian) nation did not provide any space (literally) for the emancipation and amalgamation of freedpeople into a more inclusive national identity. On one hand, "justice" to the captive nation demanded a national solution, one that would provide the black people with a country of their own, not solutions that might do justice to individuals but would obliterate the nation, thus compounding the slave traders' original crime. Nor would justice be served by depriving (white) Virginians of their country, reversing the roles of captors and captives and so sustaining the state of war between them. For Jefferson, the direct and unmediated relation between a people and its country, expressed most eloquently in his celebrations of agrarian virtue, was the foundation of American national identity.

The classic statement of Jefferson's agrarian theory comes in Query XIX of the *Notes*, immediately succeeding his discussion in XVIII of the pernicious effects of slavery on the manners and morals of Virginians.

The contrast between the images of Virginia in the two queries is striking. In XVIII ("Manners") Jefferson depicted a deeply divided state on the verge of civil war: "The whole commerce between master and slave is a perpetual exercise of the most boisterous passions, the most unremitting despotism on the one part, and degrading submissions on the other." The slaves clearly had no "amor patriae," no property in or loyalty to the country in which they labored; but slavery also had the effect of alienating masters from a direct, unmediated relation to the land, defining them instead by the despotic power they exercised over their human property.[36]

Committed to a perpetual and unjust war against a captive people, slave owners could never love their country or pursue the ways of peace as did the yeomen patriots of Query XIX ("Manufactures"). That query was ostensibly devoted to a discussion of the principle advocated by European political economists, "that every state should endeavour to manufacture for itself." Jefferson challenged this conventional wisdom, suggesting that manufactures would introduce dangerously foreign elements into the bosom of the Commonwealth. Factory operatives could not be virtuous, independent republican citizens: "Dependance begets subservience and venality"; "the mobs of great cities add just so much to the support of pure government, as sores do to the strength of the human body." Excising these corrupt, disease-prone parts of the body politic, Jefferson defined Virginia in the image of the virtuous remnant. "Those who labour in the earth are the chosen people of God," wrote Jefferson, "if ever he had a chosen people, whose breasts he has made his peculiar deposit for substantial and genuine virtue."[37] Slave owners could not claim this sort of virtuous relation to the land. Indeed, the strong implication of these passages was that the plantation, site of "the most unremitting despotism," was another, perhaps even more dangerous excrescence on the body of the Commonwealth.

Jefferson's great concern in these queries was with patriotism and public virtue.[38] Reflecting his sense of Virginia's vulnerability in the Revolution (and the poor performance of his own administration), Jefferson contrasted the internal divisions of a slaveholding oligarchy with an idealized image of a unified republic of patriotic freeholders. This imagined community was free of slaveholders and of slaves.[39] For it was only by the expatriation and colonization of the captive nation that (white) Virginians could become true patriots, enjoying the unmediated relation between a people and its territory that for Jefferson defined love of country.

Jefferson's use of the word "labour" in Query XIX evoked the familiar Lockean formula for property creation in the state of nature, a formula that could validate the claims of the first settlers of Virginia and their descendants against the proprietorial pretensions of the British crown.[40] The linking of "labour" and "virtue" in this passage also suggests a more generalized connection between Virginians collectively and the land they cultivated: agrarianism becomes synonymous with patriotism. Slaves, by contrast, could have no country, precisely because they "live and labour for another."

In a letter to Angelica Church in 1793, Jefferson put the best possible construction on the condition of his slaves, defining his role as a benevolent slaveholder as "watch[ing] for the happiness of those who labor for mine."[41] Jefferson thus reversed the classic formulation of his Declaration, with "happiness" here defined as a passive condition dependent on the will of another, not as the object of an active "pursuit." The allusion to the Declaration was probably unintended, though it perfectly parallels Jefferson's surely self-conscious reference in the *Notes*, when he proposed "to declare them a free and independant people."[42] In both cases the contrast between the activity of free Americans and the passivity of enslaved Africans is absolute. It was the difference between a people having a country within which to pursue happiness, the "immensity of land courting the industry of the husbandman" that Jefferson celebrated in Query XIX, and a people without a country.[43]

Jefferson's definition of American patriotism as the quasi-organic relation between an industrious people and a fertile continent, proceeding from the forefathers' primal appropriation of the land, anticipated romantic and racialist constructions of national identity in the nineteenth century.[44] It also reflected his concerns as a republican theorist determined to deconstruct and dismantle the old regime. The master principle of aristocracy and monarchy was that all men are created unequal, that certain privileged persons and families were entitled to impose their will (and live off the labor) of others. This was the principle that authorized enlightened Revolutionaries, in seeking to vindicate the claims of a universalized "human nature," to frame their indictment of British imperial policy in terms of the fundamental opposition between "slavery" and "freedom." Yet despotic rule destroyed public liberty, the historical claim of particular peoples to self-determination, within specific national contexts. The violation of natural rights thus became manifest when a people was divided against itself, with rulers and ruled in effect constituting distinct peoples, or when its rulers sought to divide a people from its patrimony.[45]

The American people became conscious of its national identity when the British asserted the right to give rule to their putative American subjects. For Jefferson the British threat to American liberty became suddenly conspicuous when a corrupt ministry sought to transform the feudal fiction that "all lands in England were held either mediately or immediately of the crown" into a British claim to American property. When George III increased the "terms of purchase," Jefferson explained in the *Summary View,* the fiction of royal proprietorship was exploded: it was now time to "declare that [the king] has no right to grant lands of himself." As long as his exactions were not onerous, Americans were happy to acknowledge their allegiance to the king and proud to think of themselves as Britons. But that identity was called into question when Virginians suddenly found "the acquisition of lands . . . difficult," lands which they now understood to be their own by right. "From the nature and purpose of civil institutions," Jefferson concluded, "all the lands within the limits which any particular society has circumscribed around itself are assumed by that society, and subject to their allotment only."[46]

African slaves were no part of the Virginian "society" or "people" whose claims to the American land were being jeopardized by British imperial policy. Indeed, the whole point of the patriotic resistance was to preempt the claims of a "foreign" people to the American patrimony. It was undoubtedly difficult for the more reluctant Revolutionaries to reach the conclusion that the British were in fact foreigners—that is, that they themselves were not Britons. But the foreignness of enslaved Africans, whatever the injustices committed against them, was "self-evident" to Jefferson and his countrymen. Revolutionary warfare reinforced the conviction that this captive nation was necessarily inimical, and that its freedom would entail the expropriation of the country it-self—unless these foreigners were sent away, to some other, far distant country.

The imperial crisis forced Virginians to define and defend the boundaries of their political society. The Virginian "people," Jefferson suggested, was something more than a random aggregation of inhabi-tants: its members must share common values, they must respect each other's equal rights, and they must form consensual bonds of mutual obligation. In Query VIII ("Population"), Jefferson emphasized the im-portance of harmony and homogeneity in a self-governing republic: "It is for the happiness of those united in society to harmonize as much as possible in matters which they must of necessity transact together. Civil government being the sole object of forming societies, its administra-tion must be conducted by common consent."[47]

Members of any particular society must embrace the principles that animate its constitution, and "ours perhaps are more peculiar than those of any other in the universe."[48] Virginia's constitution might be founded on universal principles (it was "a composition of the freest principles of the English constitution, with others derived from natural right and natural reason"), but it was "peculiar" to Virginia and alien to "foreign-ers" raised under monarchical regimes. Promiscuous immigration thus threatened to render Virginia "a heterogeneous, incoherent, distracted mass." Throwing off the shackles of monarchical rule, immigrants would be all too prone to "an unbounded licentiousness, passing, as is usual, from one extreme to another." Of course, this danger was much more acute in the case of slaves. In seeking release from bondage (and vengeance against their oppressors), the captive nation could hardly be expected "to stop precisely at the point of temperate liberty." By defini-tion, the "unremitting despotism" of slavery, the chronic state of war be-tween whites and blacks, precluded their amalgamation into a consen-sual community. The growing population of slaves in Virginia was therefore "a great political and moral evil."[49]

Jefferson's discussion of the problematic assimilation of immigrants points to the crucial importance of education, the intergenerational transmission of values, in his republican theory.[50] His premise was that "principles" of government, like language, passed from one generation to the next, so determining national character. Of course, immigrants and their children were to some extent educable, particularly if their numbers were limited and they were dispersed evenly throughout the country. Under these optimal conditions "importations of foreigners" could augment the "natural propagation" of the native-born population in a way that would promote the Commonwealth's economic development without jeopardizing its political unity. Regulating the flow of immigration therefore was a crucial policy question. Properly socialized, immigrants would become assimilated with and indistinguishable from the native population: intermarriage would produce a new generation of Virginians, leaving no stain or "blot in our country."[51]

Jefferson believed that each generation should be free to constitute its own government, untrammeled by the "dead hand" of the past. *"The earth belongs in usufruct to the living,"* Jefferson wrote James Madison in September 1789, in the most elaborate formulation of his doctrine. Generally celebrated as a classic statement of radical democratic theory, Jefferson's conception of generational independence—"One generation is to another as one independant nation to another"—also suggests a quasi-familial, proto-racialist definition of the "people."[52] Jefferson defined the "living" generation in terms of its relation to—and liberation from—the generation of the fathers; these generations were linked to each other by stewardship of their patrimony, the transcendentally binding obligation of "usufruct." Jefferson thus meant to establish simultaneously the absolute "independence" of a self-governing generation or people and, somewhat paradoxically, its absolute responsibility to preserve the collective estate entire for the benefit of future generations—a fundamental limitation on its freedom of action.

Jefferson's conception of Virginians as a people democratized the aristocratic principle of legally privileged, putatively immortal families with their inviolable domains. But the genealogical premise was still present in a sublimated form, with all Virginian families tied together by complex and diffuse bonds of kinship—or by the prospect of future marriages—and all sharing in the great public estate. In aristocratic societies a few families monopolized the land at the expense of all others; but families would be legally equal in republican Virginia, where the new state legislature followed Jefferson's lead in abolishing primogeniture and entail, legal devices for preserving aristocratic estates. Jefferson also sought to sustain a regime of family equality by guaranteeing easy and equitable access to public lands, now defined as the patrimony of all Virginians.[53]

Jefferson's reciprocal conceptions of Virginia as a country and of Virginians as a people thus worked to exclude the captive nation of enslaved Africans. Virginia was the country of the present generation of Virginians, the legacy of the colony's first settlers, guaranteed to their posterity by the principle of intergenerational stewardship. It was the common estate or patrimony that an arbitrary and despotic imperial government had sought to despoil and that independence had secured. It could not be the country of slaves forcibly removed from their homeland to work for others.

The power and prosperity of the new nation clearly would benefit from rapid population growth. "The present desire of America is to produce rapid population by as great importations of foreigners as possible."[54] But it was crucial that foreigners be assimilated to, and ultimately amalgamated with, the native-born population. The Virginian people could only sustain its republican character across generations if immigrants and their children were free to forge marital alliances with natives. Jefferson's conception of Virginia as a great kinship connection thus made marriage the implicit threshold to full incorporation in an inclusive, consensual citizen body. But for enslaved Africans, marriage—or, rather, its impossibility—was a boundary, not a threshold. Under the laws of Virginia, the distinction between slavery and freedom was absolute: it could not be transcended or dissolved through conjugal union. So too, according to Jefferson's understanding of the "natural" relationship between two warring nations, miscegenation was a dangerous, unnatural transgression.[55]

Jefferson's extended commentary on racial differences in Query XIV of the *Notes* makes manifest his conception of the sexual boundaries of Virginia's national identity. The discussion of difference was prefaced and framed by Jefferson's depiction of slavery as a state of war. In explaining why interracial hostility would persist even after emancipation, Jefferson cited various causes—"prejudices," "recollections," "new provocations"—including "the real distinctions which nature has made." At this point the "distinctions" were not yet invidious; they only became so when Jefferson turned from skin color, the "first difference which strikes us" and one that, whatever its source, was "fixed in nature," to standards of beauty and sexual attractiveness.[56]

That whites could claim a "greater . . . share of beauty" was self-evident to Jefferson, a judgment that was confirmed by the sexual preference of black men for white women. This supposed preference, analogous to "the preference of the Oran-ootan for the black women over those of his own species," located whites and blacks along a sexualized "great chain of being," licensing Jefferson to depict slaves as animals. "The circumstance of superior beauty, is thought worthy attention in the propagation of our horses, dogs, and other domestic animals; why not in that of man?"[57] But it should be noted that whites also participated in this sexual economy, however high on the chain they might be; indeed, as the compelling work of Annette Gordon-Reed strongly suggests, Jefferson himself later entered into a long-term miscegenous relationship with his slave Sally Hemings (DNA tests provide additional evidence they had at least one child).[58] From the "philosophical" perspective of the *Notes,* men mating (white or black) could be considered animals; so too were men at war, as "nations turn[ed] tigers . . . plundering and murdering one another."[59] Sex and war converged for Jefferson in the horrific image of a great struggle, ending only "in the extermination of the one or the other race," for possession of beautiful white women, the wives and mothers of republican Virginia.[60]

Jefferson then shifted his attention from sexual relations and family formation to the inferior "faculties of reason and imagination" that would keep the progeny of slaves from ever attaining the level of education that would permit assimilation with white Virginians. Basing his argument on comparisons with Native Americans (who lacked the great "advantages" of sustained contact with civilized Europeans) and with the white slaves of antiquity (whose condition "was much more deplorable than that of the blacks on the continent of America"), Jefferson tried to persuade himself that race was a crucial determinant in explaining the degraded condition of Virginia's slaves. Yet, as Jefferson well knew, differences rooted in nature could never adequately explain or justify the deleterious effects of conquest, captivity, and exploitation on the African nation. This is why his commentary concludes so weakly, with "a suspicion only, that the blacks, whether originally a distinct race, or made distinct by time and circumstances, are inferior to the whites in the endowments both of body and mind."[61]

Jefferson's sustained assault on the physical attributes and mental abilities of enslaved Africans helps illuminate his conception of white Virginians as a distinct "people." The presence of two peoples in one country, and their conspicuous tendency to mix, jeopardized the integrity of both. Sexual selection and family formation constituted the critical moment in the history of a people. But this was a moment of great vulnerability, when sexual liaisons could transgress and compromise the "natural" boundaries that distinguished nations at war. Jefferson's advocacy of scientifically managed breeding may have reduced "man" to the level of "domestic animals," pointing ominously toward the eugenic theories of later generations of scientific racists. But his primary intention was to secure the sexual frontier between two nations, translating his fantasy of a clear (impregnable?) boundary into a morally imperative law of nature.

For Jefferson, all the people in Virginia did not constitute the people of Virginia. His elaboration of racial distinctions, "fixed in nature" but jeopardized by myriad individual transgressions, marked the national boundary that the people of Virginia would have to defend if they meant to sustain their character as a people. "Nature" needed all the help it could get in rectifying the profoundly unnatural effects of the coinhabitance of two peoples in one country. Jefferson's formulation of the separationist imperative, predicated as it was on his "suspicion" of black inferiority, was framed in appropriately tentative, "philosophic" terms. The "lover of natural history," defined by Jefferson as someone "who views the gradations in all the races of animals with the eye of philosophy," must "excuse an effort to keep those in the department of man as distinct as nature has formed them." But there was nothing equivocal about Jefferson's revulsion against race mixing, "this blot in our country," or about the "efforts" he thought his countrymen should make to remove it.[62]

ADAM AND EVE

Virginians defined themselves as a people against the British, with whom they had once identified, by emphasizing their fealty to republican principles and the rights of man. But the definition of the national boundary between Virginians and the captive nation of enslaved Africans emphasized the local and the particular, bringing to the fore a quasi-familial, proto-racialist conception of a "people" in a natural, historic relationship to its "country." These conceptions of nationhood, cosmopolitan and particularist, may seem contradictory to us, but they were deeply, dialectically linked for Jefferson and his countrymen. Jefferson's understanding of the larger community of enslaved African Virginians as a "nation" in captivity reflected the teachings of the most enlightened treatises on the law of nature and nations; yet the idea of "nation" articulated in these treatises promoted a search for satisfying and legitimizing narratives of national origins that, like Jefferson's Saxon myth, privileged the unique history of a particular people. Jefferson's sense of Virginians as a people and Virginia as a country thus reflected the parochialism of the Anglo-American common law mind as well his imaginative effort to rationalize and reconcile the rights of warring nations.

The conjunction and confusion of what we take to be distinct intellectual traditions and the unstable and protean character of key concepts such as "nation," "race," and "people" enabled provincial Americans to envision and enact such radical and far-ranging changes in their world. They "invented" a people, or perhaps, more interestingly and ambiguously, they imagined one world made up of many distinct peoples, each with a just claim to self-rule.[63] Popular sovereignty, the revolutionary idea that legitimate authority derives from the consent of the people, may be a "fiction" or delusion.[64] Yet the most compelling work of the Revolutionary generation was much more concrete: to define and reconcile the national identities and interests of particular peoples—in America and across the world. The irony, or tragedy, of American race relations is that the very way Jefferson and other enlightened Revolutionaries defined the problem of slavery, as a state of war between two distinct peoples—as a national problem demanding a national solution—preempted and precluded the enfranchisement and assimilation of individuals. The failure of colonization schemes meant that the captive nation would not be empowered to assume its equal station in the family of nations, thus betraying the original promise and logical corollary of the American Revolution: the self-determination of all peoples.

Jefferson's conception of national identities was clearly articulated in the "Adam and Eve" letter he wrote to his protégé the young diplomat William Short in January 1793. Short had been writing to Secretary of State Jefferson from Paris, reporting and bemoaning the fate of their moderate constitutionalist friends. Convinced that the French Revolution's excesses were the inevitable, if regrettable, consequence of the great republican struggle against monarchical despotism that the American Revolution had inaugurated, Jefferson warned Short that his sentiments "would be extremely disrelished if known to your countrymen." "I know your republicanism to be pure," Jefferson concluded, "and that it is no decay of that which has embittered you against it's votaries in France, but too great a sensibility at the partial evil by which it's object has been accomplished there." But Short must be careful not to give unwitting aid and comfort to the enemies of republicanism in France or in America.[65]

The most chilling and controversial passages in the letter to Short offer an apologia for revolutionary violence. Jefferson deplored the losses of innocent life, "but I deplore them as I should have done had they fallen in battle. It was necessary to use the arm of the people, a machine not quite so blind as balls and bombs, but blind to a certain degree." The Jacobins had seen that the "experiment" in constitutional monarchy must fail and that without decisive action "the reestablishment of despotism" would necessarily follow. When they executed the king, "the Nation was with them in opinion, for however they might have been formerly for the constitution framed by the first assembly, they were come over from their hope in it, and were now generally Jacobins." Short should take the long view. "The liberty of the whole earth was depending on the issue of the contest," Jefferson reminded his young friend, "and was ever such a prize won with so little innocent blood? My own affections have been deeply wounded by some of the martyrs to this cause, but rather than it should have failed, I would have seen half the earth desolated. Were there but an Adam and an Eve left in every country, and left free, it would be better than as it now is."[66]

Jefferson confidently assumed that there was a French "people" or "Nation" capable of an enlightened understanding of its collective interests. At first, the "Nation" was "with" the Jacobins, suggesting that they still could be logically distinguished, but Jefferson concluded this crucial sentence by conflating the two, for the people "were now generally Jacobins." Jefferson imagined a similar convergence between the republican vanguard and the "people" in America.[67] Patriots in the sister republic drew inspiration from transatlantic developments. "The universal feasts, and rejoicings which have lately been had on account of the successes of the French shewed the genuine effusions of their hearts," Jefferson told Short; "99 in an hundred of our citizens" enthusiastically supported the French Revolution, including George Washington himself (who supposedly had told Jefferson to tell Short "that he considered *France as the sheet anchor of this country and its friendship as a first object*").[68]

In America as well as France, the "nation" or "people" confronted enemies. But just as the idea of "nation" denied the distinction between Jacobins and the French people—or Republicans and the American people—so opposition to the Revolution could be conceived as "foreign." The French Revolution therefore could be considered (and to an important extent it actually was) an international war, with the French nation seeking to defend its independence and integrity against the counterrevolutionary "conspiracy of kings." As Jefferson had learned during the American Revolutionary crisis, monarchical despotism divided a people against itself, perpetuating a state of war between rulers and ruled. For the Americans, and now for the French, national self-determination and republican government were inextricably linked. The genius of republicanism was to enable a nation to overcome the artificial and arbitrary divisions of the old regime, to become conscious of its collective identity and interests, and to vindicate national independence in a hostile world.

The "Adam and Eve" letter affords us an illuminating perspective on Jefferson's fundamental values as a proponent of republicanism and national self-determination, an image of his ideal world. Let there be "but an Adam and an Eve left in every country, and left free," he exhorted:

then every nation would return to first principles, and to the primal act of conjugal consent that constituted it as a distinct people.[69] Significantly, Jefferson did not imagine a return to Edenic beginnings for the whole human race: instead, he envisioned his world as a family of nations, not as the family of man. In the imagined holocaust there would be multiple survivors and multiple new beginnings.

Where would the captive nation of enslaved Africans fit in Jefferson's visionary scheme? Each nation was a great family traceable through the generations to its first parents, "an Adam and an Eve" who claimed the original, legitimate possession of its own "country." The conception of multiple origins, a staple theme in the emerging science of racial differences, was expressed here by Jefferson in national terms. And these were origins that for Jefferson's Virginia were not situated in the mists of time but in the process of settlement—the appropriation of the "country" of Virginia—that he memorialized in the *Summary View* and the *Notes on Virginia*. The coincidental conquest and captivity of the African nation was also clearly inscribed in the historical record. Yet the enslaved Africans were a people without a country: they had no rightful claims to the country of the Virginians, whatever injustices had been committed against them. Indeed, the greatest crime against the slaves was that they had been torn from their homeland, where their own Adam and Eve had founded the African nation—or race.

Within a few months of writing to Short, Jefferson began to reconsider his position on French revolutionary violence. Citizen Genet's tumultuous American tour offered Jefferson a sobering vision of how the French revolutionary contagion might spread to its sister republic; more ominously, the slave revolt in Santo Domingo showed how revolutionary slogans could jeopardize the racial order throughout the slaveholding South. Yet if Jefferson lost faith in the French Revolution, he continued to embrace the doctrine he set forth in the Adam and Eve letter—the associated ideas of national self-determination and republican self-government—throughout his career.[70] In America this doctrine enjoined separation of the two nations through the expatriation and colonization of the enslaved Africans. Had Jefferson in fact abandoned the radical nationalist principles he set forth to Short, he might have been able to imagine another solution to the problem of slavery.

COLONIZATION

Jefferson never abandoned his faith in colonization. "My sentiments have been forty years before the public," he wrote an importunate anti-slavery activist a few short weeks before his death in 1826. "Had I repeated them forty times, they would only have become the more stale and threadbare. Although I shall not live to see them consummated, they will not die with me; but living or dying, they will ever be in my most fervent prayer."[71] On his deathbed Jefferson had nothing to add to what he had written in the *Notes:* the only solution to the slavery problem was expatriation and colonization.

Jefferson's "prayer" testifies eloquently to the bankruptcy of rational expectations. The aging author of the Declaration of Independence did not have to be reminded that colonization faced increasingly formidable obstacles. The rapidly growing number of slaves was perhaps most daunting. As Jefferson told colonizationist Jared Sparks in 1824, the removal of the present slave population, which he estimated at one and a half million, might still be possible, "but six millions, (which a majority of those now living will see them attain,) and one million of these fighting men, will say, 'we will not go.'" If the slaves, sensing a momentous shift in the balance of power, might resist removal, their beleaguered masters would be equally loath to lose their precious property without fair compensation. Jefferson estimated the cost of such a massive undertaking—taking "twenty-five years for its accomplishment" (during which time the slave population would have doubled to three million) and providing for the costs of compensation, transportation, and colonization—at "thirty-six millions of dollars a year for twenty-five years," or a grand total of $900,000,000.[72]

Demographic trends, property rights, constitutional scruples, and the retarded development of public opinion mitigated against implementation of any colonization plan.[73] But Jefferson did not despair. Throughout his career he insisted that justice could be done both to the captive nation of enslaved Africans and to the property rights of Virginians by adopting a *post-nati* scheme of emancipation. First elaborated in his (unreported) amendment to the bill on slavery in the revisal of the laws, Jefferson's emancipation scheme provided that the children of slaves would be born free, stay "with their parents to a certain age, then be brought up, at the public expence, to tillage, arts or sciences, according to their geniusses, till the females should be eighteen, and the males twenty-one years of age, when they should be colonized to such place as the circumstances of the time should render most proper."[74] In 1824 Jefferson was still urging emancipation of "the afterborn, leaving them, on due compensation, with their mothers, until their services are worth their maintenance, and then putting them to industrious occupations, until a proper age for deportation." The only difference was that Jefferson now conceded that slave owners had a legitimate property interest in these "new-born infant[s]" (which he estimated at "say twelve dollars and fifty cents" each) and so were entitled to "due compensation."[75]

Jefferson's solicitude for slaveholders as individuals ("no violation of private right is proposed") in his emancipation proposal stands in stark contrast to his apparent disregard for the feelings of the slaves. "The separation of infants from their mothers . . . would produce some scruples of humanity," he acknowledged to Sparks, "but this would be straining at a gnat."[76] Jefferson's goal was not to do justice to the rights of enslaved Africans as individuals—much less to attend to the "transient" griefs of broken families.[77] In order to restore the black nation to its rights, the children of the slaves would be born free, transported to a new homeland, and declared "a free and independant people"; in effect, this rising generation constituted a "nation" distinct from its enslaved elders, who never could discharge the responsibilities of true parenthood. Infantilized by slavery, slave parents were incapable of raising their children to live free.[78]

Jefferson did not conceal the punitive aspect of his scheme for black nation making. After all, slavery itself constituted a state of war, and only by one final, massively coercive act—the forced removal of the captive nation—could a lasting peace be secured. But "who could estimate its blessed effects?" he asked Sparks. "I leave this to those who will live to see their accomplishment, and to enjoy a beatitude forbidden to my age."[79] Expatriation of the enslaved Africans would put a stop to the unjust and demoralizing exercise of despotic force against an innocent nation; it would also rid Virginia of a dangerous cancer that inevitably would destroy the Commonwealth's civic health.

Jefferson's faith in colonization did not waiver because of his horror of the only alternative he could imagine: servile insurrection and self-emancipation. Freedom for the slaves "will come," he assured Edward Coles in 1814, "whether brought on by the generous energy of our own minds; or by the bloody process of St Domingo."[80] The new black republic in the Caribbean showed how easily the wheel of fortune might turn. Narrowly averted slave insurrections in Virginia (in 1800 and 1802) and the rapid growth of the free black population under the aegis of the 1782 manumission act were ominous portents of the coming conflagration. "We are truly to be pitied," Jefferson exclaimed to his old friend Dr. Benjamin Rush in the wake of the first insurrection scare in 1800. "I am looking with anxiety to see what will be its effect on our State."[81]

The troubled history of race relations in Virginia validated Jefferson's conception of two warring nations, with a complete separation constituting the only conceivable grounds for lasting peace. But the relative weight of Jefferson's concerns shifted over time: the prospect of a just peace receded from view, while the need for racial separation came increasingly to the fore. To some extent this change in emphasis was simply the logical development of Jefferson's original formulation. After all, enslaved Africans were a hostile, dangerous enemy, and this enmity was precisely what made the claims of justice and the need to secure a lasting peace so compelling. But as long as the conditions for doing justice and securing peace remained remote, the captive nation must be effectively coerced and controlled. Coercion alone could preempt the vengeful and violent designs of a natural enemy.

Jefferson did not believe that a Hobbesian state of war was the natural, inevitable relation of distinct nations.[82] Instead, as Jefferson's favorite law of nations writers insisted, war was the ultimate sanction against violations of national right, the only means of restoring a lawful and just world order without compromising national sovereignty and self-determination. There could be no doubt that "justice," if it meant anything in the affairs of nations, was on the side of the enslaved Africans. In practice, however, a state of war had a leveling effect for republican theorists such as Jefferson, displacing the claims of justice: when the very existence of a nation was at risk, self-preservation was its highest moral imperative, whatever crimes it may have committed against its enemies. Jefferson's construction of racial differences reinforced this leveling tendency, with stereotypes of the alien "other"—perhaps less than fully human, inspired by vengeful and violent impulses—subverting and superseding his original image of an innocent people in captivity, victims of unremitting despotism.

The paradoxical effect of Jefferson's revisioning of the captive nation was to underscore both its potency, as a dangerous internal enemy, and its putatively "natural" incapacity for self-government and national self-determination. Colonization might not give rise to a truly independent black nation: "It may perhaps be doubted," Jefferson wrote in 1811, "whether many of these people would voluntarily consent to such an exchange of situation, and very certain that few of those advanced to a certain age in habits of slavery, would be capable of self-government." But Jefferson would not "discourage the experiment," for emancipation and removal would prevent a bloody race war, discharge the new nation's moral responsibility to the captive nation, and remove a dangerous cancer from the body politic.[83] If the liberated nation failed to prosper in its new homeland, this would be an unhappy, even a tragic outcome—but not one for which former slaveholders could be held responsible.

Jefferson's conception of the slaves of Virginia as natural enemies provided the conceptual framework for his "suspicion" that they were naturally inferior; his understanding of racial difference was in turn reflected in his pessimistic assessment of the future prospects of the African nation. His faith in colonization as an end in itself, in the redemption of the captive nation from bondage and its ascension to an equal and independent station in the family of nations, was also a casualty of a rapidly, radically changing world order. The wreckage of the old European balance of power in the upheavals of the French Revolutionary and Napoleonic wars blasted the hopes of Jefferson and other enlightened Revolutionaries in the progressive amelioration and increasing lawfulness of international politics. The American Revolution did not initiate the anticipated liberal republican millennium: demolition of mercantilist systems, free trade, and the liberation and self-determination of all peoples, particularly on the imperial periphery of the "civilized" world. Instead, and after only brief respite, the French Revolution inexorably drew all nations into the vortex of world war, destroying almost all of them.[84]

The shattering of Revolutionary hopes led Jeffersonians to turn away from a hopelessly corrupt and collapsing diplomatic system in an effort to isolate the American empire of liberty from Old World diseases. This was a sobering reconception of world order, or disorder, that could not accommodate a free black republic. Jefferson's scheme for black nation making in Query XIV of the *Notes* glimpsed this potential danger: after declaring the captive nation's independence, America would "extend to them our alliance and protection, till they shall have acquired strength."[85] The black nation, if truly independent, could enter into a hostile alliance that jeopardized vital American interests; indeed, this was precisely what Virginia's slaves had done—or could be understood to have done—in the Revolution, when so many escaped to British lines. The "protection" that Jefferson contemplated here was a form of control, a preemptive alliance; the "strength" required to move beyond this protectorate was relative to diplomatic exigencies and opportunities: under conditions of general peace and stability, the independent black nation could freely pursue its own line of foreign (commercial) policy without threatening American interests.

By the time of his election to the presidency in 1800, Jefferson and his followers no longer had any illusions about the new nation's role in the European balance of power. In a world that was always at war or preparing for the next war, there was no safe place for second-rank neutral powers such as the United States, much less for a new black republic. The pariah status of the self-proclaimed Republic of Haiti did not augur well for the expansion and progressive development of the international system. So too, when the Haitian contagion threatened to spread to Virginia, the limits of Jefferson's commitment to black nation making were clearly revealed. Pressed to find a new home or "receptacle" for rebellious Virginia slaves, President Jefferson considered a wide range of distant sites. Perhaps the most "probable and practicable retreat for them," he told Virginia governor James Monroe, would be the West Indies. "Inhabited already by a people of their own race and color," with "climates congenial with their natural constitution," the islands would "insulate" ex-slaves "from the other descriptions of men; nature seems to have formed these islands to become the receptacle of the blacks transplanted into this hemisphere." Indeed, "the most promising portion of them is the island of St. Domingo, where the blacks are established into a sovereignty *de facto,* and have organized themselves under regular laws and government."[86]

It is hardly surprising that Jefferson should seek to deport failed rebels to the one place in the Western Hemisphere where successful rebels exercised de facto sovereignty. As the model for slave revolts elsewhere, Haiti constituted a great potential danger; but that threat might be neutralized if, functioning as a "receptacle" for incendiary elements from the mainland, the black republic could be effectively quarantined. Far from recognizing its independence and offering a protective alliance, Jefferson proposed to intimidate Haiti by threatening to use America's preponderant power: "The possibility that these exiles might stimulate and conduct vindicative or predatory descents on our coasts, and facilitate concert with their brethren remaining here, looks to a state of things between that island and us not probable on a contemplation of our relative strength, and of the disproportion daily growing."[87] Seeking to overcome its defective (de facto) standing in the community of "civilized" states, Haiti would have powerful motives to exercise self-restraint. In the meantime it would lack the legal capacity to enter into formal alliances potentially dangerous to the United States, and there would be no legal limitations on the use of American power to exercise de facto control over the black republic.

Under the combined circumstances of incipient insurrection at home and dangerous instability abroad, Jefferson's thinking about colonization converged with the strategic imperatives of containing the Haitian Revolution. Indeed, Haiti occupied a position in Jefferson's conception of world politics analogous to that of enslaved Africans in Virginia: the enmity of both peoples was assumed, and while Jefferson acknowledged the original injustice against them, neither people could appeal to the law—under the constitution of Virginia or under the law of nations—for redress. Thus, in deporting slaves to Haiti, Jefferson would not, as his original colonization scheme promised, transform enemies, or the children of enemies, into friends. But the removal of a dangerous internal enemy would enhance the security (and improve the morals) of Virginia and its sister states. Fighting for their freedom, rebellious slaves might well overthrow a demoralized master class; but deportation would render them harmless, as they became members of a weak, unrecognized nation that would risk its very freedom by any belligerent move against the United States.

Jefferson's conception of enslaved Africans as a captive and therefore enemy nation segued into his elaboration of invidious racial distinctions in the *Notes*. As president, his efforts to imagine a place somewhere within or "beyond the limits of the United States to form a receptacle for these people" prompted similarly invidious distinctions.[88] Governor Monroe, reporting a resolution of the Virginia legislature urging the removal of insurrection-prone slaves, wondered if it might be possible to acquire sufficient land "in the vacant western territory of the United States."[89] Jefferson quickly dismissed the possibility: the expense of purchasing public lands would be prohibitive; and "questions would also arise whether the establishment of such a colony within our limits, and to become a part of our union, would be desirable to the State of Virginia itself, or to the other States—especially those who would be in its vicinity?"[90]

The impossibility of racial coexistence in one place, the premise of Jefferson's original colonization proposal, was now projected across space, as he argued against "vicinity" or neighborhood and coequal status in the American union. Colonies of freedpeople might be still more dangerous beyond the limits of the union: even in the unlikely event that either Britain to the north or Spain to the west and south should sponsor such colonies, they certainly "would not alienate the sovereignty" over their imperial domains, and the colonists therefore would become "subjects" of their respective crowns—and potential auxiliaries in future conflicts with the United States.

Up until this point in his developing argument, Jefferson's thinking was still anchored in the geopolitical framework within which he conceived colonization: the two warring nations must be extricated from their unholy embrace, each to its own country, before peace could be secured. But if Jefferson could imagine the extrication, the possibility of a lasting peace seemed to recede in time and across space. "Should we be willing to have such a colony in contact with us?" Jefferson asked Monroe, a rhetorical question that gained its force from the unspoken assumption that no peace would ever be possible between naturally inimical peoples.

The rhetorical stage was now set for one of the most extraordinary passages in the Jeffersonian canon, a passage that illuminates the powerful reciprocal connections between his ideas about race, nationhood, and international relations. "However our present interests may restrain us within our own limits," wrote Jefferson, "it is impossible not to look forward to distant times, when our rapid multiplication will expand itself beyond those limits, and cover the whole northern, if not the southern continent, with a people speaking the same language, governed in similar forms, and by similar laws." Because the spread of free republican institutions, the guarantee of perpetual peace in the American hemisphere, was predicated on the consensual union of free people and their "rapid multiplication," Jefferson could not "contemplate with satisfaction either blot or mixture"—the presence of Africans—"on that surface."[91]

Jefferson was no longer thinking in terms of a complex, progressively improving diplomatic system: instead, he envisioned an American imperium in the New World, insulated from the corruption of European politics and free from the "blot" of an alien and inimical African presence.[92] It was a vision that excluded the black nation that was supposed to follow the emancipation of Virginia's slaves. Jefferson now drew a great imaginary boundary between the European "balance of power" and the American "empire for liberty." Indelibly stained by their degraded, servile condition, Africans would never find a true home in the New World: even the successful black rebels who exercised de facto sovereignty in Santo Domingo failed to qualify as a "free and independant people."

As he imaginatively projected enslaved Africans beyond Virginia and, ultimately, beyond the limits of the civilized world, Jefferson defined the black nation in increasingly racialist and naturalistic terms. The original historical narrative that Jefferson had sketched in the Declaration of Independence, the narrative that made emancipation and colonization morally imperative, was superseded by the geopolitician's "realistic" assessment of pervasive security threats to the American republic and the natural philosopher's scientific observations about "fixed" racial differences that were grounded in nature—and beyond the kind of redemption in history that the American Declaration promised to oppressed peoples everywhere. The black nation therefore did not gain an independent, equal standing in the family of nations: instead, it became a "race," an order of mankind fated by its natural incapacities to remain beyond the limits of the civilized world.

Searching for a "receptacle" for this dangerous and degraded race, Jefferson became less concerned with "justice" among nations than with the political and moral hygiene of his beloved Virginia. Virginia's civic well-being was Jefferson's paramount, passionate concern, when (in 1814) he urged his young neighbor Edward Coles not to free his slaves and "abandon" his country. Jefferson was convinced that the descendants of Africans, unlike the descendants of the great family of European nations, could never be assimilated with the Virginians. Freed from bondage, they could only be "pests in society by their idleness, and the depredations to which this leads them"; marked by their skin color, Africans were perpetual aliens, foreigners by nature. Their only escape was through race mixing, a transgression of natural boundaries that jeopardized the very survival of Virginia: the "amalgamation" of the blacks "with the other color produces a degradation to which no lover of his country, no lover of excellence in the human character can innocently consent."[93] For Jefferson, racial purity and national identity thus became inextricably linked.

"KNELL OF THE UNION"

The collapse of the European diplomatic system and the resulting efforts of Jefferson and his successors to insulate the New World from the corruptions of the Old that culminated in the Monroe Doctrine of 1824 subverted any reasonable prospect for the liberation, colonization, and nationhood of enslaved African Americans. The feeble experiments in colonization actually undertaken in (British) Sierra Leone and (American) Liberia were clearly destined to perpetual clienthood under paternalistic imperial regimes: they would serve as "receptacles" for redundant freedpeople, entrepôts for metropolitan trading interests, and missionary outposts for Christian civilization. Jefferson's "just God," the God who would restore an oppressed people to its national rights, presided over a world that no longer existed.

Yet if Jefferson's solution to the slavery problem was rendered obso-

lete by revolutionary changes in world politics (and corresponding conceptual changes), the failure to take effective steps to end slavery in Virginia and other slaveholding states threatened to destroy the American
union. Indeed, that failure reflected a fundamental confusion about
who should assume responsibility for compensating owners of slave
property as well as for the considerable costs of transportation and colonization. The very definition of American and Virginian national identity was implicated in the resulting political, constitutional, and conceptual impasse.

When Jefferson first elaborated his colonization plans in the *Notes on
Virginia,* he assumed that Virginians alone would bear whatever costs
his project entailed. The genius of his *post-nati* emancipation scheme
was that it would preempt the imposition of high taxes on nonslave-
holders and slaveholders alike to finance compensation for valuable
slave property. By contrast, all Virginians had a national interest in and
responsibility for removal of the emancipated slaves. With ratification of
the new federal Constitution, this responsibility was no longer so clear-
cut. A rebellious slave population jeopardized the security of the union
as a whole; Virginia and its sister states no longer had direct authority
over commercial and political relations with the larger world or access to
revenues generated by federal import duties or the sale of public lands in
the new national domain. If slavery, then, was a "national"—that is, an
American—problem, its solution demanded action by the federal government, acting on behalf of the whole union.

At the same time Jefferson and his fellow southerners insisted that
slavery was a domestic institution, governed and protected by state law.
Any emancipation scheme that threatened to interfere with slavery
where it was already established thus could be construed as an assault on
the integrity of the state constitutions and private property rights that
secured republican liberty.[94] Thus, true advocates of freedom from other
states would eschew any initiative that could be construed as outside or
"foreign" interference: they would not even talk about dismantling the
institution, for this was strictly and sacredly a concern for the states.
When the separate states finally determined that the moment for emancipation was ripe, the crucial test for states with few or no slaves would
be their willingness to share the financial burdens. "And from what fund

are these expenses to be furnished?" Jefferson asked in his letter to Jared Sparks. "Why not from that of the lands which have been ceded by the very States now needing this relief? And ceded on no consideration, for the most part, but that of the general good of the whole." The "object" was undoubtedly "more important to the slave States," Jefferson conceded, but it "is highly so to the others also, if they were serious in their arguments on the Missouri question."[95]

Jefferson now assumed that every slave owner had a right to compensation for the loss of property—and that the federal government would do the compensating. Nonslaveholding northerners probably would balk at the massive intersectional transfer of wealth that full compensation would entail, but Jefferson's *post-nati* scheme would constitute a radical reduction in costs. "The estimated value of the new-born infant is so low, (say twelve dollars and fifty cents,) that it would probably be yielded by the owner gratis, and would thus reduce the six hundred millions of dollars, the first head of expense, to thirty-seven millions and a half; leaving only the expenses of nourishment while with the mother, and of transportation." Slave owners "probably" would yield even this relatively trivial compensation, but they must do so voluntarily.[96] After all, as Jefferson told Congressman John Holmes during the Missouri crisis, "the cession of that kind of property, for so it is misnamed, is a bagatelle which would not cost me a second thought, if, in that way, a general emancipation and *expatriation* could be effected."[97] Yet it was a "bagatelle" that carried enormous symbolic weight in the context of the sectional divisions the Missouri debates exposed.

Accustomed to thinking of the federal government as a hostile, "foreign" power, southerners believed that the federal tariff shifted southern wealth into the coffers of greedy northern bankers and manufacturers.[98] Southerners risked beggaring themselves by emancipating their slaves, further eroding their already tenuous position in the intersectional struggle for control of the federal government. Enlightened southerners might well acknowledge, as Jefferson did to Holmes, that there could be no just claim to human property. But Jefferson warned that the durability of the union, based on intersectional equity, constitutional compromises, and respect for states' rights, required that nonslaveholding northerners act as if slaveholders' property were sacred and inviolable.

It became suddenly, startlingly clear to Jefferson during the Missouri crisis that his cherished union, riven by a "geographical line," was on the verge of collapse.[99] America would become the image of Europe, as the union's warring fragments struggled for advantage. "This momentous question"—would the new, slaveholding state of Missouri be permitted to join the union?—"like a fire-bell in the night, awakened and filled me with terror," he exclaimed in his April 1820 letter to Holmes. "I considered it at once as the knell of the Union." The determination of northern restrictionists to limit the spread of slavery signaled belligerent intentions against the South. Instead of assisting southerners in their ongoing struggle against a dangerous internal enemy by working toward "a general emancipation and *expatriation,*" these northerners sought to confine and concentrate America's slave population in the states where slavery was already established.[100]

Jefferson's response to the Missouri crisis did not mean that he had abandoned his lifelong opposition to slavery. The central issue, he insisted, was the nature of the union itself, and the equal rights of member states—Virginia as well as Missouri—to draft their own constitutions and then govern themselves without outside interference. Jefferson would have been outraged at the suggestion that his states' rights principles were designed to perpetuate and expand an "empire of slavery." Yet the institution of slavery was clearly at the front of Jefferson's mind as he scanned the ideological horizon for deviations from constitutional orthodoxy. The conception of slavery as an institutionalized state of war, and of enslaved Africans as a captive nation, did not diminish over the years. Old Republicans like Jefferson recoiled at the horrors of race war that they thought any weakening of the institution would unleash. In the *Arator* essays (1813), John Taylor of Caroline captured this sense of foreboding: "The history of parties in its utmost malignity is but a feint mirror for reflecting the consequences of a white and a black party. If badges and names have been able to madden men in all ages, up to robbery and murder in their most atrocious forms, no doubt can exist of the consequences of placing two nations of distinct colours and features on the same theatre, to contend, not about sounds and signs, but for wealth and power."[101] The rapid growth of the slave population and, perhaps more ominously, of the free black population, pointed toward a shifting balance of forces and the imminence of servile insurrection.

Prohibiting the export and "diffusion" of slaves to Missouri and other new western states thus would aggravate Virginia's security dilemma, hastening the day when the cold war of slavery turned hot. Surely good republicans in the North could grasp the southern states' predicament. "We have the wolf by the ear," as he told Holmes, "and we can neither hold him, nor safely let him go."[102] Virginia's very existence was at risk. The loss of effective power in an increasingly hostile central government jeopardized states' rights and sectional interests: with ostentatious solicitude for poor slaves, restrictionists would disarm the slave states, putting a "dagger" into the hands of their enemies.[103]

Jefferson remained adamantly opposed to slavery: the very existence of the institution embroiled his beloved commonwealth in a perpetual war that was degrading and demoralizing—and that Virginia ultimately might lose. Yet Jefferson was equally adamantly antislave, and his loathing of the black enemy was only exacerbated by the apparent futility of efforts to seek peace through "a general emancipation and *expatriation*." The intensity of this loathing became an increasingly formidable obstacle to even imagining, much less fulfilling, the original promise of colonization: the creation of a "free and independant" black nation. If they stayed in Virginia, freedpeople would use the "dagger" against their former masters, for whatever else they were by "nature," these black people were natural enemies. In the end, it did not matter where former slaves were sent, for the enmity of the black nation was as indelibly "fixed" as the skin color of its people.

The bankruptcy of Jefferson's colonization scheme became fully apparent in his advocacy of diffusion. "All know that permitting the slaves of the South to spread into the West will not add one being to that unfortunate condition," he assured his old Revolutionary comrade the marquis de Lafayette. Opening the West to slavery "will increase the happiness" of existing slaves, "and by spreading them over a larger surface, will dilute the evil everywhere, and facilitate the means of getting finally rid of it, an event more anxiously wished by those on whom it presses than by the noisy pretenders to exclusive humanity."[104] Jefferson believed that emancipation would be facilitated by diffusion, he told Holmes, "by dividing the burden on a greater number of coadjutors."[105]

Diffusion would make slavery a national problem, not a narrowly and dangerously sectional one. The financial "burden" of solving the problem, through a general emancipation and expatriation, also would be more widely diffused. Until that glorious epoch finally arrived—and a "revolution in public opinion" would have to take place first[106]—slaves would be better treated, "happier," less prone to revolt. Perhaps more importantly, the racial balance would be favorable everywhere to the continuing security and dominion of the white nation. Ironically, enthusiasts such as Jefferson conjured up a bright image of diffusion as a panacea that would both preempt a bloody race war and renew the bonds of affectionate union among patriotic Americans, an image that would inspire a later generation of proslavery apologists. Why not embrace the means of diffusion—the spread of slavery across the continent—and eschew Jefferson's end—justice to the captive nation through colonization and expatriation?

The Missouri crisis tested Jefferson's commitment to colonization. In a practical sense diffusion represented the negation of expatriation and colonization: the captive nation would be broken up, and individual slaves would be dispersed across the country, not sent to some new homeland. (Of course, this was precisely what was already happening in slaveholding America, before anyone thought to call it "diffusion"—or to imagine that it would lead to the institution's ultimate extinction.) As an alternative to the idea of unceasing conflict between hostile nations, diffusion—for all the sins its exponents sought to disguise or deny—did focus attention on the welfare of slaves as individuals.

Perhaps the Missouri debates could have led Jefferson to a new understanding of the slavery problem. Had Jefferson pursued the logic of diffusion, he might have abandoned his nationalist perspective; someone so profoundly opposed to slavery in principle and so convinced that great injustices had been done the African people surely would have resisted the seductions of proslavery. He might then have been forced, despite everything he had always thought about the slavery problem, to consider doing the right thing by individual slaves, one after another, until at least some of the damage was undone. In doing so, Jefferson might have come to envision the possibility of a genuine amalgamation, a mixing and blending of two nations into one; or rather, he might have acknowledged the genealogical ties that already linked white families and black families at Monticello and across the country. And perhaps he could have recognized his own mixed-race children.

But Jefferson remained true to the tenets of his nationalist faith. For him, capitulation to restrictionism would have been "treason against the hopes of the world," a reversal of the outcome of the American Revolution.[107] Pulling back from the precipice, Americans preserved the union and kept the spirit of the Revolution alive—however attenuated it might be. There was still reason to hope, as Jefferson did until his dying days, that the unfinished business of the Revolution would still be accomplished. When the proud author of the American Declaration of Independence died on its fiftieth anniversary, another declaration, establishing the captive nation of enslaved Africans as a separate "free and independant people," was yet to be enacted. But "nothing is more certainly written in the book of fate," wrote Jefferson in his *Autobiography,* the book of his own life, "than that these people are to be free."[108]

4 July 1826

THOMAS JEFFERSON was too old and feeble to accept an invitation to come to Washington, D.C., to help commemorate the fiftieth anniversary of American independence on 4 July 1826. His letter to Roger C. Weightman on 24 June declining the invitation was the last one he ever wrote. Could he have traveled, Jefferson told Weightman, he would have been delighted to join in the celebration at Washington, to "have met and exchanged there congratulations personally with the small band, the remnant of that host of worthies, who joined with us on that day, in the bold and doubtful election we were to make for our country, between submission or the sword." Jefferson proudly identified himself with the generation that had created the new American nation, exulting in his own role as author of the Declaration of Independence. The American Revolution had been an epochal moment in world history, he proclaimed, "the signal of arousing men to burst the chains under which monkish ignorance and superstition had persuaded them to bind themselves, and to assume the blessings and security of self-government."[1]

The new nation was founded on the self-evident principles Jefferson set forth in the Declaration. But it could only survive and prosper if those principles remained vital for each successive generation. "After half a century of experience and prosperity," Jefferson could still say that his fellow citizens "continue to approve the choice we made."

> That [republican] form which we have substituted, restores the free right to the unbounded exercise of reason and freedom of opinion. All eyes are opened, or opening, to the rights of man.

The general spread of the light of science has already laid open to every view the palpable truth, that the mass of mankind has not been born with saddles on their backs, nor a favored few booted and spurred, ready to ride them legitimately, by the grace of God. These are grounds of hope for others.

Americans must cherish their nationhood so that other peoples could hope to secure their own.

Jefferson's empire was manifest in his vision of progressive enlightenment that would ultimately encompass "the mass of mankind," bringing freedom to oppressed peoples everywhere—including enslaved Africans, returned at last to their own "country." Paradoxically, however, the expanding regime of freedom depended on the cultivation of national distinctions, on a self-conscious kinship of a single people across generations. This consciousness of national identity set Americans apart, if not above, the rest of mankind. As descendants of Revolutionary fathers who had risked everything when they rejected "submission" and chose the "sword," Americans knew they were a special people, the only people on earth who had shown that they were capable of governing themselves.

From our disenchanted modern perspective, the contradiction between Jefferson's imperial goals and the language of nationhood seems glaring. Nationalism, many cosmopolitans have come to believe, is worse than a last refuge for scoundrels: it is the irrational antithesis to the enlightened consciousness of global interdependence that our shrinking world requires. From our superior vantage nationalism appears to be a problem, if not the problem—something for right-minded statesmen to transcend (and for academics to demystify and deconstruct), so that we can get on with mankind's business. But Jefferson looked through the other end of history's telescope: nationhood was the solution to the local tyrannies of the old regime, the threshold to full, equal, and consensual participation in the modern world. His vision of a republican empire in turn provided the framework for his conception of the American nation. The coming into existence of this liberty-loving, self-governing people was an epochal moment in the history of political civilization, the "signal" for all other peoples to burst their chains.

Jefferson envisioned an empire without a metropolis, a republican regime without concentrations of power or privilege, a consensual union of self-governing states. Such an empire could only be sustained by a united, virtuous people, sharing common principles, drawn together by common interests, tied by bonds of affection and love. To preserve their liberties and secure their union, Americans must never forget who they were. "For ourselves," Jefferson enjoined his friends in Washington, "let the annual return of this day forever refresh our recollections of these rights, and an undiminished devotion to them."

With our wise hindsight, the tensions and contradictions between Jeffersonian means and ends, between the claims of nationhood and "the rights of man," seem striking. Surely Jefferson himself, in the recurrent moments of crisis recounted in this book, was acutely aware of these contradictions. Yet, even though his faith was often and sorely tested, he remained convinced to his dying day, 4 July 1826, that the Revolution had been worth the sacrifices it entailed: American nationhood was not simply a boon to colonists seeking to evade onerous tax burdens but a great benefit to mankind.

What became of his vision? Jefferson's empire, the federal union that sustained slavery and imploded in a bloody war, is long gone; the nation he helped create in order to secure that union has been transformed beyond recognition. Was the American Revolution therefore pointless? Was the Revolutionaries' faith in progress and improvement naive, self-deluding, or hypocritical? Whatever our inclinations, we cannot escape the questions. In asking them, we put ourselves back into the imperial framework within which Jefferson first envisioned our national history.

Notes

ABBREVIATIONS

JMP William T. Hutchinson, William M. E. Rachal, et al., eds.
The Papers of James Madison: Congressional Series. 17 vols. Chicago
Charlottesville, Va., 1959–91.

L&B Andrew A. Lipscomb and Albert Ellery Bergh, eds. *The Writings of
Thomas Jefferson.* 20 vols. Washington, D.C., 1903–4.

Lib. Cong. Library of Congress, Washington, D.C.

Notes Thomas Jefferson. *Notes on the State of Virginia.* Ed. William
Peden. Chapel Hill, N.C., 1954.

TJ Thomas Jefferson

TJP Julian Boyd et al., eds. *The Papers of Thomas Jefferson.* 27 vols. to
date. Princeton, N.J., 1950—.

TJW Merrill D. Peterson, ed. *Jefferson Writings.* New York, 1984.

INTRODUCTION: JEFFERSON'S EMPIRE

1. The Declaration of Independence as Adopted by Congress, 4 July 1776,
TJP 1:429–33, at 429.

2. TJ, Second Inaugural Address, 4 March 1805, *TJW,* 518–23, at 519.

3. TJ to Dr. Joseph Priestley, 21 March 1801, in L&B, 10:227–30, at 229.

4. TJ, First Inaugural Address, 4 March 1801, *TJW,* 492–96, at 493.

5. "He is without a doubt the man of the millennium," according to film-
maker Ken Burns, quoted in an Associated Press story, "Tourist Sites Hope
Jefferson Film Brings Visitors," Charlottesville *Daily Progress,* 5 Feb. 1997. The
classic study is Peterson, *Jefferson Image in the American Mind;* on TJ's role in
the early development of his image, see McDonald, "Jefferson and America:
Episodes in Image Formation." For TJ's standing in the American pantheon,
see Onuf, "Scholars' Jefferson"; Ellis, *American Sphinx,* 3–23; Maier, *American
Scripture,* ix–xxi, 154–215; Lewis and Onuf, "American Synecdoche."

6. TJ to Roger C. Weightman, 24 June 1826, in L&B, 16:181–82, at 182. For
an appreciation of TJ's imperial vision, written in the wake of a world war
against totalitarian regimes, see Boyd, "Jefferson's 'Empire of Liberty.'"

7. For a critique focused on foreign policy, see Tucker and Hendrickson,
Empire of Liberty, esp. 157–71.

8. Foster et al., "Jefferson Fathered Slave's Last Child." On the relationship, see Gordon-Reed, *Thomas Jefferson and Sally Hemings.* For the impact of race and slavery on TJ's reputation, see French and Ayers, "Strange Career of Thomas Jefferson." The implications of the DNA study for our understanding of TJ, slavery, and race relations are explored in Lewis and Onuf, *Sally Hemings and Thomas Jefferson.*

9. *Notes,* Query XVIII ("Manners"), 162.

10. For Peterson's "mortifying confession" that TJ "remains for me, finally, an impenetrable man," see his *Jefferson and the New Nation,* viii.

11. Burstein, "Problem of Jefferson Biography." Burstein's *Inner Jefferson* is a particularly revealing portrait. I am indebted to TJ's biographers, particularly to Peterson's *Jefferson and the New Nation* and Malone's *Jefferson and His Time.*

12. TJ to Roger C. Weightman, 24 June 1826, in L&B, 16:181–82, at 181. For TJ's moral vision, see Helo, "Jefferson's Republicanism and Slavery," and Yarbrough, *American Virtues.*

13. Boorstin, *Lost World of Thomas Jefferson.*

14. Malone, *Jefferson the Virginian;* Wilson, "Jefferson and the Republic of Letters." For the problem of Anglo-American provincial culture, see Greene, "Search for Identity."

15. See Ceaser, *Reconstructing America,* 19–65.

16. On nationalism, see Gellner, *Nations and Nationalism;* Hobsbawm, *Nations and Nationalism since 1780;* Anderson, *Imagined Communities;* Greenfield, *Nationalism: Five Roads to Modernity.* On British (and greater British) national identity, see Colley, *Britons;* on the United States, see Onuf, "Federalism, Republicanism, and Sectionalism," and Waldstreicher's *In the Midst of Perpetual Fetes.*

17. See Onuf and Onuf, *Federal Union, Modern World.*

18. The Declaration of Independence as Adopted by Congress, 4 July 1776, *TJP* 1:429–33, at 429.

19. Pagden, *Lords of All the World,* quotation at 157.

20. TJ's "original Rough draft" of the Declaration of Independence, *TJP* 1:423–28, at 427.

21. For discussion of the key texts in the debate over TJ's "republicanism" and "liberalism," see Onuf, "Scholars' Jefferson," 675–84.

22. Onuf, *Republican Legacy in International Thought.*

23. See Mayer, *Constitutional Thought of Jefferson.*

24. TJ, First Inaugural Address, 4 March 1801, *TJW,* 492–96, at 493–94, 493.

25. TJ to John Holmes, 22 April 1820, in L&B, 15:248–50, at 250. The brief quotations in the following paragraph are from this letter, at 250, 249.

26. For the early American union, see Hendrickson, *Ideological Origins of American Internationalism.*

27. The phrase is from TJ to John Taylor of Caroline, 4 [misdated 1] June 1798, in L&B, 10:44–47, at 46.

28. For a redefinition of American nationhood in a way that transcends the Anglo-American "*ethnocultural* identity" of TJ's "First Republic," see Lind,

Next American Nation, quotation at 27. I am skeptical that national identity can be so neatly calibrated to the successive "republics" Lind describes. See note 16 above.

29. TJ to James Madison, 6 Sept. 1789, *TJP* 15:392–98, at 395.

30. Morgan, *Inventing the People.*

31. For the "revolution of 1800," see TJ to Judge Spencer Roane, 6 Sept. 1819, in L&B, 15:212–16, at 212.

32. For the sentimental TJ, see Burstein, *Inner Jefferson.* Fliegelman, *Declaring Independence,* and Burstein, *Sentimental Democracy,* track sentimental themes through the larger culture.

33. *Notes,* Query XIV ("Laws"), 138.

34. TJ, First Inaugural Address, 4 March 1801, *TJW,* 492–96, at 494.

35. The Declaration of Independence as Adopted by Congress, 4 July 1776, *TJP* 1:429–33, at 431.

1. "WE SHALL ALL BE AMERICANS"

1. TJ Speech to Jean Baptiste Ducoigne, [ca. 1] June 1781, *TJP* 6:60–64, at 60. On TJ's sponsorship of Clark's unsuccessful expedition, see Malone, *Jefferson the Virginian,* 333–36.

2. *Notes,* 59–60, and Query IX ("Aborigines"), 93.

3. See Sheehan, *Seeds of Extinction.* See also Sheehan, "Indian Problem in the Northwest"; Pearce, *Savages of America;* Berkhofer, *White Man's Indian;* and Lerner, "Reds and Whites: Rights and Wrongs."

4. Hantman and Dunham, "Enlightened Archaeologist."

5. TJ to William Ludlow, 6 Sept. 1824, in L&B, 16:74–75.

6. TJ, First Inaugural Address, 4 March 1801, *TJW,* 492–96, at 494.

7. TJ, Second Inaugural Address, 4 March 1805, ibid., 518–23, at 520.

8. Declaration of Independence as Adopted by Congress, July 4, 1776, *TJP* 1:429–33, at 429.

9. TJ Speech to Jean Baptiste Ducoigne, [ca. 1] June 1781, ibid., 6:60–64, at 60, 61, 60–61.

10. Draft of Instructions to the Virginia Delegates in the Continental Congress (MS Text of *A Summary View*), [July 1774], ibid., 121–37, at 134, 133.

11. Refutation of the Argument That the Colonies Were Established at the Expense of the British Nation [after 19 Jan. 1776], *TJP* 1:277–85. On charters as "evidence of [colonial] rights," see Reid, *Authority of Rights,* 159–68.

12. TJ to John Adams, 11 June 1812, in Cappon, *Adams-Jefferson Letters* 2:305–8, at 307. For TJ's response to this speech given by Outacity on the eve of his departure for England in 1762, see Malone, *Jefferson the Virginian,* 60–61.

13. *Notes,* Query VI ("Productions Mineral, Vegetable, and Animal"), 63, 62. During his vice presidency TJ took extraordinary pains to vindicate the authenticity of Logan's speech. See app. 4 in ibid., 226–58, and Malone, *Jefferson and the Ordeal of Liberty,* 346–56.

14. See Hutchins, *Constitution and the Tribes,* particularly chaps. 4 and 6 on

the differences between Washington's and TJ's Indian diplomacy. See also Sheehan, *Seeds of Extinction*, 152, on TJ's tendency to "infantilize the Indian."

15. *Notes,* Query XI ("Aborigines"), 93. For another discussion of "wolves" and "sheep," suggesting that those who, like the Indians, "live without government" enjoyed "an infinitely greater degree of happiness than those who live under European governments," see TJ to Edward Carrington, 16 Jan. 1787, *TJP* 11:48–50, at 49.

16. *Notes,* Query XI ("Aborigines"), 93.

17. TJ to Chastellux, 7 June 1785, *TJP* 8:185–86, at 186.

18. On Indians as "aristocrats," see Lerner, "Reds and Whites: Rights and Wrongs," 149–50.

19. See Fliegelman, *Prodigals and Pilgrims,* chap. 5 ("Affectionate Unions and the New Voluntarism," 123–54, and Lewis, "Republican Wife."

20. Declaration of Independence as Adopted by Congress, 4 July 1776, *TJP* 1:429–33, at 429, 431.

21. For TJ's misogyny and a suggestion that his sentimental celebration of female virtue and republican family life may have proceeded from and expressed more tormented feelings (particularly about his mother), see Lockridge, *On the Sources of Patriarchal Rage.* For TJ as a sentimentalist, see Burstein, *Inner Jefferson.*

22. TJ to John Page, 5 Aug. 1776, *TJP* 1:485–86.

23. In 1813 TJ still argued that the British were responsible for retarding the progress of civilization in Indian country. "On the commencement of our present war," he wrote Baron Alexander von Humboldt, "we pressed on them [the Indians] the observance of peace and neutrality, but the interested and unprincipled policy of England has defeated all our labors for the salvation of these unfortunate people. They have seduced the greater part of the tribes within our neighborhood, to take up the hatchet against us, and the cruel massacres they have committed on the women and children of our frontiers taken by surprise, will oblige us now to pursue them to extermination, or drive them to new seats beyond our reach" (TJ to von Humboldt, 6 Dec. 1813, in L&B, 14:20–25, at 23).

24. TJ to Chastellux, 7 June 1785, *TJP* 8:185–86, at 185.

25. Ibid. On TJ's word lists, see Sheehan, *Seeds of Extinction,* 54–56, and Boorstin, *Lost World of Jefferson,* 75–80.

26. *Notes,* Query VI ("Productions Mineral, Vegetable, and Animal"), 58, 59, 61. In the 1787 edition of the *Notes,* TJ included as an appendix Commentaries by Charles Thomson, secretary of Congress, confirming his position on the Indians' potency and potential (ibid., 199–202). See also Sheehan, *Seeds of Extinction,* 66–88, and Boorstin, *Lost World of Jefferson,* 81–88. For TJ as a democratic theorist, focusing on this query, see Matthews, *Radical Politics of Jefferson,* 53–65; for the implications of TJ's turn to natural philosophy in his argument against the degeneracy thesis, see Ceaser, *Reconstructing America,* 19–53.

27. TJ to Chastellux, 7 June 1785, *TJP* 8:185–86, at 185.

28. *Notes,* Query VI ("Productions Mineral, Vegetable, and Animal"), 59–60.

29. Ibid., 60; Memorandums on a Tour from Paris to Amsterdam, Strasburg, and Back to Paris, 3 March–22 April 1788, *TJW,* 629–58, at 652.

30. *Notes,* Query VI, 60.

31. TJ, Second Inaugural Address, 4 March 1805, *TJW,* 518–23, at 520.

32. Memorandums on a Tour from Paris to Amsterdam, Strasburg, and Back to Paris, 3 March–22 April 1788, ibid., at 651–52.

33. On the "noble savage," see Sheehan, *Seeds of Extinction,* 89–116.

34. Stuart, *Half-way Pacifist.*

35. Declaration of Independence as Adopted by Congress, 4 July 1776, *TJP* 1:429–33, at 431.

36. Merrell, "Declarations of Independence"; White, *Middle Ground;* Calloway, *Revolution in Indian Country;* Hinderaker, *Elusive Empires;* Hutchins, *Constitution and the Tribes.*

37. As George Washington wrote in 1784, "Men in these times, talk with as much facility of fifty, a hundred, and even 500,000 Acres as a Gentleman formerly would do of 1000 acres" (Washington to Jacob Read, 3 Nov. 1784, in Fitzpatrick, *Writings of Washington* 27:486). See Onuf, *Statehood and Union,* 33–36.

38. Edward Countryman interprets the history of the Revolution in the West in terms of just such a transformation, from a colonial old regime to the new republican dispensation ("Indians, the Colonial Order, and the Revolution"). On land policy, see Abernethy, *Western Lands and the Revolution;* Malone, *Jefferson the Virginian,* 247–60; Onuf, *Origins of the Federal Republic,* 75–102; Notes and Documents Relating to the Transylvania and Other Claims and Bills for Establishing a Land Office, editorial notes, *TJP* 2:64–66, 133–38. TJ was not troubled by the mode in which Indian titles had been liquidated: "That the lands of this country were taken from them by conquest, is not so general a truth as is supposed. I find in our historians and records, repeated proofs of purchase, which cover a considerable part of the lower country; and many more would doubtless be found on further search." In his original manuscript TJ acknowledged that "these purchases were sometimes made with the price in one hand and the sword in the other." But more transactions set a higher standard, perhaps indicative of the Virginians' moral progress: "The upper country we know has been acquired altogether by purchases made in the most unexceptionable form" (*Notes,* 96, 281 n. 4).

39. Virginia Constitution [29 June 1776], *TJP* 1:377–86, at 383.

40. Onuf, *Origins of the Federal Republic,* 76–83. On the land companies, see Livermore, *Early American Land Companies.* Membership lists may be found in the Jefferson Papers, Lib. Cong., 7:1164 (Vandalia), 1166 (Indiana and Illinois-Wabash).

41. This was the recommendation of "Cincinnatus," *Mote Point of Finance.*

42. Remonstrance of 14 Dec. 1779 (drafted by George Mason), in Hening, *Statutes at Large* 10:557–59.

43. Smith, *Virgin Land,* 15–18, 132–44; McCoy, *Elusive Republic.*

44. For the old regime in Indian country, see Jones, *License for Empire,*

36–119. See also De Vorsey, *Indian Boundary in the Southern;* Alden, *John Stuart and the Southern Frontier;* White, *Middle Ground,* 205–365; Hinderaker, *Elusive Empires,* 134–75; Richter, "Native Peoples and the Eighteenth-Century Empire."

45. "And no purchases of Land shall be made of the *Indian* Natives but on behalf of the Publick, by authority of the General Assembly" (Virginia Constitution [29 June 1776], *TJP* 1:377–86, at 383).

46. The language is TJ's and may be found both in the Virginia Constitution and in successive drafts of the Declaration (ibid., 377–78 [Constitution as Adopted] and 419, 425, 431 [Composition Draft, Original Rough Draft, and Declaration as Adopted]).

47. The references to "Mercenaries" and "Savages" are to the Declaration as Adopted, ibid., 431; the passage on "fellow-subjects" appears only in TJ's Original Rough Draft, ibid., 425.

48. The point of these reforms in the land system, TJ later explained, was "to make an opening for the aristocracy of virtue and talent, which nature has wisely provided for the direction of the interests of society," thus replacing the "aristocracy of wealth" that had flourished under British rule. Before independence "the transmission of this [landed] property from generation to generation in the same name raised up a distinct set of families who, being privileged by law in the perpetuation of their wealth were thus formed into a Patrician order, distinguished by the splendor and luxury of their establishments. From this order too the king habitually selected his Counsellors of State, the hope of which distinction devoted the whole corps to the interests & will of the crown" (TJ, *Autobiography* [1821], in *TJW,* 3–101, at 32). Holly Brewer has recently shown that these reforms had a much greater effect than historians have generally recognized ("Entailing Aristocracy in Colonial Virginia").

49. Nor could frontier squatters and speculators be allowed to form their own states: these "banditii and adventurers" would form "Establishments not only on dissimilar principles to those which form the basis of our Republican Constitutions, but such as might eventually prove destructive to them" (Virginia Delegates to Gov. Benjamin Harrison, 1 Nov. 1783, in Burnett, *Letters of the Members* 7:365).

50. See Countryman, "Indians, the Colonial Order, and the Revolution."

51. For TJ and many of his fellow Virginians, the protracted agitation by the land companies against Virginia's jurisdiction cemented the connection between the defense of charters, resistance to a strong central government, and hostility to native rights. The most important assaults on the charter included Paine, *Public Good,* and Wharton, *Plain Facts.* In their efforts to reach some kind of settlement with the federal government, Wharton and his land company associates continued to argue against Virginia's charter claims long after the cession was completed, thus reinforcing the link between land speculation and solicitude for native rights.

52. Philbrick, *Laws of Illinois Territory,* introduction; Onuf, *Statehood and Union,* 44–66.

53. Craig, *Olden Time* 2:406–28. The commissioners' position was based on a congressional report adopted on 15 Oct. 1783 (Ford, *Journals of Congress* 25:681–93).

54. Chief Justice John Marshall's "discovery doctrine," set forth in the landmark case of *Johnson v. McIntosh* (1823), reaffirmed state titles as the foundation of federal title, thus turning back the last serious land company challenge to the charter claims of Virginia and other ceding states on behalf of the Indians' original property rights. See Robertson, "*Johnson v. M'Intosh.*" Cf. Hutchins, *Constitution and the Tribes,* chap. 9.

55. See, for instance, Horsman, *Expansion and American Indian Policy,* 40–45; Prucha, *American Indian Treaties,* 42–48.

56. Stanley Elkins and Eric McKitrick emphasize the connection between Federalist Indian policy in the Northwest and Anglo-American diplomatic relations; British evacuation of their forts in the region, according to the terms of the Jay Treaty (1794), was crucial to the pacification of the frontier (Elkins and McKitrick, *Age of Federalism,* 436–39).

57. See Banning, *Jeffersonian Persuasion.*

58. [Taylor], *Definition of Parties,* 12. See Shalhope, *John Taylor of Caroline.* For TJ's appreciation of Taylor's polemical efforts, see TJ to James Madison, 1 Sept. 1793, *TJP* 27:6–8, at 8; TJ to Madison, 15 May 1794, *JMP* 15:332–33, at 333. On Federalist Indian policy in this period, see Sheehan, "Indian Problem in the Northwest."

59. [Taylor], *Definition of Parties,* 4, 12.

60. Ibid., 12, 13.

61. Ibid., 4, 13.

62. Ibid., 14.

63. [Taylor], *Enquiry into the Tendency of Certain Public Measures,* 85.

64. TJ, First Inaugural Address, 4 March 1801, *TJW,* 492–96, at 494, 493.

65. TJ to Kitchao Geboway, 27 Feb. 1808, in L&B, 16:425–27, at 426. My understanding of "philanthropy" is indebted to Bernard Sheehan: ultimately, "hating Indians could not be differentiated from hating Indianness"; "philanthropy had in mind the disappearance of an entire race" (*Seeds of Extinction,* 277, 278). See Lerner, "Reds and Whites: Rights and Wrongs," 166–70. For a critical account of TJ's Indian policy during his presidency, see Hutchins, *Constitution and the Tribes,* chap. 6.

66. TJ to the Chiefs of the Wyandots, Ottawas, Chippewas, Powtewatamies, and Shawanese, 10 Jan. 1809, in L&B, 16:461–65, at 462–63; TJ to Captain Hendrick, the Delawares, Mohicans, and Munries, 21 Dec. 1808, ibid., 450–54, at 453.

67. TJ to the Chiefs of the Ottawas, Chippewas, Powtowatamies, Wyandots, and Senecas of Sandusky, 22 April 1808, ibid., 428–32, at 428.

68. TJ to Captain Hendrick, the Delawares, Mohicans, and Munries, 21 Dec. 1808, ibid., 450–54, at 451.

69. Ibid., at 453. See also TJ to the Chiefs of the Shawanee Nation, 19 Feb. 1807, ibid., 421–25, at 424: "When the white people first came to this land, they

were few, and you were many: now we are many, and you few; and why? because, by cultivating the earth, we produce plenty to raise our children, while
yours, during a part of every year, suffer for want of food, are forced to eat un-
wholesome things, are exposed to the weather in your hunting camps, get diseases and die. Hence it is that your numbers lessen."

70. TJ to the Chiefs of the Wyandots, Ottawas, Chippewas, Powtewatamies
and Shawanese, 10 Jan. 1809, ibid., 461–65, at 463.

71. TJ to Captain Hendrick, the Delawares, Mohicans, and Munries, 21
Dec. 1808, ibid., 450–54, at 452.

72. TJ to the Chiefs of the Ottawas, Chippewas, Powtowatamies, Wyandots, and Senecas of Sandusky, 22 April 1808, ibid., 428–32, at 429.

73. TJ to My Children, Chiefs of the Chickasaw Nation, Mingkey, Mataha,
and Tishohanta, 7 March 1805, ibid., 410–12, at 411–12. See also TJ to the
Chiefs of the Ottawas, Chippewas, Powtowatamies, Wyandots, and Senecas of
Sandusky, 22 April 1808, ibid., 428–32, at 429: "Whenever you find it your interest to dispose of a part to enable you to improve the rest, and to support
your families in the meantime, we are willing to buy, because our people increase fast."

74. TJ sought to accelerate the liquidation of Indians' property rights by
promoting their indebtedness. See TJ to Governor William H. Harrison, 27
Feb. 1803, ibid., 10:368–73, at 370: "When these debts get beyond what the individuals can pay, they become willing to lop them off by a cession of lands";
"they will in time either incorporate with us as citizens of the United States, or
remove beyond the Mississippi." Modern commentators understandably find
this strategy abhorrent. (Hutchins, *Constitution and the Tribes,* chap. 6, charges
that "Jefferson advocated debt ensnarement, to place the Creeks under the ex-
ploitative control of the U.S. government.") But TJ's Indian messages did not
disguise the mechanism at work, nor could he escape the discipline of debt in
his own private life and public career. On debt, see Sloan, *Principle and Interest;*
on TJ as manipulator, see Lewis, "'The Blessings of Domestic Society.'"

75. TJ to Captain Hendrick, the Delawares, Mohicans, and Munries, 21
Dec. 1808, in L&B, 16:450–54, at 452. TJ made the same suggestion to the
Cherokee in 1803, through Benjamin Hawkins, the U.S. agent: "In truth, the
ultimate point of rest and happiness for them is to let our settlements and
theirs meet and blend together, to intermix, and become one people" (TJ to
Benjamin Hawkins, 18 Feb. 1803, ibid., 10:360–65, at 363).

76. TJ to the Chiefs of the Upper Cherokees, 4 May 1808, ibid., 16:432–35,
at 434. For the context of this message, see McCloughlin, "Jefferson and
Cherokee Nationalism," 564–65.

77. TJ to the Miamis, Powtewatamies, Delawares, and Chippeways, 21 Dec.
1808, in L&B, 16:438–40, at 439. On the mixing of whites and Indians, see
Lerner, "Reds and Whites: Rights and Wrongs," 163–64, and Jordan, *White
over Black,* 477–81.

78. TJ to the Wolf and People of the Mandan Nation, 30 Dec. 1806, *TJW,*

564–66, at 564; TJ to My Children, White-hairs, Chiefs, and Warriors of the Osage Nation, 16 July 1804, in L&B, 16:405–10, at 406.

2. REPUBLICAN EMPIRE

1. TJ, Second Inaugural Address, 4 March 1805, in Richardson, *Messages and Papers of the Presidents* 1:378–82, at 379.

2. TJ, First Inaugural Address, 4 March 1801, ibid., 321–24, at 322.

3. For Antifederalists and the problem of size, see Matson and Onuf, *A Union of Interests*, 128–34. On "virtue," see Montesquieu, *Spirit of the Laws*, pt. 1, bk. 3, chap. 3, pp. 22–24. In response, Federalists cited another passage (in bk. 9, chap. 1, p. 131) in which Montesquieu asserted that a "federal republic" combined the "internal advantages of republican government and the external force of monarchy."

4. TJ to Monsieur [François] d'Ivernois, 6 Feb. 1795, in L&B, 9:297–301, at 299–300. In this letter TJ recapitulates the main points of Madison's essay; see Cooke, *Federalist*, no. 10, 56–65.

5. See especially Tucker and Hendrickson, *Empire of Liberty*, 125–56. For another critical account, emphasizing "the bankruptcy of Jefferson's commercial ideology, diplomacy and policy," see Ben-Atar, *Origins of Jeffersonian Commercial Diplomacy*, quotation at 170. For the Louisiana Crisis, and citations, see Onuf, "Expanding Union," 50–56.

6. See Pagden, *Lords of All the World*, 156–200, and Pocock, "States, Republics, and Empires." On the conceptual history of federalism and union, see Onuf and Onuf, *Federal Union, Modern World*. For are conceptualization of the history of European states-systems, see Deudney, "Philadelphian System," and Deudney, "Binding Sovereigns." For a history of the American federal union as a states-system, see Hendrickson, *Ideological Origins of American Internationalism*.

7. For a skeptical account of the Americans' protestations of loyalty and their identification with the empire, appropriately emphasizing their opportunistic character, see Tucker and Hendrickson, *Fall of the First British Empire*, 199–209.

8. On increasingly divergent conceptions of empire and the imperial constitution before the Revolution, see Knorr, *British Colonial Theories;* Koebner, *Empire;* Greene, *Peripheries and Center;* Reid, *Constitutional History of the Revolution.*

9. I am indebted to Burstein, *Sentimental Democracy,* chap. 5, for these citations and the following discussion. Burstein's book offers an account of how Americans fashioned a collective identity by drawing liberally—and "romantically"—from British sources, including ideas about empire. My understanding of the origins of American nationalism has been strongly influenced by Waldstreicher, *In the Midst of Perpetual Fetes.*

10. Stiles, *United States Elevated to Glory,* 50.

11. See Weinberg, *Manifest Destiny;* Van Alstyne, *Rising American Empire;* DeConde, *This Affair of Louisiana;* Horsman, *Race and Manifest Destiny.* For a typology of "empire" that focuses on transhistorical "generic features," see Meinig, *Continental America,* 170–96, quotation at 179. Meinig writes: "To recast the history of Anglo-American expansionism into imperial terms is merely one basic shift in perspective that can help Euro-Americans gain a clearer view of our national past" (196). For the way urban boosters reconciled metropolitan aspirations with a republican conception of empire, see Cronon, *Nature's Metropolis,* 41–46. John Wright, Chicago's leading booster, insisted in 1869 that his city "is no monopolist. . . . She rejoices in the truth that we constitute no ordinary nation, but a constellation of sovereign, free and independent States, which fact of art itself tends to create many centres, while nature, in these immense vallies of thousands of miles, has ordained sites for many great cities" (as quoted in ibid., 45).

12. Pagden, *Lords of All the World.*

13. "Vision of the Paradise . . . ," *United States Magazine,* March 1779, as cited in Burstein, *Sentimental Democracy,* chap. 5.

14. "Cassius," *New Jersey Journal,* 31 Oct. 1787, in Kaminski, *Documentary History of the Ratification* 3:143.

15. Pagden, *Lords of All the World,* 178–200.

16. Enthusiastic Revolutionaries asserted that conflicts within and among the American provinces were themselves a function of a corrupt British administration. Gordon Wood has linked this rhetoric to a republican discourse of "moral reformation" that focused on civic decay and corruption in provincial societies (*Creation of the American Republic,* 91–124). I contend here that the patriots' republican discourse was also, and perhaps primarily, an imperial discourse: appropriating the language of British oppositionists, Americans imagined an imperial regime within which they could claim equal rights and benefits.

17. Minutes of the Board of Visitors, University of Virginia, 4 March 1825, *TJW,* 479.

18. *TJP* 1:429–33, at 429. For the "liberalism" of the Declaration, see Sheldon, *Political Philosophy of Jefferson.* "It may thus be seen," Sheldon writes, "that Jefferson has adapted the language of Lockean liberalism, created originally for individual men in the state of nature, to the needs of revolutionary colonies in a federated empire of equal and independent states" (49–50).

19. Onuf, "Declaration of Independence for Diplomatic Historians." For an example of how diplomatic history written with a consciousness of the problematic distinction between "domestic" and "foreign" can challenge and revise conventional assumptions in early American political history, see Lewis, *American Union and the Problem of Neighborhood.*

20. The primary definition of "federal" in the *OED* is "of or pertaining to a covenant, compact, or treaty." See Pocock, "States, Republics, and Empires." On the importance of treaties in Revolutionary thought, see Onuf and Onuf, *Federal Union, Modern World,* 109–13.

21. TJ's notes on debates in Congress, 7 June 1776, *Autobiography,* 6 Jan. 1821, *TJW,* 15.

22. McLaughlin, "Background of American Federalism"; Onuf, *Origins of the Federal Republic;* Greene, *Peripheries and Center.*

23. On the turn to natural rights—and the quest for union within the empire—see Conrad, "Putting Rights Talk in Its Place," 260–61. Confusion about the role and authority of Congress as putative successor to the British crown's prerogative powers suggests continuities in Revolutionary constitutionalism that the decision for independence has obscured (Marston, *King and Congress*).

24. Onuf and Onuf, *Federal Union, Modern World.* The idea that the United States was a prototype for a "more perfect" world order was fashionable among world federalists such as James Brown Scott during the era of the League of Nations; see Scott, *United States of America.*

25. See Colley, *Britons.* For the recent literature on British identity, see Gould, "A Virtual Nation." For the American case, see Greene, *Intellectual Construction of America,* 95–129; Greene, "Empire and Identity"; Breen, "Ideology and Nationalism."

26. On the reciprocal development of regional and national identities, see Onuf, "Federalism, Republicanism, and the Origins of Sectionalism." The classic analysis of this "character," one that emphasizes associational activity, is Tocqueville, *Democracy in America,* esp. 1:191–98.

27. TJ, Draft of Instructions to the Virginia Delegates in the Continental Congress (MS Text of *A Summary View*), [July 1774], *TJP* 1:121–41, at 133.

28. Ibid., 122; Bland, *Colonel Dismounted,* 319. For "the right of migration," see Reid, *Authority of Rights,* 118–20. For the Bland-TJ connection, see Gutzman, "Old Dominion, New Republic," chap. 1.

29. TJ, Draft of Instructions, *TJP* 1:122–23.

30. Ibid., 129.

31. Ibid., 135.

32. See, for instance, Ellis, *American Sphinx,* 59: "His several arguments for American independence all were shaped around a central motif, in which the imperfect and inadequate present was contrasted with a perfect and pure future"; these were the "personal cravings" of a "young man" who failed to grow up. For the editing of the Declaration, see Maier, *American Scripture,* 97–153.

33. I am indebted to Wood's *Radicalism of the Revolution* for my understanding of republicanism.

34. TJ's "original Rough draught" of the Declaration of Independence, *TJP* 1:423–28, at 426–27.

35. The Declaration of Independence as Adopted by Congress, 4 July 1776, ibid., 429–33, at 429, 432.

36. Ibid., 429.

37. Malone, *Jefferson the Virginian,* 169–96. On the relation between TJ's "cosmopolitanism" and his "deep loyalties" to Virginia, see Greene, "Intellectual Construction of Virginia," quotations at 250, and Gutzman, "Old Dominion, New Republic." On Virginia expansionists in the colonial period, see Eg-

nal, *A Mighty Empire,* 87–101, and Breen, *Tobacco Culture,* 180–86, 204–10. For the liberal political economic vision of "Virginia nationalists" in the early republic, see Appleby, "'Agrarian Myth' in the Early Republic," and Appleby, *Capitalism and a New Social Order.*

38. *Notes,* Query I ("Boundaries"), 4.

39. Ibid. See Seelye, *Beautiful Machine.*

40. *Notes,* Query II ("Rivers"), 15.

41. TJ, Draft of Instructions, *TJP* 1:133. "Laborers" was "farmers" in the printed version of the *Summary View,* ibid., n. 35, 137.

42. The Constitution as Adopted by the Convention, [29 June 1776], ibid., 383; Third Draft by TJ, [before 13 June], ibid., 363. See Onuf, *Origins of the Federal Republic,* 75–102.

43. For the text of the Ordinance, adopted by Congress on 23 April 1784, and commentary, see Onuf, *Statehood and Union,* 46–49.

44. On "permeable" boundaries, see Onuf and Onuf, *Federal Union, Modern World,* 135–39.

45. For the literature on the *Notes,* see Onuf, "Scholars' Jefferson," 682.

46. TJ's "ward republics" took this principle of territorial fission to its logical extreme, "distributing to every one exactly the functions he is competent to . . . , dividing and subdividing these republics from the great national one down through all its subordinations, until it ends in the administration of every man's farm by himself" (TJ to Joseph C. Cabell, 2 Feb. 1816, in L&B, 14:417–23, at 421).

47. Hirschman, *Passions and the Interests;* Pagden, *Lords of All the World,* 156–77. For Jeffersonian political economy, see McCoy, *Elusive Republic.* On mercantilism, see Crowley, *Privileges of Independence.*

48. On TJ's "agrarianism," see Marx, *Machine in the Garden,* and Bender, *Toward an Urban Vision,* 4–7, 21–25.

49. *Notes,* Queries XIX and III, 165, 17.

50. Onuf, *Statehood and Union,* 5–15.

51. *Notes,* Query XIX ("Manufactures"), 165.

52. Ibid., and Query XXII ("Public Revenue and Expences"), 175.

53. "Were I to indulge my own theory, I should wish them [the Americans] to practice neither commerce nor navigation, but to stand with respect to Europe precisely on the footing of China. . . . But this is theory only, and a theory which the servants of America are not at liberty to follow" (TJ to G. K. van Hogendorp, 13 Oct. 1785, *TJP* 8:631–34, at 633). For similar sentiments, see also TJ to George Washington, 15 March 1784, ibid., 7:25–27.

54. *Notes,* Query XXII, 174.

55. Peterson, "Jefferson and Commercial Policy." For more critical accounts, see Crowley, *Privileges of Independence,* 156–63 and passim, and Ben-Atar, *Origins of Jeffersonian Commercial Diplomacy.*

56. *Notes,* 175.

57. [Madison], "Foreign Influence," *Aurora* (Philadelphia), 23 Jan. 1799,

JMP 17:214–20, at 218. In 1803, when the Federalist threat had passed, TJ discounted Madison's concerns: "The great mass of our people are agricultural; and the commercial cities, though, by the command of newspapers, they make a great deal of noise, have little effect in the direction of the government" (TJ to Mr. Pictet, 5 Feb. 1803, in L&B, 10:355–57, at 356). Significantly, however, TJ still posited a fundamental divide between vicious cities, which were centers of "foreign influence," and the virtuous countryside: city people "are as different in sentiment and character from the country people as any two distinct nations, and are clamorous against the order of things established by the agricultural interest." It is also interesting that TJ, like Madison, asserted here that the press remained under Federalist (foreign) control, even though it was the proliferation of Republican newspapers that made his election possible.

58. TJ's Draft of the Kentucky Resolutions, Oct. 1798, *TJW,* 449–56, at 454. Not surprisingly, in view of later developments, TJ's reference to "nullification" (453) has elicited the most scholarly commentary, but it was the threat of war that most compellingly expressed his sense of desperation.

59. Taylor, *Tyranny Unmasked,* 141.

60. Constitutional historian Andrew C. Lenner has shown that both Federalists and Republicans invoked law of nations doctrine throughout the formative party battles of the 1790s. In the subsequent era of Republican ascendancy, the law of nations justified a radically circumscribed definition of federal authority and a correspondingly robust conception of state sovereignty. In times of crisis southerners would invoke Vattel and the other great treatise writers when their enemies sought to consolidate power and encroach on the reserved rights and vital interests of their states. The recourse to international law by patriotic southerners who sought to uphold the principles of self-determination and state equality was particularly conspicuous in the Missouri controversies (Lenner, *Federal Principle in American Politics*).

61. For an elaboration of this theme, see Onuf, "Federalism, Republicanism, and Sectionalism."

62. For "the reign of witches," see TJ to John Taylor, 4 [misdated, 1] June 1798, in L&B, 10:44–47, at 46; for "monocrats," see TJ to William B. Giles, 31 Dec. 1795, ibid., 9:317. In the latter letter TJ also described Federalists as "the British and anti-republican party" (316).

63. First Inaugural Address, 4 March 1801, in Richardson, *Messages and Papers of the Presidents* 1:322. TJ returned to this theme in his letter to Pictet, cited in n. 57 above: "Every man being at his ease, feels an interest in the preservation of order, and comes forth to preserve it at the first call of the magistrate."

64. TJ elaborated this partisan sociology in his letter to Elbridge Gerry, 13 May 1797, in L&B, 9:380–86, quotation at 383: "Foreign and false citizens now constitute the great body of what are called our merchants, fill our sea ports, are planted in every little town and district of the interior country."

65. First Inaugural Address, 4 March 1801, in Richardson, *Messages and Papers of the Presidents* 1:322–23.

3. THE REVOLUTION OF 1800

1. TJ to Judge Spencer Roane, 6 Sept. 1819, in L&B, 15:212–16, at 212. For a discussion of these constitutional issues in the context of Virginia's republican tradition, see Gutzman, "Old Dominion, New Republic." On TJ, Old Republicans, and the Court, see also Malone, *Sage of Monticello*, 345–61; Mayer, *Constitutional Thought of Jefferson*, 277–91. On Roane, see Huebner, "Consolidation of State Judicial Power." The "Hampden" essays, nos. 1–4, are reprinted in Gunther, *Marshall's Defense of McCulloch*, 107–54.

2. Roane thought his essays "relate[d] to a subject as cardinal, in my judgment, as that which involved our Independence" (Spencer Roane to TJ, 22 Aug. 1819, Jefferson Papers, Lib. Cong.). TJ's response suggested that Roane should look first to 1800.

3. TJ to Roane, 6 Sept. 1819, in L&B, 15:212–16, at 212.

4. TJ to John Dickinson, 6 March 1801, ibid., 10:216–18, at 217.

5. See Elkins and McKitrick, *Age of Federalism*. See also Buel, *Securing the Revolution*, and Sharp, *American Politics in the Early Republic*.

6. For further discussion, see Smith, *Freedom's Fetters*. For TJ's life in this period, see Malone, *Jefferson and the Ordeal of Liberty*, 359–506. For crucial documents, see *JMP*, vol. 17.

7. Monroe to George W. Erving, 4 April 1800, in Hamilton, *Writings of Monroe* 3:172–73.

8. James Monroe to TJ, 16 June 1798, ibid., 125–28, at 126.

9. TJ to Joseph Priestley, March 21, 1801, in L&B, 10:227–30, at 229.

10. TJ, First Inaugural Address, 4 March 1801, *TJW*, 492–96, at 493–94. For the importance of "spiritedness" in the people, see Yarbrough, *American Virtues*, 132–40 and passim.

11. TJ to Judge William Johnson, 12 June 1823, in L&B, 15:439–52, at 443–44.

12. "In truth," TJ wrote Samuel Kercheval, "the abuses of monarchy had so much filled all the space of political contemplation, that we imagined everything republican which was not monarchy. We had not yet penetrated to the mother principle, that 'governments are republican only in proportion as they embody the will of their people, and execute it.' Hence, our first constitutions had really no leading principles in them" (TJ to Samuel Kercheval, 12 July 1816, ibid., 32–44, at 32–33).

13. TJ to Samuel Kercheval, 12 July 1816, ibid., 35. The reference was to constitutional reform in Virginia and TJ's attitude toward the 1776 state constitution. It was in this letter that TJ famously attacked excessive reverence for constitutions: "Some men look at constitutions with sanctimonious reverence, and deem them like the ark of the covenant, too sacred to be touched. They ascribe to the men of the preceding age a wisdom more than human, and suppose what they did to be beyond amendment. I knew that age well; I belonged to it, and labored with it. It deserved well of its country. It was very like the present,

but without the experience of the present; and forty years of experience in government is worth a century of book-reading; and this they would say themselves, were they to rise from the dead" (40).

14. TJ to Roane, 6 Sept. 1819, ibid., 212–16, at 212.

15. The historical literature on the "revolution of 1800" is rich and controversial. Students of the so-called first party system emphasized the surprisingly smooth transition to Republican rule, so calling into question the "revolution"'s radicalism. Richard Hofstadter portrays TJ as an inveterately optimistic apostle of "conciliation" and "absorption" whose moderate policies enabled the deposed Federalists to survive as a viable, if not quite loyal, opposition. TJ's "notion that the animating principle behind Federalism had been a passion for monarchy, however delusive it had been, led to the comforting conclusion that the last nail had now been driven into the coffin of the hereditary principle, and hence that the country had reached a unanimity deep enough" (Hofstadter, *Idea of a Party System,* 151, 168). The suggestion that Republican fears were exaggerated, if not delusional, runs through the scholarship of republican revisionists. See especially Howe, "Republican Thought and Political Violence"; Banning, *Jeffersonian Persuasion;* Elkins and McKitrick, *Age of Federalism.* Critics of the revisionists take TJ's professions more seriously. See Sisson, *American Revolution of 1800,* and, particularly, Appleby, *Capitalism and a New Social Order.* Most recently, Joanne B. Freeman has shifted attention away from institutional and ideological development to the highly volatile political culture of the new national political elite. She depicts the 1800 election as "An Honor Dispute of Grand Proportions" in chap. 5 of "Affairs of Honor." Because TJ and other leaders could not acknowledge their own partisanship, they were prone to identify their personal honor with the national interest. For the political culture of the "revolutionary gentry," see Wiebe, *Opening of American Society,* pt. 1 (pp. 1–125).

16. Levy, *Jefferson and Civil Liberties.*

17. "Correspondence between George Nicholas, Esq., of Kentucky, and the Hon. Robert G. Harper," *Virginia Argus,* 15 Nov. 1799; Page, *Address to the Freeholders,* 11.

18. TJ to Thomas Pinckney, 29 May 1797, in L&B, 9:388–91, at 389.

19. Pendleton, *Address of the Honorable Edmund Pendleton,* 12.

20. Nicholas, *A Letter from George Nicholas,* 21.

21. For TJ's attitude to parties, see McDonald, "Jefferson and America: Episodes in Image Formation," esp. chap. 1 ("Political Invention"). For TJ's ambivalent ideas about executive power—combining "*both* radical Whig scorn for imperial government *and* the [Bolingbrokean] ideal of the patriot king," see Ketcham, *Presidents above Party,* 100–113, quotation at 106.

22. TJ to Francis Hopkinson, 13 March 1789, *TJP* 14:649–51, at 650.

23. TJ to George Washington, 9 Sept. 1792, ibid., 24:351–60, at 353, 355. On this letter, see Burstein, *Inner Jefferson,* 212–15; on TJ's understanding of Hamilton, see Freeman, "Slander, Poison, Whispers, and Fame."

24. TJ to George Washington, 9 Sept. 1792, *TJP* 24:351–60, at 352. See Sloan, *Principle and Interest,* chap. 4 ("Errors of Political Life"), 125–64. For Republican ideology and its crucial role in leading TJ to see the error of his ways, see Banning, *Jeffersonian Persuasion;* on assumption, see esp. 137–47.

25. TJ to William B. Giles, 31 Dec. 1795, in L&B, 9:314–18, at 317.

26. TJ to Edmund Randolph, 3 Feb. 1794, ibid., 279–80, at 280.

27. [Taylor], *Definition of Parties,* 15. For Taylor's thought, see Shalhope, *John Taylor of Caroline.*

28. Bailyn, *Ideological Origins of the Revolution,* 144–59; Wood, "Conspiracy and the Paranoid Style."

29. "What is become of the Soveriegn People?" Walter Jones asked James Madison. "They, poor Souls, were told *they* had formed a Government—that a due number of checks and balances were provided—they confide in the Magic of these checks & balances—they indulge an Apathy to public Concerns & Information—they persue, with extreme avidity, the objects of Self Interest and Self injoyment, in which are Swallowed up their Benevolence & public Spirit" (Jones to Madison, 15 May 1796, *JMP* 16:359–62, at 361).

30. TJ to Aaron Burr, 17 June 1797, in L&B, 9:400–404, at 403.

31. Banning, *Jeffersonian Persuasion,* 128–32.

32. TJ to Sullivan, Feb. 9, 1797, in L&B, 9:376–79, at 378.

33. TJ to Elbridge Gerry, 13 May 1797, ibid., 380–86, at 383.

34. [Taylor], *Enquiry into the Tendency of Certain Public Measures,* 22.

35. Ibid., 24.

36. James Madison to TJ, 23 April 1796, *JMP* 16:335–36, at 335. See also Madison to TJ, 1 May 1796, ibid., 342–44, at 343.

37. James Madison to James Monroe, 20 Dec. 1795, ibid., 168–71, at 169.

38. TJ to Phillip Mazzei, 24 April 1796, in L&B, 9:335–37, at 335–36.

39. [Madison], "Foreign Influence," *Aurora* (Philadelphia), 23 Jan. 1799, in *JMP* 17:214–20, at 218–19.

40. On "these foreign and false citizens [who] now constitute the great body of what are called our merchants," see TJ to Elbridge Gerry, 13 May 1797, in L&B, 9:380–86, at 383. At TJ's urging Edmund Pendleton wrote a pamphlet that developed the party's semiofficial line on all these issues ("a ruinous debt," "an army of 50,000 mercenaries," and "an enormous patronage, [that] will subject America to executive despotism"), *Address of the Honorable Edmund Pendleton,* 5.

41. [Madison], "Foreign Influence," *Aurora* (Philadelphia), 23 Jan. 1799, in *JMP* 17:214–20, at 219–20.

42. James Monroe to TJ, 16 June 1798, in Hamilton, *Writings of Monroe* 3:125–28, at 126.

43. Kettner, *Development of American Citizenship,* 213–47; Smith, *Civic Ideals.*

44. Amendments to the Constitution, 28 Sept. 1789, in Veit, Bowling, and Bickford, *Creating the Bill of Rights,* Article the Third (adopted as First Amendment), 3.

45. Banning, *Sacred Fire of Liberty,* 281–90; Banning, *Jefferson and Madison,* chap. 1 ("Parchment Barriers and Fundamental Rights") and documentary appendix, 125–58. See also Finkelman, "Between Scylla and Charybdis," esp. 129–32.

46. "The jealousy of the subordinate governments is a precious reliance. . . . The declaration of rights will be the text whereby they will try all the acts of the federal government" (TJ to Madison, March 15, 1789, *TJP* 14:659–63, at 660).

47. On "gangrene," see TJ to John Melish, 13 Jan. 1813, ibid., 13:206–13, at 209.

48. *Notes,* Query XVIII ("Manners"), 163. For a clear statement of the natural right of self-preservation, see TJ to Edmond Charles Genet, 17 June 1793: "By our treaties with several of the belligerant powers, which are a part of the laws of our land, we have established a State of peace with them. But without appealing to treaties, we are at peace with them all by the law of nature. For by nature's law, man is at peace with man, till some aggression is committed, which, by the same law, authorizes one to destroy another as his enemy" (*TJP* 26:297–300, at 299–300). On the significance of law of nations treatises in TJ's composition of the *Notes,* see Ferguson, *Law and Letters in American Culture,* 42–50.

49. Nicholas Onuf shows that "levels" thinking in international relations theory is a republican legacy. My understanding of "republicanism" in international thought—and in American federalism—is indebted to Onuf, *Republican Legacy in International Thought.* See also Onuf and Onuf, *Federal Union, Modern World.* For these themes in TJ's thought, see Mayer, *Constitutional Thought of Jefferson,* esp. chaps. 5–7 (on the election of 1800, Bill of Rights, and federalism).

50. TJ to Gideon Granger, 13 Aug. 1800, in L&B, 10:166–70, at 168.

51. Virginia Resolutions, in the House of Delegates, 21 Dec. 1798, *JMP* 17:184–90, at 189. For TJ's draft of the Kentucky Resolutions, Oct. 1798, see *TJW,* 449–56. For an interpretation of the Resolutions that emphasizes civil liberties and discounts the significance of states' rights, see Koch and Ammon, "Virginia and Kentucky Resolutions." Cf. Gutzman, "A Troublesome Legacy."

52. TJ to Peregrine Fitzhugh, Esq., 23 Feb. 1798, in L&B, 10:1–4, at 3.

53. Page, *Address to the Freeholders,* 19.

54. [Madison], "Political Reflections," *Aurora* (Philadelphia), 23 Feb. 1799, in *JMP* 17:237–43, at 242.

55. Nicholas, *Letter from George Nicholas,* 23.

56. Ibid., 21.

57. TJ to Col. William Duane, 28 March 1811, in L&B, 13:28–29, at 29.

58. John Taylor to TJ, 15 Feb. 1799, Jefferson Papers, Lib. Cong.

59. [Tucker], *Letter to a Member of Congress,* 2. James Madison underscored the danger of loose construction: "Indeed such an unbridled spirit of construction as has gone forth in sundry instances, would bid defiance to any possible parchment securities against Usurpation" (Madison to TJ, 15 March 1800, *JMP* 17:372–73, at 373). See Powell, "Original Understanding of Original Intent."

60. TJ to Thomas Paine, 18 March 1801, in L&B, 10:223–25, at 224: "The return of our citizens from the phrenzy into which they had been wrought, partly by ill conduct in France, partly by artifices practised on them, is almost entire, and will, I believe, become quite so." See also Pendleton, *Address of the Honorable Edmund Pendleton:* Foreign "relations ought to be explained in an artless, sincere, and unprejudiced mode, that the people may understand them, and that the existing passions which produce error may be assuaged, since the people can only thus discern truth, and by so doing preserve liberty" (19).

61. TJ to Madison, 26 April 1798, *JMP* 17:120–22, at 120.

62. TJ to Thomas Lomax, 12 March 1799, in L&B, 10:123–25, at 123–24.

63. For the way opposition printers sustained the Republican cause—at a time when the party's "leaders" were virtually immobilized—see Pasley, *"Tyranny of Printers."* Pasley suggests that TJ and his elite colleagues never fully appreciated the crucial role of the printers in the "revolution of 1800," both because of their disdain for socially inferior artisans and because of their ambivalence about partisan activity. By identifying themselves with the "nation" as a whole, Republicans could mystify their relation to specific constituencies and downplay their own agency—and that of lower-level part operatives—in rallying voters. See also Pasley, "'A Journeyman, Either in Law or Politics.'" On the proliferation of Republican newspapers in the wake of the Sedition Act, see also Smith, "Crisis, Unity, and Partisanship," chap. 7.

64. [Tucker], *Letter to a Member of Congress,* 47.

65. TJ to Edmund Pendleton, 2 April 1798, in L&B, 10:19–22, at 22. See also TJ to Samuel Smith, 22 Aug. 1798, ibid., 55–59, at 56: these principles "are the same, I am sure, with those of the great body of the American people."

66. "A Republican," "Prospect on the Rariton," *Aurora,* 19 March 1799.

67. On "the Tory interest," see TJ to Pendleton, 2 April 1798, in L&B, 9:19–22, at 21–22.

68. Banning, *Jeffersonian Persuasion,* esp. chap. 9 ("The Principles of Ninety-Eight"). For nationalism, see Onuf, "Federalism, Republicanism, and Sectionalism," and Waldstreicher, *In the Midst of Perpetual Fetes.*

69. [Madison], "Foreign Influence," *Aurora* (Philadelphia), 23 Jan. 1799, in *JMP* 17:214–20, at 216.

70. Nicholas, *Letter from George Nicholas,* 20.

71. Declaration of Independence as Adopted by Congress, 4 July 1776, *TJP* 1:429–33, at 429.

72. *Observations on the Alien and Sedition Laws,* 19, 9. On the importance of natural law principles—and particularly this first law—in Federalist jurisprudence, see Lenner, "A Tale of Two Constitutions."

73. TJ to Gerry, 13 May 1797, in L&B, 9:380–86, at 385.

74. TJ to Joseph Priestley, 21 March 1801, ibid., 10:227–30, at 229.

75. TJ to James Lewis, Jr., 9 May 1798, ibid., 36–38, at 37.

76. TJ to John Taylor, 26 Nov. 1798, ibid., 63–67, at 64.

77. TJ to Elbridge Gerry, 26 Jan. 1799, ibid., 74–86, at 82.

78. See Kuroda, *Origins of the Twelfth Amendment.*

79. See Sharp, *American Politics in the Early Republic,* 250–75. See also Malone, *Jefferson and the Ordeal of Liberty,* 484–506.

80. See TJ to John Taylor of Caroline, 1 June 1798, in L&B, 10:44–47, warning against the "evils of scission" (46), and Taylor's response, 25 June 1798, Jefferson Papers, Lib. Cong.: "If the mass of our citizens are now republican, will submission to anti-republican measures, encrease that mass?"

81. TJ to Gov. Thomas McKean, 9 March 1801, in L&B, 10:221–22, at 221.

82. "For the National Intelligencer," "LETTER from a respectable citizen to a Member of Congress, on the ELECTION of a PRESIDENT," *National Intelligencer,* 21 Jan. 1801.

83. "ARISTIDES," "ON THE ELECTION OF A PRESIDENT, No. II," ibid., 5 Jan. 1801.

84. "ELECTION OF A PRESIDENT," ibid., 16 Feb. 1801.

85. Ibid.

86. Ibid. On the imaginative transcendence of time and distance, see Waldstreicher, *In the Midst of Perpetual Fetes,* esp. 183–92 ("1800: A Different Kind of Revolution").

87. TJ to Joseph Priestley, 21 March 1801, in L&B, 10:227–30, at 229–30.

88. TJ to John Dickinson, 6 March 1801, ibid., 216–18, at 217.

89. Ibid.

90. See "An Old Inhabitant of Columbia: to Editor of the *National Intelligencer,*" *National Intelligencer,* 16 Feb. 1801: "Though opposed, on principle, to Mr. Jefferson, so long as the voice of my country remained unexpressed, I could not hesitate a moment in considering him as our executive magistrate, as soon as that voice was expressed in a fair and unequivocal manner. . . . To what motive can this persevering hostility to the election of Mr. Jefferson be ascribed? Do those who entertain it sincerely believe that in expressing it, they speak the sentiments of their constituents?"

91. TJ to Col. James Monroe, 7 March 1801, in L&B, 10:218–21, at 219, 218.

92. TJ to Joel Barlow, 14 March 14, 1801, ibid., 222–23, at 222; see also TJ to Thomas Paine, 18 March, ibid., 223–25, for similar sentiments.

93. Hofstadter, *Idea of a Party System,* 150–55.

94. TJ to William B. Giles, 23 March 1801, in L&B, 10:238–40, at 240.

95. TJ, First Inaugural Address, *TJW,* 492–96, at 493–94.

96. TJ to Paine, 18 March 1801, in L&B, 10:223–24, at 223–24.

4. FEDERAL UNION

1. TJ to James Donaldson, 7 Feb. 1820, Jefferson Papers, Lib. Cong.

2. For Tallmadge's amendment, 13 and 15 Feb. 1819, see *Annals of Congress,* 15th Cong., 2d sess. (House), 1166, 1170. The standard work is Moore, *Missouri Controversy.* On TJ's response, see Malone, *Sage of Monticello,* 328–61. Cf. Miller, *Wolf by the Ears,* 221–52.

3. TJ to Nelson, 12 March 1820, in L&B, 15:238–39, at 238.

4. TJ to former Congressman John Holmes [of Massachusetts], 22 April 1820, ibid., 248–50, at 249.

5. For TJ's "voice"—and the tension, if not contradiction, between an accommodating, concessive tone and the imperatives of partisanship—see Dawidoff, "Man of Letters," and Wilson, "Jefferson and the Republic of Letters." See also Onuf, "Scholars' Jefferson." For TJ's letter writing (and reading), see Burstein's *Inner Jefferson*.

6. Adams to TJ, 23 Nov. 1819, in Cappon, *Adams-Jefferson Letters* 2:548–50, at 548.

7. For TJ's nautical imagery, see Burstein, *Inner Jefferson*, 85–86.

8. TJ to Adams, 10 Dec. 1819, in Cappon, *Adams-Jefferson Letters* 2:548–50, at 548–49. For an account of this correspondence, see Ellis, *Passionate Sage: The Character of John Adams*, 113–42; on Missouri, see ibid., 138–42. Not surprisingly Adams was "utterly averse to the admission of Slavery into the Missouri Territory" (Adams to William Tudor, 20 Nov. 1819, quoted in ibid., 140). But Adams tactfully avoided such assertions in his correspondence with TJ, optimistically suggesting that the controversy might "follow the other Waves under the Ship and do no harm" (Adams to TJ, 21 Dec. 1819, in Cappon, *Adams-Jefferson Letters* 2:550–51, at 551). It is apparent, however, that Adams could not understand why TJ was so upset by the Missouri affair. Taking a longer view of the nation's prospects, Adams assumed the role of a "Cassandra," predicting that "this mighty Fabric [would be rent] in twain, or perhaps into a leash" by the disunionist schemes of "another Hamilton" or "another Burr"; in the end, there might be "as many Nations in North America as there are in Europe" (ibid.). But TJ did not believe that rogue spirits such as Burr or Hamilton could ever endanger the union again; the whole point of his analysis was that union was threatened from within, not by separatists but rather by neo-Federalist consolidationists who sought to destroy states' rights. The Missouri crisis resulted from rejection of the settlers' efforts to join the union, and not from any original intention of theirs to break away from it. Finally, Adams could broach the possibility of the Europeanization of North America with philosophical equanimity; such a prospect was abhorrent to TJ. TJ did not respond to this letter; perhaps Adams's rather whimsical, humorously pompous language ("mighty Fabric" and "leash" of independent nations, suggesting a pack of dogs and evoking a conventional view of the state of nature where the "dogs of war" were unleashed) was sufficient to tell TJ that Adams was not taking him seriously.

9. TJ to Holmes, 22 April 1820, in L&B, 15:248–50, at 250. On this letter, see Finkelman, "Jefferson and Slavery," 211–12.

10. TJ to Adams, 22 Jan. 1821, in Cappon, *Adams-Jefferson Letters* 2:569–70, at 569. For another reference to "our Holy Alliance of restrictionists," see TJ to Joseph Cabell, 31 Jan. 1821, in L&B, 15:310–13, at 311. TJ was urging expeditious action on his cherished plans for the University of Virginia—a place where Vir-

ginia boys would not be seduced by restrictionist principles, as he supposed was happening at Princeton, where "more than half [the students] were Virginians."

11. TJ to the Marquis de La Fayette, 26 Dec. 1820, in L&B, 15:299–302, at 301. At this point he had concluded that the controversy was a "wave," not a "breaker": "The boisterous sea of liberty indeed is never without a wave, and that from Missouri is now rolling towards us, but we shall ride over it as we have over all others" (ibid., 300–301).

12. TJ to Charles Pinckney, Sept. 30, 1820, ibid., 279–81, at 280. For a discussion of partisan motives that offers substantiation for this perception, see Moore, *Missouri Controversy,* 66–83.

13. TJ to Adams, 22 Jan. 1821, in Cappon, *Adams-Jefferson Letters* 2:569–70, at 570. For a slightly earlier, more circumspect formulation of these concerns, see TJ to Albert Gallatin, 26 Dec. 1820, *TJW,* 1447–50.

14. Miller, *Wolf by the Ears,* 231–32. Merrill Peterson writes that the controversy "threw Jefferson into the deepest political malaise of his entire life" (*Jefferson and the New Nation,* 997). Peterson, Malone, Miller, and Sheldon all suggest that TJ's "malaise" was attributable at least in part to his concerns about the consolidationist tendencies of the Marshall Court (exacerbated by *McCulloch v. Maryland* [1819] but dating back to the early days of his presidency), banks, the protective tariff, and a variety of other issues that seemed ominously interrelated. See Peterson, *Jefferson and the New Nation,* 988–1004 (noting TJ's own disastrous financial affairs in these years); Miller, *Wolf by the Ears,* 226–31 (emphasizing TJ's concern that the South-West axis that had dominated American politics was in jeopardy); and Sheldon, *Political Philosophy of Jefferson,* 135–40 (arguing that "the emancipation of slaves occupied a lower position than either his personal lifestyle or the ideal [agrarian] republic for which he had risked his life and fortune" [139]). TJ's zeal for state's rights "bordered on fanaticism," concedes Malone, the friendliest of biographers (*Sage of Monticello,* 356). For a revisionist account of TJ and Missouri, calling into question his malaise and suggesting his "strategic" use of exaggerated language to achieve political goals, see Leibiger, "Thomas Jefferson and the Missouri Crisis," 127.

15. For the antebellum response to TJ's ambiguous legacy on slavery restriction, see Peterson, *Jefferson Image in the American Mind,* 189–226, esp. at 189–94.

16. TJ to Hon. Mark Langdon Hill, 5 April 1820, in L&B, 15:242–43, at 243.

17. TJ to William Short, 13 April 1820, to John Holmes, 22 April 1820, to Charles Pinckney, 30 Sept. 1820, ibid., 247, 249–50, 280–81.

18. TJ to William Short, 4 Aug. 1820, ibid., 257–64, at 263. For the relation of Latin American developments to the politics—and theoretical premises—of American federalism, see Lewis, *American Union and the Problem of Neighborhood.*

19. TJ to William Short, 4 Aug. 1820, in L&B, 15:257–64, at 263.

20. TJ to Charles Pinckney, 30 Sept. 1820, ibid., 279–81, at 281.

21. TJ to Rush, 20 Oct. 1820, ibid., 281–84, at 283.

22. Ibid., 283–84. See also TJ to Albert Gallatin, 26 Dec. 1820, *TJW,* 1450: "Should this scission take place, one of it's most deplorable consequences would be it's discouragement of the efforts of the European nations in the re-generation of their oppressive and Cannibal governments."

23. TJ to Charles Pinckney, 30 Sept. 1820, in L&B, 15:279–80, at 280.

24. Ibid.; TJ to William Short, 13 April 1820, ibid., 243–48, at 247.

25. TJ to John Holmes, 22 April 1820, ibid., 248–50, at 250.

26. TJ to M. Barbé de Marbois, 14 June 1817, ibid., 129–31, at 130–31.

27. See Onuf and Onuf, *Federal Union, Modern World.*

28. TJ to John Jacob Astor, 9 Nov. 1813, in L&B, 13:432–34, at 433; see also TJ to Astor, 24 May 1812, ibid., 150–53.

29. TJ to Sen. John Breckinridge, 12 Aug. 1803, ibid., 10:407–11, at 409–10.

30. TJ rehearsed the alternative scenario in an anxious letter to Robert R. Livingston, written before the crisis was resolved, 18 April 1802: "The day that France takes possession of N. Orleans fixes the sentence which is to restrain her forever within her low water mark. It seals the union of two nations who in conjunction can maintain exclusive possession of the ocean. From that moment we must marry ourselves to the British fleet and nation" (*TJW,* 1104–7, at 1105). It is curious that TJ, the notorious Anglophobe, should here not just imagine an ad hoc alliance (thus responding to diplomatic exigencies in a way that "realists" so admire) but should talk of a lasting "union" between the two nations that could be described as a "marriage."

31. For an earlier expression of this theme, see TJ to James Madison, 30 Jan. 1787, *JMP* 9:247–52: Americans could never be brought to "cut the throats of their brothers and sons." Here was the most powerful argument against enforc-ing restriction, "Wilberforce" wrote in the Richmond *Enquirer,* 6 Jan. 1820: "With what face could we march to the slaughter of our brothers and children, resisting by armed force the invasion of unlicensed power?"

32. Scholars have lavished considerable attention on the "radical" implica-tions of TJ's making each rising generation "sovereign" with respect to its pred-ecessors. In his letter to Madison of 6 Sept. 1789, *TJP* 15:392–98, at 395, TJ wrote that "between society and society, or generation and generation, there is no municipal obligation, no umpire but the law of nature." This was, TJ ex-plained, precisely the condition of independent states under international law: "By the law of nature, one generation is to another as one independant nation to another." The passing on, from generation to generation, of an enormous public debt constituted a de facto "state of war" (disguised by the forms of mu-nicipal law) between the dead (who squandered the common wealth with which they had been entrusted) and the living. But TJ's manifesto should not be construed as a "declaration of war" between the generations: to the contrary, the constitutional protection against the accumulation of such debts that he urged on Madison and his congressional colleagues would preempt all grounds of future contention along generational lines. Generational equity was thus

analogous to state equality: it would facilitate the "union" of fathers and sons by eliminating all artificial obstructions to their natural harmony and affection. The antitype of TJ's affectionate, familial regime was aristocracy, the institutional embodiment of intergenerational inequity and the corrupt foundation of the European old regime. TJ was thus extending and elaborating what he took to be the fundamental principle of the American Revolution, the principle that defined the difference between Europe and America; he was not advocating redistributionist policies, nor was he seeking to provide a theoretical rationale for evading his own debts to (largely foreign) creditors. See Sloan, "'The Earth Belongs in Usufruct to the Living,'" and the fuller treatment in his *Principle and Interest*. For the kind of intergenerational relations TJ hoped would emerge in Virginia and in the new nation generally, see Hellenbrand, *Unfinished Revolution*. The natural relationship of father and son—recapitulated in the classroom in the relationship between mentor and student—constituted TJ's paradigm for affectionate union.

33. The tension between TJ's plans for education and his conception of the minimal state was suggested to me by Robert A. Gross of the College of William and Mary.

34. TJ to Joseph Cabell, 2 Feb. 1816, to Samuel Kercheval, 12 July 1816, to Kercheval, 5 Sept. 1816, in L&B, 14:417–23, 15:32–44, 70–73. See also Matthews, *Radical Politics of Jefferson*, 77–95.

35. TJ to Kercheval, 12 July 1816, in L&B, 15:32–44, at 38.

36. TJ to Cabell, 2 Feb. 1816, ibid., 14:417–23, at 421.

37. Onuf and Onuf, *Federal Union, Modern World*, 74–91; Onuf, *Republican Legacy in International Thought*, esp. chap. 8 ("Levels"). For another view, portraying TJ as a sovereignty theorist, see Antholis, "Liberal Democratic Theory and Sovereignty," esp. chap. 4 ("Thomas Jefferson and the American Dissolution of Sovereignty"). Though I think Antholis confuses effects with causes, I have found his analysis very suggestive. Antholis suggests that TJ did not "dissolve" sovereignty by transmuting it into the "fiction" of popular sovereignty but rather by discovering it—and seeking to give it efficacy—everywhere, in the claims of distinct generations or in the various levels of self-government. On popular sovereignty, see Morgan, *Inventing the People*.

38. TJ to Kercheval, 5 Sept. 1816, in L&B, 15:70–73, at 72. The "sacred compact" argument was subsequently elaborated by "An American" in "Missouri Question," no. 5, Richmond *Enquirer*, 13 Jan. 1820.

39. On the salience of the law of nations for Jeffersonian federalism, see Lenner, "John Taylor and Federalism."

40. On New England separatism in this period, see Banner, *To the Hartford Convention*. For TJ's animus toward New England, see Shalhope, "Thomas Jefferson's Republicanism," 539–42.

41. The negotiators at Ghent were awaiting the "result, not of the Congress of Vienna, but of Hartford," TJ wrote his old friend M. Correa de Serra, 27 Dec. 1814, in L&B, 14:221–25, at 225.

42. See TJ to Pres. James Monroe, 11 June 1823, ibid., 15:435–39, at 435: "The matter which now embroils Europe, the presumption of dictating to an independent nation [in this case, Naples] the form of its government, is so arrogant, so atrocious, that indignation, as well as moral sentiment, enlists all our partialities and prayers in favor of one, and our equal execrations against the other."

43. TJ to Lafayette, 14 Feb. 1815, ibid., 14:245–55, at 251.

44. TJ, First Inaugural Address, 4 March 1801, *TJW,* 492–96, at 493.

45. Before the outbreak of war, TJ discussed the possibility of "a separate treaty between her [Britain] and your Essex men" (TJ to Gen. Henry Dearborn, 14 Aug. 1811, in L&B, 13:72–74, at 73).

46. This unnatural dependency would put Massachusetts in the anomalous and untenable position of Britain's remaining American colonies. On the Jeffersonian reliance on America's agricultural productivity as a key to an effective foreign policy, see McCoy, *Elusive Republic,* and Stagg, *Mr. Madison's War.*

47. The quotations in the previous two paragraphs are all from TJ to James Martin, 20 Sept. 1813, in L&B, 13:381–84, at 382–83.

48. If war should break out between Massachusetts and the union, "it would be a contest of one against fifteen," TJ wrote James Martin, 20 Sept. 1813, ibid., 383. For further comments on the "defection of Massachusetts" and the "factionists of Boston," see TJ to William Short, 28 Nov. 1814, to John Melish, 10 Dec. 1814, ibid., 14:211–18, at 217, 219–21, at 221.

49. TJ to William Short, 28 Nov. 1814, ibid., 211–18, at 217–18.

50. TJ discounts the "danger from the defection of Massachusetts" in his letter to Short, ibid., 217.

51. TJ to Baron Alexander von Humboldt, 6 Dec. 1813, ibid., 20–25, at 22.

52. TJ to John Melish, 13 Jan. 1813, ibid., 13:206–13, at 209.

53. TJ to Dr. John Crawford, 2 Jan. 1812, ibid., 117–19, at 119.

54. TJ to Horatio G. Spafford, March 17, 1814, ibid., 14:118–20, at 120. For an earlier discussion of this point, emphasizing the role of state governments in preserving liberty, see TJ to Destutt de Tracy, 26 Jan 1811, ibid., 13:13–21, at 19: "The true barriers of our liberty in this country are our State governments; and the wisest conservative power ever contrived by man, is that of which our Revolution and present government found us possessed. Seventeen distinct States, amalgamated into one as to their foreign concerns, but single and independent as to their internal administration, regularly organized with a legislature and governor resting on the choice of the people, and enlightened by a free press, can never be so fascinated by the arts of one man, as to submit voluntarily to his usurpation." TJ's brief for the extended republic was, of course, a recapitulation of James Madison's *Federalist* No. 10: "The influence of factious leaders may kindle a flame within their particular States, but will be unable to spread a general conflagration through the other States" (Cooke, *Federalist,* 64).

55. TJ to Dr. Elijah Griffith, 28 May 1809, in L&B, 12:285–86, at 285.

56. TJ to Dearborn, 17 March 1815, ibid., 14:287–89, at 288–89.

57. Ibid., 289.

58. TJ to John Holmes, 22 April 1820, ibid., 15:248–50, at 249.

59. TJ to Albert Gallatin, 16 June 1817, ibid., 131–35, at 135.

60. TJ to Henry Dearborn, 17 March 1815, ibid., 14:287–89, at 287, 288.

61. TJ to William H. Crawford, 11 Feb. 1815, P.S. of 26 Feb., ibid., 240–44, at 244.

62. For the analogy of the union to "the planetary system," see TJ to John Melish, Dec. 10, 1814, ibid., 219–21, at 221.

63. TJ to Col. William Duane, 28 March 1811, ibid., 13:25–31, at 28–29. See Brown, *Republic in Peril.*

64. Kent Co., Del., Democratic-Republicans to TJ, 13 Jan. 1807, Jefferson Papers, Lib. Cong.

65. New York General Republican Committee to TJ, received 16 Dec. 1806, ibid.

66. Chenango Co., N.Y., Republicans to TJ, 19 Jan. 1807, ibid.

67. Young Men of Democratic Principles, Philadelphia, to TJ, 1 Dec. 1806, ibid.

68. Maryland Legislature to TJ, 3 Jan. 1807, ibid.

69. See Abernethy, *Burr Conspiracy.* See also Malone, *Jefferson the President: Second Term,* 215–88. For the geopolitical context, see Lewis, *American Union and the Problem of Neighborhood,* 31–32 and passim; see also Onuf, "Expanding Union." For a spirited defense of Burr (and an attack on TJ's motives for pursuing him), see Kennedy, *Jefferson, Hamilton, and Burr.* Kennedy argues that TJ's "amoebic imperialism" was designed to promote slave state expansionism; Burr's (presumably widely known) hostility to slavery made his motives suspect in administration circles.

70. Ohio General Assembly Address in support of TJ's administration, 6 Dec. 1806, Jefferson Papers, Lib. Cong.

71. Chenango Co., N.Y., Republicans to TJ, 19 Jan. 1807, ibid. See also Orange Co., N.Y., Republicans to TJ, 27 Dec. 1806, ibid.: "The finances of our nation are in so flourishing a state . . . [because] they have not been lavished upon '*every speck of War,*' but are still in reserve for real and not imaginary dangers."

72. "Wars of ambition are the offspring of Monarchy; they are incompatible with the genius and the spirit of our excellent constitution. When freemen are summoned to the field of battle it should be to defend and not to sacrifice their happiness and liberties" (New York General Committee to TJ, received 16 Dec. 1806, ibid.).

73. Kent Co., Del., Democratic-Republicans to TJ, 13 Jan. 1807, ibid.: Many of the addresses emphasized the "difference between . . . [the Europeans'] Situation and our own." See the Young Men of Democratic Principles, Philadelphia, to TJ, 1 Dec. 1806, ibid.

74. Proclamation of 27 Nov. 1806, in Richardson, *Messages and Papers of the Presidents* 1:404–5, at 404.

75. See TJ's Notes (on procedure to be followed against conspirators), 25 Nov. 1806, Jefferson Papers, Lib. Cong., including a list of letters to be written to officials at Pittsburgh, Marietta, Louisville, New Orleans, and other locations.

76. TJ to Gov. William C. C. Claiborne at New Orleans, 20 Dec. 1806, ibid.

77. Malone, *Jefferson the President: Second Term*, 291–370.

78. TJ to Isaac Weaver, Jr., 7 June 1807, in L&B, 11:219–21, at 220–21. For similar sentiments, see TJ to M. Dupont de Nemours and TJ to Marquis de la Fayette, both 14 July 1807, ibid., 275–76, 277–79.

79. TJ to Gov. William C. C. Claiborne, 3 Feb. 1807, ibid., 150–51, at 151.

80. Young Men of Democratic Principles, Philadelphia, to TJ, 1 Dec. 1806, Jefferson Papers, Lib. Cong.

81. TJ to James Bowdoin, 2 April 1807, in L&B, 11:183–86, at 185.

82. Malone, *Jefferson the President: Second Term*, 237–38, 360–62.

83. TJ to Gov. John Langdon, 22 Dec. 1806, Jefferson Papers, Lib. Cong. For such a prediction, see a pamphlet by Joseph Hamilton Daveiss (the Federalist U.S. attorney in Kentucky and a leading opponent of the Burr conspiracy in that state), *Essay on Federalism*, 46: "The farther a state government is removed from the national centre, the less it hears, and sees, and feels, of that government, and the less interest it takes in its concerns. You must, therefore, expect the federative cord to weaken as it is stretched and extended."

84. TJ to William B. Giles, 20 April 1807, in L&B, 11:187–91, at 187.

85. TJ to Charles Clay, 11 Jan. 1807, ibid., 132–33, at 133.

86. TJ to Gov. Edward Tiffin, 2 Feb. 1807, ibid., 146–47, at 147. On Ohio's "patriotism and public spirit," see also TJ to Sec. of War (Henry Dearborn), 27 Oct. 1807, ibid., 385–86.

87. See TJ to Gen. John Shee (Philadelphia Republican Militia), 14 Jan. 1807, to Capt. Charles Christian (Saratoga Rangers), 14 Jan. 1807, declining offers to mobilize: "I am ever unwilling that it [peace] should be disturbed, until greater and more important interests call for an appeal to force" (ibid., 140–41, 141–42, quotations at 140).

88. TJ's Sixth Annual Message, 2 Dec. 1806, in Richardson, *Messages and Papers of the Presidents* 1:405–10, at 410.

89. TJ's First Annual Message, 8 Dec. 1801, ibid., 326–32, at 327.

90. TJ to William Short, 3 Oct. 1801, in L&B, 10:284–88, at 287.

91. See Onuf and Onuf, *Federal Union, Modern World*, 179–82.

92. TJ to Dr. James Brown, 27 Oct. 1808, in L&B, 12:182–85, at 185.

93. Ibid., 183–84.

94. TJ, Second Inaugural Address, 4 March 1805, in Richardson, *Messages and Papers of the Presidents* 1:378–82, at 379.

95. The Declaration of Independence as Adopted by Congress, *TJP* 1:429–33, quotations at 429–30. For TJ and the Declaration, see Ellis, *American Sphinx*, 24–63, and Maier, *American Scripture*, 97–153. For the political history

of independence, see Rakove, *Beginnings of National Politics,* 87–110. For TJ's sentimental conception of union, see Wills, *Inventing America,* esp. 259–319, and Fliegelman, *Declaring Independence.* See also the suggestive comments in Wood, "Trials and Tribulations of Jefferson." TJ, writes Wood, "always conceived of his 'empire of liberty' as one of like principles, not like boundaries"; his "contempt for the modern state" was predicated on "his extraordinary faith in the natural sociability of people" (408). For a discussion of TJ's *Summary View of the Rights of British America* (1774) that underscores its federalist premises and nationalist intentions, see Conrad, "Putting Rights Talk in Its Place." Conrad's reading of this crucial text provides important clues to TJ's concerns in the Declaration.

96. TJ's Original Rough Draft of the Declaration, *TJP* 1:423–28, quotations at 427, 426, 427. On the "Authority of Migration," see Reid, *Authority of Rights,* 114–23. For the expatriation idea in Revolutionary Virginia, see Gutman, "Old Dominion, New Republic," chap. 1.

97. TJ's Original Rough Draft of the Declaration, *TJP* 1:423–28, at 427. On the importance of treaties for Anglo-American imperial reformers, see Onuf and Onuf, *Federal Union, Modern World,* 108–13.

98. See, for example, Becker, *Declaration of Independence,* 213: "Congress omitted this passage [on the slave trade] altogether. I am glad it did. One does not expect a declaration of independence to represent historical events with the objectivity and exactitude of a scientific treatise; but here the discrepancy between the fact and the representation is too flagrant." Though Wills, in *Inventing America,* 65–75, challenges the conventional understanding (I believe mistakenly) that TJ "resented changes in his document only, or even principally, because this clause was omitted," he agrees that the document was much improved by this excision (quotation at 74).

99. *Autobiography,* 6 Jan. 1821, *TJW,* 1–101, quotations above and in subsequent paragraph at 18. TJ claimed that these comments were transcriptions of notes he had taken "while these things were going on" (24).

100. Freeman, "Slander, Poison, Whispers, and Fame."

101. TJ's Original Rough Draft of the Declaration, *TJP* 1:423–28, at 426.

102. *Autobiography,* in *TJW,* 18.

103. It should be noted that Charles Francis Adams, grandson of TJ's Revolutionary colleague John Adams, endorsed TJ's position in a letter of 4 July 1862 to his son Charles, then in the field with the Union army: "Eighty-six years ago our ancestors staked themselves in a contest of a far more dangerous and desperate character. The only fault they committed was in omitting to make it more general and complete. Had they consented to follow Thomas Jefferson to the full extent of his first draught of the Declaration, they would have added little to the seven years severity of their struggle and would have entirely saved the present trials from their children" (Ford, *Cycle of Adams Letters* 1:162). I am indebted to Richard Samuelson for this citation.

104. TJ's Original Rough Draft of the Declaration, *TJP* 1:423–28, at 426.

105. TJ to Hugh Nelson, 12 March 1820, to Charles Pinckney, 30 Sept. 1820, in L&B, 15:238–399, at 238, 279–80, at 280.

106. TJ to John Holmes, 22 April 1820, ibid., 248–50, at 250.

107. Ibid.

108. TJ to William Short, 13 April 1820, ibid., 243–48, at 248.

109. TJ to Maria Cosway, 12 Oct. 1786, *TJP* 10:443–55, at 450, 451.

110. For these years, see Peterson, *Jefferson and the New Nation*, 97–240.

111. Onuf, *Statehood and Union*, 44–54. See also the editorial note and documents on the 1784 Ordinance in *TJP* 6:581–617.

112. Report of the Committee, 1 March 1784, *TJP* 6:604. The ban on settlers with hereditary titles was omitted in the ordinance adopted by Congress on 23 April (ibid., 613–15).

113. For TJ's geopolitical concerns in the 1784 ordinance, see Berkhofer, "Jefferson and the Origins of the Territorial System."

114. For TJ's misgivings about these revisions, see Onuf, *Statehood and Union*, 50–56. See ibid., 60–64, for the text of the Northwest Ordinance. James Monroe, who played a key role in the revision process, reassured TJ that the "most important principles" of his plan were "preserv'd" in Congress's new "colonial" system (Monroe to TJ, May 11, 1786, *TJP* 9:510–12, at 511).

115. For this compromise tradition, see Knupfer, *Union As It Is*.

116. For an engaging portrait of Madison in his retirement years that substantiates this contrast with TJ, see McCoy, *Last of the Fathers*. Madison responded "with far greater equanimity" to the settlement of the Missouri controversy "than many other prominent Virginians"—including his friend TJ (quotation at 113).

117. Draft of the Kentucky Resolutions, October 1798, *TJW*, 449–56, at 453.

118. Madison may have been protesting too much, in dissociating himself from the legacy of 1798—and, implicitly, from TJ. See Gutzman, "A Troublesome Legacy."

119. See Carpenter, *South as a Conscious Minority*, and McCardell, *Idea of a Southern Nation*.

120. See the speech by Sen. Richard M. Johnson of Kentucky, 1 Feb. 1820, in *Annals of Congress*, 16th Cong., 1st sess., 350, explaining what TJ "meant" by saying "all men are created equal": "The meaning of this sentence is defined by its application; that all communities stand upon an equality; that Americans are equal with Englishmen, and have the right to organize such government for themselves as they shall choose, whenever it is their pleasure to dissolve the bonds which unite them to another people. The same principle applied to Missouri will defeat the object of gentlemen who advocate this restriction."

121. TJ to William Short, 13 April 1820, in L&B, 15:243–48, at 248.

5. "TO DECLARE THEM A FREE AND
INDEPENDANT PEOPLE"

1. *Notes,* Query XVIII ("Manners"), 163. TJ originally drafted the *Notes* in 1781–82; the first English edition was published in London in 1787. See Wilson, "Jefferson and the Republic of Letters."

2. *Notes,* Query XIV ("Laws"), 143.

3. TJ to Benjamin Banneker, 30 Aug. 1791, *TJP* 22:97–98; TJ to Henri Gregoire, 25 Feb. 1809, in L&B, 12:254–55.

4. On TJ and slavery, see Boorstin, *Lost World of Jefferson,* esp. 59–108; McColley, *Slavery and Jeffersonian Virginia;* Jordan, *White over Black,* esp. 429–81 ("Thomas Jefferson: Self and Society"); Cohen, "Jefferson and the Problem of Slavery"; Freehling, "Founding Fathers and Slavery"; Davis, *Slavery in the Age of Revolution,* esp. 169–84 ("Jefferson's Uncertain Commitment"); Diggins, "Slavery, Race, and Equality"; Miller, *Wolf by the Ears;* Matthews, *Radical Politics of Jefferson,* 53–75; Haskell, "Capitalism and the Humanitarian Sensibility"; Freehling, *Road to Disunion,* 121–43 ("Conditional Termination in the Early Republic"); Wilson, "Jefferson and the Character Issue"; Finkelman, "Jefferson and Slavery"; Stanton, "'Those Who Labor for My Happiness'"; Boulton, "American Paradox"; O'Brien, *Long Affair;* Ellis, *American Sphinx,* 144–52; Ellis, "Jefferson's Cop-Out," Gordon-Reed, *Thomas Jefferson and Sally Hemings;* Ceaser, *Reconstructing America,* 19–65; Helo, "Jefferson's Republicanism and Slavery." For historiographical discussions, see French and Ayers, "Strange Career of Jefferson"; Onuf, "Scholars' Jefferson"; Finkelman, "Thomas Jefferson and Slavery II: Historians and Myths"; Gordon-Reed, *Jefferson and Hemings;* Wilentz, "Life, Liberty, and the Pursuit of Jefferson."

5. *Notes,* Query XVIII, 162–63. For a meditation on this Query and on the *Notes* generally, see Simpson, "Ferocity of Self." Simpson suggests that "Jefferson sees rebellion as virtually fore-ordained": "Calling into question the very possibility of the self as an independent entity, it is in a sense a text counter to the Declaration" (75, 76). See also Simpson, *Mind and the American Civil War,* 22–29.

6. Nussbaum, *Concise History of the Law of Nations,* 150–64; Onuf and Onuf, *Federal Union, Modern World,* 10–19. On TJ and the law of nations, see Lang, *Foreign Policy and the Early Republic,* 127–56 ("The Jeffersonian Approach"); for the argument that law of nations treatises by Hugo Grotius and other publicists provided the organizing structure of the *Notes,* see Ferguson, *Law and Letters in American Culture,* 42–50.

7. *Notes,* Query XVIII, 163.

8. For the classic statement on slavery as a state of war, see Locke, *Two Treatises of Government,* Second Treatise, chap. 4 ("Of Slavery"), 324–26.

9. TJ to John Holmes, 22 April 1820, in L&B, 15:248–50, at 249.

10. Vattel, *Law of Nations* 1.1. For Vattel's influence, see Fenwick, "Authority of Vattel."

11. *Notes,* Query XIV, 138. The quotations in the next two paragraphs are also from this passage.

12. The Declaration of Independence as Adopted by Congress, 4 July 1776, *TJP* 1:429.

13. *Autobiography,* dated 6 Jan.–29 July 1821, *TJW,* 44.

14. TJ to Jared Sparks, 4 Feb. 1824, in L&B, 16:8–14, at 9.

15. Bailyn, *Ideological Origins of the Revolution,* 232–46 and passim. On the connection between the rhetoric of slavery and the collective identity of Anglo-Americans, see Breen, "Ideology and Nationalism on the Eve of the Revolution."

16. Blackstone, *Commentaries on the Laws of England* 1:112.

17. Breen, "Ideology and Nationalism on the Eve of the Revolution"; Greene, "Search for Identity"; Greene, *Intellectual Construction of America,* 129: "In both America and England . . . the continuing authority of European culture operated powerfully to prevent observers from developing a fully positive identification of the societies of colonial British America during the first three-quarters of the eighteenth century." Reid's *Constitutional History of the Revolution* shows that the ideological struggle of the imperial crisis is best understood as a great debate within the British constitutional tradition. For the development of British identity in this period, see Colley, *Britons.*

18. Onuf and Onuf, *Federal Union, Modern World,* 108–13.

19. On *The Summary View,* see Conrad, "Putting Rights Talk in Its Place." See also Anthony Lewis, "Jefferson's *Summary View* as a Chart of Political Union," *WMQ* 5 (1948), 34–51. For the text of the essay, see "A Native and Member of the House of Burgesses" [TJ], *Summary View.*

20. *Summary View,* 243, 251.

21. Ibid., 253, 256, 244, 256.

22. Ibid., 243. TJ subsequently failed to incorporate the expatriation right in Congress's Declaration on the Causes and Necessity of Taking Up Arms, [6 July 1775]; see TJ's Draft, *TJP* 1:214. TJ returned to this theme once again in his *Autobiography,* in *TJW,* 9: "Expatriation . . . [was] a natural right, and acted on as such, by all nations, in all ages." Unfortunately, "in this doctrine . . . I had never been able to get any one to agree with me but Mr. Wythe." See Colbourn, *Lamp of Experience,* 158–84 ("Thomas Jefferson and the Rights of Expatriated Men"); Reid, *Authority of Rights,* 118–20; Ellis, *American Sphinx,* 32–34, 52; Gutzman, "Old Dominion, New Republic," chap. 1.

23. *Summary View,* 252. See the "Address of the House of Burgesses to the King in Opposition to the Slave Trade," 1 April 1772, in Van Schreeven et al., *Revolutionary Virginia* 1:85–88: "The importation of Slaves into the Colonies from the Coast of *Africa* hath long been considered as a Trade of great Inhumanity, and, under its present Encouragement, we have too much Reason to fear will endanger the very Existence of your Majesty's *American* Dominions" (87).

24. *Summary View,* 252. "Enfranchisement" is TJ's term. It is highly unlikely

that he contemplated extending the franchise to freedpeople in Virginia. Perhaps the word choice reflects TJ's larger theme in *Summary View*, that the very existence of a "free people" depends on their right to exercise legislative powers. As TJ would soon make clear, in order to be "enfranchised," slaves would not only have to be liberated but also expatriated to a "country" of their own.

25. TJ's "original Rough draught" of the Declaration of Independence, n.d., *TJP* 1:426. For the drafting of the Declaration, see Maier, *American Scripture*; see 146–47 on the excised passage on the slave trade.

26. Maier, *American Scripture*, 143–53; Wills, *Inventing America*, 65–75.

27. TJ's draught of the Declaration, *TJP* 1:425, 424. For allegiance and protection in pre-Revolutionary polemics, see Kettner, *Development of American Citizenship*, 165–72.

28. See Holton, "Rebel against Rebel."

29. Yarbrough, *American Virtues*: "All that the Declaration requires is that blacks be restored to their natural liberty to form themselves into a distinct people. They do not have the right to join an existing polity unless that people chooses to admit them" (10). See also Jaffa, *Crisis of the House Divided*, 378–81.

30. Boorstin, *Lost World of Jefferson*, 68–98; Jordan, *White over Black*, 435–57; Miller, *Wolf by the Ears*, 46–59; Boulton, "American Paradox"; Ceaser, *Reconstructing America*, 19–65.

31. TJ to Edward Coles, 25 Aug. 1814, *TJW*, 1343–46, at 1344. TJ was explaining why he and Col. Richard Bland had failed to persuade their fellow burgesses to legalize individual manumissions and thus take a small first step toward emancipation: "It was not easy to carry them to the whole length of the principles which they invoked for themselves."

32. *OED*.

33. On the Americans' "volitional" conception of citizenship, see Kettner, *Development of American Citizenship*, 173–209, and Smith, *Civic Ideals*. On the development of American nationalism, see Breen, "Ideology and Nationalism on the Eve of the Revolution"; Onuf, "Federalism, Republicanism, and Sectionalism"; and especially Waldstreicher, *In the Midst of Perpetual Fetes*.

34. For TJ's moral philosophy, see Helo, "Jefferson's Republicanism and Slavery." In chap. 2, "The Notion of the Moral Sense in Jefferson's Thinking," Helo persuasively challenges the conventional notion that TJ's acknowledgment of a universal moral sense was the foundation of his conception of equality (see Wills, *Inventing America*, 223–28; Matthews, *Radical Politics of Jefferson*, 60–62). Helo writes: "Equality could be taken as an eternal moral principle in the sense that no man could be deemed as moral without free will. The very concept of free will naturally required the principal equality between the free agents as far as they were deemed independent willing beings in the first place. . . . Here arises the notion of active citizenship as equivalent to the notion of civic personality on each man's self-understanding." Expanding the sphere of moral action "within the historical circumstances of general inequality" depended on recognizing legitimate claims to national self-determination:

the self-government of a people was the threshold of moral agency. Helo describes TJ's moral thinking as "a special kind of modernized, although much less Christianized, version of Aristotelianism." Greene historicizes American Revolutionary conceptions of "equality" in "All Men Are Created Equal."

35. TJ to William Gordon, 16 July 1788, *TJP* 13:363–64. See also Finkelman, "Jefferson and Slavery," 193. For these difficult years in TJ's life, see Malone, *Jefferson the Virginian*, 314–69, and Peterson, *Jefferson and the New Nation*, 166–240.

36. *Notes*, Query XVIII, 162, 163.

37. Ibid., Query XIX, 164–65. For political economic thought in this period, see McCoy, *Elusive Republic*. Joyce Appleby cautions against exaggerating TJ's commitment to an agrarian way of life; see her essays "'Agrarian Myth'" and "What Is Still American in Jefferson's Political Philosophy?" Although I endorse Appleby's interpretation of TJ's political economy, I would emphasize the significance of the agrarian idea for his conception of national identity. For a balanced discussion, see Yarbrough, *American Virtues*. Yarbrough suggests that "for eighteenth-century Americans . . . independence meant not self-sufficiency but avoiding those activities and jobs that placed one person under the command of another" (76). I would only add that independence was as much the desideratum for the republic as for the republican. On Jeffersonian pastoralism, see Marx, *Machine in the Garden*, and the corrective by Wilson, "American Agricola."

38. See Yarbrough, *American Virtues*, esp. 55–101.

39. Simpson comments: "The pastoral vision in the nineteenth Query of the *Notes on Virginia*—may we infer?—represents Jefferson's necessary repression of the immediately preceding vision of the slave culture of Virginia" ("Ferocity of Self," 77).

40. Locke, *Two Treatises*, Second Treatise, chap. 5, para. 28, p. 329: "Whatsoever [man] . . . removes out of the State that Nature hath provided, and left it in, he hath mixed his *Labour* with, and joyned to it something that is his own, and thereby makes it his *Property*."

41. TJ to Angelica Church, 27 Nov. 1793, *TJP* 27:449–50, at 449. For TJ as a slaveholder, see Stanton, "'Those Who Labor for My Happiness.'"

42. See Lewis, "Happiness."

43. *Notes*, Query XIX, 164.

44. See Appleby, *Without Resolution*, 21: "As with the Afro-Americans, the differences of the Indians—in this case their willed preference to retain their native ways—eliminated them from the grand human destiny which the American nation had come to embody. It was a grim testimony to Jefferson's commitment to uniformity"—and to the "master passion" of his generation: "to erect republics for white men." See also MacLeod, "Toward Caste": "Southern whites preserved their commitment to republicanism by formally reading blacks out of the polity" (231). The classic study on this theme is Morgan, *American Slavery, American Freedom*.

45. Breen emphasizes the "logical link . . . between England's newly aggressive nationalism and the dramatic popular appeal of natural rights liberalism" in "Ideology and Nationalism on the Eve of the Revolution," 35–36. See also Sheldon, *Political Philosophy of Jefferson,* 41–52. Sheldon writes: "It may thus be seen that Jefferson has adapted the language of Lockean liberalism, created originally for individual men in the state of nature, to the needs of revolutionary colonies in a federated empire of equal and independent states." Americans embraced "natural rights liberalism" as they sought to define and secure their rights collectively; little "adapting" was necessary when Americans appropriated this doctrine from influential treatises on the law of nature and of nations (49–50). For Locke's significance in developing the "modern" natural rights doctrine that TJ found so congenial in conceptualizing political society and the society of nations, see Zuckert, *Natural Rights and the New Republicanism.*

46. *Summary View,* 254–55.

47. *Notes,* Query VIII, 84.

48. Ibid.

49. Ibid., 84–85, 87; the reference to "unremitting despotism" is from ibid., Query XVIII, 162.

50. See Kett, "Education," and Yarbrough, *American Virtues,* 125–32. On the problem of generations, see Hellenbrand, *Unfinished Revolution.* Hellenbrand writes: "The success of Jefferson's family-nation . . . thus depended on the careful screening of all applicants for utopia and the scrupulous education of those people already on board" (117).

51. *Notes,* Query VIII, 83, 84, 87.

52. TJ to James Madison, 6 Sept. 1789, *TJP* 15:392–98, at 392, 395. On this letter, see Sloan, "'The Earth Belongs to the Living,'" and Sloan, *Principle and Interest.*

53. Bill to Enable Tenants in Fee Tail to Convey Their Lands in Fee Simple [14 Oct. 1776] and A Bill Directing the Course of Descents [adopted 30 Nov. 1785], *TJP* 1:560–62, 2:391–93. These were two of the four acts, TJ proudly recalled in his *Autobiography* (in *TJW,* 44), that formed "a system by which every fibre would be eradicated of antient or future aristocracy" (the other two were his bills for religious freedom and for general education). See Brewer, "Entailing Aristocracy in Colonial Virginia."

54. *Notes,* Query VIII, 83.

55. Jordan, *White over Black,* 461–75 (on TJ) and 542–69 (on miscegenation and colonization).

56. *Notes,* Query XIV ("Laws"), 138. See Fliegelman, *Declaring Independence,* 189–95.

57. *Notes,* Query XIV, 138.

58. Foster et al., "Jefferson Fathered Slave's Last Child." By themselves the DNA tests cannot prove TJ's paternity, as Dr. Foster has taken pains to emphasize: they demonstrate a match between Eston Hemings's descendants and a line of Jefferson descendants traceable to TJ's uncle. Another Jefferson male

could have been responsible for this match. The probability of such an alternative scenario is very low, however, as the documentary research of staff members at the Thomas Jefferson Memorial Foundation has demonstrated. The case for TJ's paternity was already very strong before the DNA tests were undertaken. See Gordon-Reed, *Thomas Jefferson and Sally Hemings.*

59. The reference is to Britain and France; TJ to Robert R. Livingston, 9 Sept. 1801, in L&B, 10:277–84, at 280.

60. *Notes,* Query XIV, 138.

61. Ibid., 143, 140, 141, 143.

62. Ibid., 143. The reference for "this blot . . . " is in Query VIII, 87.

63. For an extraordinary example of such imagining, see "Celadon," *Golden Age,* 10, 12: enslaved Africans "shall in the proper season be set at liberty. —A tract of land will be allowed them [and] . . . they will by degrees form a State of their own"; "and in all those vast spaces westward to the great ocean, there may be seats hereafter for sundry foreign nations." In addition to future states for freed people ("Nigrania") and native Americans ("Savagenia"), "there may be a French, a Spanish, a Dutch, an Irish, an English, &c. yea, a Jewish State here in process of time. —And all of them united in brotherly affection, will at last form the most potent empire on the face of the earth."

64. Morgan, *Inventing the People.*

65. TJ to William Short, 3 Jan. 1793, *TJP* 25:14–17, at 15.

66. Ibid., 14. "What Jefferson is telling Short," Conor Cruise O'Brien argues, "is that no atrocity the French Revolutionaries could possibly commit could shake his faith in the French Revolution. Anything the French revolutionaries might choose to do—up to massacring the entire French population, minus two—would *ipso facto* represent Freedom. It is difficult to resist the conclusion [and O'Brien does not] that the twentieth-century statesman whom the Thomas Jefferson of January 1793 would have admired most is Pol Pot" (*Long Affair,* 150). Joseph Ellis reaches a similar verdict in *American Sphinx:* "Such an extreme version of what might be called revolutionary realism, which conjures up comparisons to the twentieth-century radicals in the Lenin or Mao mold, exposes a chilling side of Jefferson's character that seems so thoroughly incongruous with his temperament and so resolutely ideological" (127). Not surprisingly, the "Adam and Eve" letter has proved something of an embarrassment to TJ's modern-day defenders; Matthews ignores it altogether in his *Radical Politics of Jefferson.*

67. Banning, *Jeffersonian Persuasion.*

68. TJ to William Short, 3 Jan. 1793, *TJP* 25:14–17, at 14, 15.

69. Ibid., 25:14.

70. Cf. O'Brien, *Long Affair,* who suspects that TJ's "living faith [in the Revolution] actually died in the late summer of 1793" (288).

71. TJ to James Heaton, 20 May 1826, *TJW,* 1516. Unlike James Madison, TJ never joined the American Colonization Society. Madison was a strong supporter of the ACS from its founding in 1817; he served as its president from 1833

until his death in 1836. See Tyler-McGraw, "Jefferson and the Colonization Society."

72. TJ to Jared Sparks, 4 Feb. 1824, in L&B, 16:8–14, at 13, 9–10. Sparks, the recently installed editor of the *North American Review,* had sent TJ his review of "The Sixth Annual Report of the Colonization Society."

73. Jordan, *White over Black,* 542–69. See also Lewis, "Problem of Slavery in Southern Discourse." For TJ's colonization plans, see Finkelman, "Jefferson and Slavery," 198–201.

74. *Notes,* Query XIV, 137–38.

75. TJ to Jared Sparks, 4 Feb. 1824, in L&B, 16:8–14, at 10, 11.

76. Ibid., 12, 13.

77. *Notes,* Query XIV, 139.

78. See also TJ to Edward Coles, 25 Aug. 1814, *TJW,* 1343–46, at 1345: slaves were "by their habits rendered as incapable as children of taking care of themselves, and are extinguished promptly wherever industry is necessary for raising young."

79. TJ to Jared Sparks, 4 Feb. 1824, in L&B, 16:8–14, at 13.

80. TJ to Edward Coles, 25 Aug. 1814, *TJW,* 1343–46, at 1345.

81. TJ to Benjamin Rush, 23 Sept. 1800, in L&B, 10:173–76, at 176. See also Egerton, *Gabriel's Rebellion;* McColley, *Slavery and Jeffersonian Virginia,* 91–113.

82. Stuart, *Half-Way Pacifist.* TJ proclaimed in his Second Inaugural, 4 March 1805, that "we act on that conviction, that with nations as with individuals our interests soundly calculated will ever be found inseparable from our moral duties" (in Richardson, *Messages and Papers of the Presidents* 1:378–82, at 378).

83. TJ to John Lynch, 21 Jan. 1811, in L&B, 13:10–13, at 12.

84. Perkins, *Creation of a Republican Empire;* Onuf and Onuf, *Federal Union, Modern World,* 149–84.

85. *Notes,* Query XIV, 138.

86. TJ to Gov. James Monroe, 24 Nov. 1801, in L&B, 10:294–98, at 296–97. On TJ's posture toward Haiti, see Zuckerman, "Power of Blackness."

87. TJ to Gov. James Monroe, 24 Nov. 1801, in L&B, 10:294–98, at 297.

88. Ibid., 295.

89. James Monroe to TJ, 15 June 1801, in Hamilton, *Writings of Monroe* 3:292–95, at 293.

90. TJ to Gov. James Monroe, 24 Nov. 1801, in L&B, 10:294–98, at 295.

91. Ibid., 296.

92. Lewis, *American Union and the Problem of Neighborhood;* Onuf, "Expanding Union," 52–56; Onuf and Onuf, *Federal Union, Modern World,* 149–53.

93. TJ to Edward Coles, 25 Aug. 1814, *TJW,* 1343–46, at 1345.

94. Lewis, "Problem of Slavery in Southern Discourse."

95. TJ to Jared Sparks, 4 Feb. 1824, in L&B, 16:8–14, at 11.

96. Ibid.

97. TJ to John Holmes, 22 April 1820, ibid., 15:248–50, at 249.

98. These concerns are fully rehearsed in Taylor, *Tyranny Unmasked*. See generally Carpenter, *South as a Conscious Minority*. For the impact of the tariff on South Carolina politics, see Freehling, *Prelude to Civil War*.

99. TJ to John Holmes, 22 April 1820, to Hon. Mark Langdon Hill, 5 April 1820, in L&B, 15:248–50, at 249, and 243–44, at 243.

100. TJ to Holmes, 22 April 1820, ibid., 248–50, at 249.

101. Taylor, *Arator*, no. 28, 177. Colonizationist Robert Goodloe Harper echoed Taylor in 1823: "The alarming danger of cherishing in our bosom a distinct nation, which can never become incorporated with us, while it rapidly increases in numbers, and improves in intelligence; learning from us the arts of peace and war, the secret of its own strength, and the talent of combining and directing its force, a nation which must ever be hostile to us, from feeling and interest, because it can never incorporate with us, nor participate in the advantages which we enjoy; the danger of such a nation in our bosom, needs not be pointed out to any reflecting mind." Quoted in [Sparks], "Sixth Annual Report."

102. TJ to John Holmes, 22 April 1820, in L&B, 15:248–50, at 249. The original "ear" is mistranscribed here as "ears."

103. TJ to John Adams, 22 Jan. 1821, in Cappon, *Adams-Jefferson Letters* 2:570.

104. TJ to the Marquis de La Fayette, 26 Dec. 1820, in L&B, 15:299–302, at 301. See Miller, *Wolf by the Ears*, 234–42.

105. TJ to John Holmes, 22 April 1820, in L&B, 15:248–50, at 250.

106. TJ to James Heaton, 20 May 1826, *TJW,* 1516. On TJ's procrastination on the slavery issue, see Finkelman, "Jefferson and Slavery," 207–10.

107. TJ to John Holmes, 22 April 1820, in L&B, 15:248–50, at 250.

108. *Autobiography* (1821), in *TJW,* 44.

EPILOGUE: 4 JULY 1826

1. TJ to Roger C. Weightman, 24 June 1826, in L&B, 16:181–82. For TJ's last days, see Malone, *The Sage of Monticello,* 479–99. On the letter to Weightman and its literary sources, see Adair, "Rumbold's Dying Speech." See also Appleby, "Jefferson and His Complex Legacy," and McDonald, "Jefferson and America: Episodes in Image Formation."

Bibliography

ABBREVIATIONS

JER   *Journal of the Early Republic*
WMQ   *William and Mary Quarterly*, 3d series

PRIMARY SOURCES

Annals of the Congress of the United States, 1789–1824. 42 vols. Washington, D.C., 1834–56.

Blackstone, William. *Commentaries on the Laws of England.* 4 vols. 1765–69; rept. London, 1821.

Bland, Richard. *The Colonel Dismounted.* 1764; rept. in Bernard Bailyn, ed. *Pamphlets of the American Revolution,* 292–354. Cambridge, Mass., 1965.

Boyd, Julian, et al., eds. *The Papers of Thomas Jefferson.* 27 vols. to date. Princeton, N.J., 1950—.

Burnett, Edmund Cody, ed. *Letters of the Members of the Continental Congress.* 8 vols. Washington, D.C., 1921–36.

Cappon, Lester J., ed. *The Adams-Jefferson Letters.* 2 vols. Chapel Hill, N.C., 1959.

"Celadon." *The Golden Age: or, Future Glory of North-America Discovered.* N.p., 1785.

"Cincinnatus, Lucius Quintus." *The Mote Point of Finance, or The Crown Lands Equally Divided.* Broadside. Philadelphia, 30 Dec. 1779.

Cooke, Jacob E., ed. *The Federalist.* Middletown, Conn., 1961.

Craig, Neville, ed. *The Olden Time.* 2 vols. Cincinnati, 1876.

Daviess, Joseph Hamilton. *An Essay on Federalism.* [Frankfort, Ky, 1810?].

Fitzpatrick, John C., ed. *The Writings of George Washington.* 39 vols. Washington, D.C., 1931–44.

Ford, Worthington Chauncey, ed. *A Cycle of Adams Letters, 1861–1865.* 2 vols. Boston, 1920.

——. *Journals of the Continental Congress.* 34 vols. Washington, D.C., 1904–37.

Gunther, Gerald, ed. *John Marshall's Defense of McCulloch v. Maryland.* Stanford, Calif., 1969.

Hamilton, Stanislaus Murray, ed. *The Writings of James Monroe.* 7 vols. New York, 1898–1903.

Hening, William Waller, comp. *The Statutes at Large: Being a Collection of All the Laws of Virginia, from the First Session of the Legislature, in the Year 1619.* 13 vols. Richmond, etc., 1809–23.

Hutchinson, William T., William M. E. Rachal, et al., eds. *The Papers of James Madison: Congressional Series.* 17 vols. Chicago and Charlottesville, Va., 1959–91.

Jefferson, Thomas. *Notes on the State of Virginia,* ed. William Peden. Chapel Hill, N.C., 1954.

——. Papers. Manuscripts Division, Library of Congress.

[——.] *A Summary View of the Rights of British America. Set Forth in Some Resolutions Intended for the Inspection of the Present Delegates of the People of Virginia. Now in Convention.* Williamsburg, Va., 1774; rept. in Van Schreeven et al. *Revolutionary Virginia* 1:240–56.

Kaminski, John P., et al., eds. *The Documentary History of the Ratification of the Constitution.* 16 vols. to date. Madison, Wis., 1976—.

Lipscomb, Andrew A., and Albert Ellery Bergh, eds., *The Writings of Thomas Jefferson,* 20 vols. Washington, D.C., 1903–4.

Locke, John. *Two Treatises of Government.* Ed. Peter Laslett. 1960; rev. ed., Cambridge, 1963.

Montesquieu, baron de [Charles de Secondat]. *The Spirit of the Laws.* 1748; ed. and trans. Anne M. Cohler et al., Cambridge, 1989.

Nicholas, George. *A Letter from George Nicholas of Kentucky, to His Friend in Virginia. Justifying the Conduct of the Citizens of Kentucky, as to Some of the Late Measures of the General Government.* Philadelphia, 1799.

Observations on the Alien and Sedition Laws of the United States. Washington, Pa., 1799.

Page, John. *Address to the Freeholders of Gloucester County, at Their Election of a Member of Congress . . . April 24, 1799.* Richmond, 1799.

Paine, Thomas. *Public Good: Being an Examination into the Claims of Virginia to Vacant Western Territory.* Philadelphia, 1780.

Pendleton, Edmund. *An Address of the Honorable Edmund Pendleton, of Virginia, to the American Citizens, on the Present State of Our Country.* Boston, 1799.

Peterson, Merrill D., ed. *Jefferson Writings.* New York, 1984.

Richardson, James D., ed. *A Compilation of the Messages and Papers of the Presidents, 1789–1902.* 12 vols. Washington, D.C., 1903–6.

[Sparks, Jared.] "The Sixth Annual Report of the American Society for Colonizing the Free People of Color of the United States." *North American Review* 42 (1824): 40–90.

Stiles, Ezra. *The United States Elevated to Glory and Honour.* Worcester, Mass., 1785.

Taylor, John. *Arator. Being a Series of Agricultural Essays, Practical and Political: In Sixty-Four Numbers.* Ed. M. E. Bradford. 1818; rept. Indianapolis, 1977.

[——.] *Definition of Parties; or, The Political Effects of the Paper System Considered.* Philadelphia, 1794.

[——.] *An Enquiry into the Principles and Tendency of Certain Public Measures.* Philadelphia, 1794.

——. *Tyranny Unmasked.* 1821; ed. F. Thornton Miller, Indianapolis, 1992.

Tocqueville, Alexis de. *Democracy in America.* 2 vols. Trans. Francis Bowen, 1862; ed. Phillips Bradley, New York, 1945.

[Tucker, St. George.] *A Letter to a Member of Congress; Respecting the Alien and Sedition Laws.* N.p., 1799.

Van Schreeven, William J., Robert L. Scribner, and Brent Tarter, eds. *Revolutionary Virginia: The Road to Independence.* 7 vols. Charlottesville, Va., 1973–83.

Vattel, Emmerich de. *The Law of Nations or The Principles of Natural Law Applied to the Conduct and to the Affairs of Nations and of Sovereigns.* 1758; trans. Charles G. Fenwick, Washington, D.C., 1916.

Veit, Helen E., Kenneth R. Bowling, and Charlene Bangs Bickford, eds. *Creating the Bill of Rights: The Documentary Record from the First Federal Congress.* Baltimore, 1991.

Wharton, Samuel. *Plain Facts: Being an Examination into the Rights of the Indian Nations of America.* Philadelphia, 1781.

SECONDARY SOURCES

Abernethy, Thomas P. *The Burr Conspiracy.* New York, 1954.

——. *Western Lands and the American Revolution.* 1937; rept. New York, 1959.

Adair, Douglass. "Rumbold's Dying Speech, 1685, and Jefferson's Last Words on Democracy, 1826." In Adair, *Fame and the Founding Fathers,* 192–202. Ed. Trevor Colbourn. New York, 1974.

Alden, John. *John Stuart and the Southern Colonial Frontier: A Study of Indian Relations, War, Trade, and Land Problems in the Southern Wilderness, 1754–1775.* Ann Arbor, Mich., 1944.

Anderson, Benedict. *Imagined Communities: Reflections on the Origin and Spread of Nationalism.* 1983; rev. ed., London and New York, 1991.

Antholis, William John. "Liberal Democratic Theory and the Transformation of Sovereignty." Ph.D. diss., Yale University, 1993.

Appleby, Joyce. "The 'Agrarian Myth' in the Early Republic." In Appleby, *Liberalism and Republicanism,* 253–76.

——. *Capitalism and a New Social Order: The Republican Vision of the 1790s.* New York, 1984.

——. "Jefferson and His Complex Legacy." In Onuf, *Jeffersonian Legacies,* 1–16.

——. *Liberalism and Republicanism in the Historical Imagination.* Cambridge, Mass., 1992.

——. "What Is Still American in Jefferson's Political Philosophy?" In Appleby, *Liberalism and Republicanism,* 291–319.

——. *Without Resolution: The Jeffersonian Tensions in American Nationalism.*

An Inaugural Lecture Delivered before the University of Oxford on 25 April 1991. Oxford, 1992.

Bailyn, Bernard. *The Ideological Origins of the American Revolution.* Cambridge, Mass., 1967.

Banner, James M., Jr. *To the Hartford Convention: The Federalists and the Origins of Party Politics in Massachusetts, 1789–1815.* New York, 1970.

Banning, Lance. *Jefferson and Madison: Three Conversations from the Founding.* Madison, Wis., 1995.

———. *The Jeffersonian Persuasion: Evolution of a Party Ideology.* Ithaca, N.Y., 1978.

———. *The Sacred Fire of Liberty: James Madison and the Founding of the Federal Republic.* Ithaca, N.Y., 1995.

Becker, Carl L. *The Declaration of Independence: A Study in the History of Political Ideas.* 1922; rept. New York, 1958.

Ben-Atar, Doron S. *The Origins of Jeffersonian Commercial Diplomacy.* New York, 1993.

Bender, Thomas. *Toward an Urban Vision: Ideas and Institutions in Nineteenth Century America.* Lexington, Ky., 1975.

Berkhofer, Robert F., Jr. "Jefferson, the Ordinance of 1784, and the Origins of the American Territorial System." *WMQ* 29 (1972): 231–62.

———. *The White Man's Indian: Images of the American Indian from Columbus to the Present.* New York, 1978.

Boorstin, Daniel J. *The Lost World of Thomas Jefferson.* 1948; rept. Chicago, 1981.

Boulton, Alexander O. "The American Paradox: Jeffersonian Equality and Racial Science." *American Quarterly* 47 (1995): 467–92.

Boyd, Julian P. "Thomas Jefferson's 'Empire of Liberty.'" *Virginia Quarterly Review* 24 (1948): 538–54.

Breen, T. H. "Ideology and Nationalism on the Eve of the American Revolution: Revisions *Once More* in Need of Revising." *Journal of American History* 84 (1997): 13–39.

———. *Tobacco Culture: The Mentality of the Great Tidewater Planters on the Eve of Revolution.* Princeton, N.J., 1985.

Brewer, Holly. "Entailing Aristocracy in Colonial Virginia: 'Ancient Feudal Restraints' and Revolutionary Reform." *WMQ* 54 (1997): 307–46.

Brown, Roger H. *The Republic in Peril: 1812.* New York, 1964.

Buel, Richard, Jr. *Securing the Revolution: Ideology in American Politics, 1789–1815.* Ithaca, N.Y., 1972.

Burstein, Andrew. *The Inner Jefferson: Portrait of a Grieving Optimist.* Charlottesville, Va., 1995.

———. "The Problem of Jefferson Biography." *Virginia Quarterly Review* 70 (1994): 403–20.

———. *Sentimental Democracy: The Evolution of America's Romantic Self-Image.* New York, 1999.

Calloway, Colin G. *The American Revolution in Indian Country: Crisis and Diversity on Native American Communities.* New York, 1995.

Carpenter, Jesse T. *The South as a Conscious Minority, 1789–1861: A Study in Political Thought.* 1930; rept. Columbia, S.C., 1990.

Ceaser, James W. *Reconstructing America: The Symbol of America in Modern Thought.* New Haven, 1997.

Cohen, William. "Thomas Jefferson and the Problem of Slavery." *Journal of American History* 56 (1969): 503–26.

Colbourn, H. Trevor. *The Lamp of Experience: Whig History and the Intellectual Origins of the American Revolution.* Chapel Hill, N.C., 1965.

Colley, Linda. *Britons: Forging the Nation, 1707–1837.* New Haven, 1992.

Conrad, Stephen A. "Putting Rights Talk in Its Place: The *Summary View* Revisited." In Onuf, *Jeffersonian Legacies,* 254–80.

Countryman, Edward. "Indians, the Colonial Order, and the Social Significance of the American Revolution." *WMQ* 53 (1996): 342–62.

Cronon, William. *Nature's Metropolis: Chicago and the Great West.* New York, 1991.

Crowley, John E. *The Privileges of Independence: Neomercantilism and the American Revolution.* Baltimore, 1993.

Davis, David Brion. *The Problem of Slavery in the Age of Revolution, 1770–1823.* Ithaca, N.Y., 1975.

Dawidoff, Robert. "Man of Letters." In Peterson, *Jefferson: A Reference Biography,* 181–98.

DeConde, Alexander. *This Affair of Louisiana.* New York, 1976.

Deudney, Daniel. "Binding Sovereigns: Authorities, Structures, and Geopolitics in Philadelphian Systems." In Thomas J. Biersteker and Cynthia Weber, eds., *State Sovereignty as Social Construct,* 190–239. Cambridge, 1996.

———. "The Philadelphian System: Sovereignty, Arms Control, and Balance of Power in the American States-Union, ca. 1787–1861." *International Organization* 49 (1995): 191–228.

De Vorsey, Louis, Jr. *The Indian Boundary in the Southern Colonies, 1763–1775.* Chapel Hill, N.C., 1961.

Diggins, John P. "Slavery, Race, and Equality: Jefferson and the Pathos of the Enlightenment." *American Quarterly* 28 (1976): 206–26.

Egerton, Douglas R. *Gabriel's Rebellion: The Virginia Slave Conspiracies of 1800 and 1802.* Chapel Hill, N.C., 1993.

Egnal, Marc. *A Mighty Empire: The Origins of the American Revolution.* Ithaca, N.Y., 1988.

Elkins, Stanley, and Eric McKitrick. *The Age of Federalism.* New York, 1993.

Ellis, Joseph J. *American Sphinx: The Character of Thomas Jefferson.* New York, 1997.

———. "Jefferson's Cop-Out." *Civilization* 3 (Dec. 1996–Jan. 1997): 46–53.

———. *The Passionate Sage: The Character and Legacy of John Adams.* New York, 1993.

Fenwick, Charles G. "The Authority of Vattel." *American Political Science Review* 7 (1913): 370–424.

Ferguson, Robert A. *Law and Letters in American Culture.* Cambridge, Mass., 1984.

Finkelman, Paul. "Between Scylla and Charybdis: Anarchy, Tyranny, and the Debate over a Bill of Rights." In Ronald Hoffman and Peter J. Albert, eds., *The Bill of Rights: Government Proscribed,* 103–74. Charlottesville, Va., 1997.

———. "Jefferson and Slavery: 'Treason against the Hopes of the World.'" In Onuf, *Jeffersonian Legacies,* 181–221.

———. "Thomas Jefferson and Slavery II: Historians and Myths." In Finkelman, *Slavery and the Founders: Race and Liberty in the Age of Jefferson,* 138–67. Armonk, N.Y., 1996.

Fliegelman, Jay. *Declaring Independence: Jefferson, Natural Language, and the Culture of Performance.* Stanford, Calif., 1993.

———. *Prodigals and Pilgrims: The American Revolution against Patriarchal Authority.* Cambridge, 1982.

Foster, Eugene, et al., "Jefferson Fathered Slave's Last Child." *Nature* 196 (5 Nov. 1998): 27–28.

Freehling, William W. "The Founding Fathers and Slavery." *American Historical Review* 77 (1972): 81–93. Rev. as "The Founding Fathers, Conditional Antislavery, and the Nonradicalism of the American Revolution." In Freehling, *The Reintegration of American History,* 12–33. New York, 1994.

———. *Prelude to Civil War: The Nullification Controversy in South Carolina, 1816–1836.* New York, 1965.

———. *The Road to Disunion: Secessionists at Bay, 1776–1854.* New York, 1990.

Freeman, Joanne B. "Affairs of Honor: Political Combat and Political Culture in the Early American Republic." Ph.D. diss., University of Virginia, 1997.

———. "Slander, Poison, Whispers, and Fame: Jefferson's 'Anas' and Political Gossip in the Early Republic." *JER* 15 (1995): 25–57.

French, Scot A., and Edward L. Ayers. "The Strange Career of Thomas Jefferson: Race and Slavery in American Memory, 1943–1993." In Onuf, *Jeffersonian Legacies,* 418–56.

Gellner, Ernest. *Nations and Nationalism.* Ithaca, N.Y., 1983.

Gordon-Reed, Annette. *Thomas Jefferson and Sally Hemings: An American Controversy.* Charlottesville, Va., 1997.

Gould, Eliga H. "A Virtual Nation: Greater Britain and the Imperial Legacy of the American Revolution." *American Historical Review* 104 (1999): 476–89.

Greene, Jack P. "All Men Are Created Equal: Some Reflections on the Character of the American Revolution." In Greene, *Imperatives, Behaviors, and Identities,* 236–67.

———. "Empire and Identity." In Marshall, *The Eighteenth Century,* 208–30.

———. *Imperatives, Behaviors, and Identities: Essays in Early American Cultural History.* Charlottesville, Va., 1992.

———. *The Intellectual Construction of America: Exceptionalism and Identity from 1492 to 1800.* Chapel Hill, N.C., 1993.

———. "The Intellectual Construction of Virginia." In Onuf, *Jeffersonian Legacies*, 225–53.

———. *Peripheries and Center: Constitutional Development in the Extended Polities of the British Empire and the United States, 1607–1788.* Athens, Ga., 1986.

———. "Search for Identity: An Interpretation of the Meaning of Selected Patterns of Social Response in Eighteenth-Century America." In Greene, *Imperatives, Behaviors, and Identities*, 143–73.

Greenfield, Liah. *Nationalism: Five Roads to Modernity.* Cambridge, Mass., 1992.

Gutzman, Constantine [Kevin R.]. "Old Dominion, New Republic: Making Virginia Republican, 1776–1840." Ph.D. diss., University of Virginia, 1999.

———. "A Troublesome Legacy: James Madison and 'The Principles of '98.'" *JER* 15 (1995): 569–89.

Hantman, Jeffrey L., and Gary Dunham. "The Enlightened Archaeologist." *Archaeology* 46 (May/June 1993), 44–49.

Haskell, Thomas L. "Capitalism and the Origins of the Humanitarian Sensibility, Part I." *American Historical Review* 90 (1985): 339–61.

Hellenbrand, Harold. *The Unfinished Revolution: Education and Politics in the Thought of Thomas Jefferson.* Newark, Del., 1990.

Helo, Ari. "Thomas Jefferson's Republicanism and the Problem of Slavery." Ph.D. diss., University of Tampere (Finland), 1999.

Hendrickson, David C. *The Ideological Origins of American Internationalism, 1754–1861.* New York, forthcoming.

Hinderaker, Eric. *Elusive Empires: Constructing Colonialism in the Ohio Valley, 1673–1800.* New York, 1997.

Hirschman, Albert O. *The Passions and the Interests: Political Arguments for Capitalism before Its Triumph.* Princeton, N.J., 1977.

Hobsbawm, E. J. *Nations and Nationalism since 1780.* Cambridge, 1990.

Hofstadter, Richard. *The Idea of a Party System: The Rise of Legitimate Opposition in the United States, 1780–1840.* Berkeley, Calif., 1969.

Holton, Woody. "Rebel against Rebel: Enslaved Virginians and the Coming of the American Revolution." *Virginia Magazine of History and Biography* 105 (1997): 157–92.

Horsman, Reginald. *Expansion and American Indian Policy, 1783–1812.* East Lansing, Mich., 1967.

———. *Race and Manifest Destiny: The Origins of American Racial Anglo-Saxonism.* Cambridge, Mass., 1981.

Howe, John R., Jr. "Republican Thought and the Political Violence of the 1790s." *American Quarterly* 19 (1967): 147–65.

Huebner, Timothy B. "The Consolidation of State Judicial Power: Spencer Roane, Virginia Legal Culture, and the Southern Judicial Tradition." *Virginia Magazine of History and Biography* 102 (1994): 47–72.

Hutchins, Francis G. "The Constitution and the Tribes." Manuscript in author's possession.

Jaffa, Harry V. *Crisis of the House Divided: An Interpretation of the Issues in the Lincoln-Douglas Debates.* 1959; rept. Chicago, 1982.

Jones, Dorothy V. *License for Empire: Colonialism by Treaty in Early America.* Chicago, 1982.

Jordan, Winthrop. *White over Black: American Attitudes toward the Negro, 1550–1812.* Chapel Hill, N.C., 1968.

Kennedy, Roger G. *Jefferson, Hamilton, and Burr.* New York, 1999.

Ketcham, Ralph. *Presidents above Party: The First American Presidency, 1789–1829.* Chapel Hill, N.C., 1984.

Kett, Joseph. "Education." In Peterson, *Jefferson: A Reference Biography,* 233–51.

Kettner, James. *The Development of American Citizenship, 1608–1870.* Chapel Hill, N.C., 1978.

Knorr, Klaus E. *British Colonial Theories, 1570–1850.* Toronto, 1944.

Knupfer, Peter B. *The Union As It Is: Constitutional Unionism and Sectional Compromise, 1787–1861.* Chapel Hill, N.C., 1991.

Koch, Adrienne, and Harry Ammon. "The Virginia and Kentucky Resolutions: An Episode in Jefferson's and Madison's Defense of Civil Liberties." *WMQ* 5 (1948): 145–76.

Koebner, Richard. *Empire.* Cambridge, 1961.

Konig, David Thomas, ed. *Devising Liberty: Preserving and Creating Freedom in the New American Republic.* Stanford, Calif., 1995.

Kuroda, Tadahisa. *The Origins of the Twelfth Amendment: The Electoral College in the Early Republic, 1787–1804.* Westport, Conn., 1994.

Lang, Daniel G. *Foreign Policy and the Early Republic: The Law of Nations and the Balance of Power.* Baton Rouge, La., 1985.

Leibiger, Stuart. "Thomas Jefferson and the Missouri Crisis: An Alternative Interpretation." *JER* 17 (1997): 121–30.

Lenner, Andrew C. *The Federal Principle in American Politics.* Madison, Wis., forthcoming.

——. "John Taylor and the Origins of American Federalism." *JER* 17 (1997): 399–423.

——. "A Tale of Two Constitutions: Nationalism in the Federalist Era." *American Journal of Legal History* 40 (1996): 72–105.

Lerner, Ralph. "Reds and Whites: Rights and Wrongs." In Lerner, *The Thinking Revolutionary: Principle and Practice in the New Republic,* 139–73. Ithaca, N.Y., 1987.

Levy, Leonard W. *Jefferson and Civil Liberties: The Darker Side.* 1963; rept. Chicago, 1989.

Lewis, Anthony. "Jefferson's *Summary View* as a Chart of Political Union." *WMQ* 5 (1948): 34–51.

Lewis, James E., Jr. *American Union and the Problem of Neighborhood: The*

United States and the Collapse of the Spanish Empire, 1783–1829. Chapel Hill, N.C., 1998.

Lewis, Jan. "'The Blessings of Domestic Society': Thomas Jefferson's Family and the Transformation of American Politics." In Onuf, *Jeffersonian Legacies,* 109–46.

——. "Happiness." In Jack P. Greene and J. R. Pole, eds., *The Blackwell Encyclopedia of the American Revolution.* Oxford, 1991, 641–47.

——. "The Problem of Slavery in Southern Discourse." In Konig, *Devising Liberty,* 265–97.

——. "The Republican Wife: Virtue and Seduction in the Early Republic." *WMQ* 44 (1987): 689–721.

Lewis, Jan, and Peter Onuf. "American Synecdoche: Thomas Jefferson as Image, Icon, Character, and Self." *American Historical Review* 103 (1998): 125–36.

——, eds. *Sally Hemings and Thomas Jefferson: History, Memory, and Civic Culture.* Charlottesville, Va., 1999.

Lind, Michael. *The Next American Nation: The New Nationalism and the Fourth American Revolution.* New York, 1995.

Livermore, Shaw. *Early American Land Companies: Their Influence on Corporate Development.* New York, 1939.

Lockridge, Kenneth A. *On the Sources of Patriarchal Rage.* New York, 1992.

Maier, Pauline. *American Scripture: Making the Declaration of Independence.* New York, 1997.

Malone, Dumas. *Jefferson and His Time.* 6 vols. Boston, 1948–81. Vol. 1, *Jefferson the Virginian* (1948); vol. 2, *Jefferson and the Rights of Man* (1951); vol. 3, *Jefferson and the Ordeal of Liberty* (1962); vol. 4, *Jefferson the President: First Term, 1801–1805* (1970); vol. 5, *Jefferson the President: Second Term, 1805–1809* (1974); vol. 6, *The Sage of Monticello* (1981).

Marshall, P. J., ed., *The Eighteenth Century.* Vol. 2 of William Roger Louis, ed., *The Oxford History of the British Empire.* Oxford, 1998.

Marston, Jerrilyn Greene. *King and Congress: The Transfer of Political Legitimacy, 1774–1776.* Princeton, N.J., 1987.

Marx, Leo. *The Machine in the Garden.* New York, 1964.

Matson, Cathy D., and Peter S. Onuf. *A Union of Interests: Political and Economic Thought in Revolutionary America.* Lawrence, Kans., 1990.

Matthews, Richard K. *The Radical Politics of Thomas Jefferson: A Revisionist View.* Lawrence, Kans., 1984.

Mayer, David N. *The Constitutional Thought of Thomas Jefferson.* Charlottesville, Va., 1994.

McCardell, John. *The Idea of a Southern Nation.* New York, 1979.

McCloughlin, William G. "Thomas Jefferson and the Beginning of Cherokee Nationalism, 1806 to 1809." *WMQ* 32 (1975): 547–80.

McColley, Robert. *Slavery and Jeffersonian Virginia.* 1964; 2d ed., Urbana, Ill., 1973.

McCoy, Drew R. *The Elusive Republic: Political Economy in Jeffersonian America.* Chapel Hill, N.C., 1980.

——. *The Last of the Fathers: James Madison and the Republican Legacy.* New York, 1989.

McDonald, Robert M.S. "Jefferson and America: Episodes in Image Formation." Ph.D. diss., University of North Carolina, 1998.

McLaughlin, Andrew. "The Background of American Federalism." *American Political Science Review* 12 (1918): 215–40.

MacLeod, Duncan J. "Toward Caste." In Ira Berlin and Ronald J. Hoffman, eds., *Slavery and Freedom in the Age of the American Revolution*, 217–36. Charlottesville, Va., 1983.

Meinig, D. W. *Continental America, 1800–1867.* Vol. 2 of *The Shaping of America: A Geographical Perspective on 500 Years of History.* New Haven, 1993.

Merrell, James H. "Declarations of Independence: Indian-White Relations in the New Nation." In Jack P. Greene, ed., *The American Revolution: It Character and Limits*, 197–223. New York, 1987.

Miller, John Chester. *The Wolf by the Ears: Thomas Jefferson and Slavery.* New York, 1977.

Moore, Glover. *The Missouri Controversy, 1819–1821.* Lexington, Ky., 1953.

Morgan, Edmund S. *American Slavery, American Freedom: The Ordeal of Colonial Virginia.* New York, 1975.

——. *Inventing the People: The Rise of Popular Sovereignty in England and America.* New York, 1988.

Nussbaum, Arthur. *A Concise History of the Law of Nations.* 1947; rev. ed., New York, 1954.

O'Brien, Conor Cruise. *The Long Affair: Thomas Jefferson and the French Revolution, 1785–1800.* Chicago, 1996.

Onuf, Nicholas Greenwood. *The Republican Legacy in International Thought.* Cambridge, 1998.

Onuf, Peter S. "A Declaration of Independence for Diplomatic Historians." *Diplomatic History* 22 (1998): 71–83.

——. "The Expanding Union." In Konig, *Devising Liberty*, 50–80.

——. "Federalism, Republicanism, and the Origins of American Sectionalism." In Edward L. Ayers et al., *All over the Map: Rethinking American Regions*, 11–37. Baltimore, 1996.

——. *The Origins of the Federal Republic: Jurisdictional Conflicts in the United States, 1775–1787.* Philadelphia, 1983.

——. "The Scholars' Jefferson," *WMQ* 50 (1993): 671–99.

——. *Statehood and Union: A History of the Northwest Ordinance.* Bloomington, Ind., 1987.

——, ed. *Jeffersonian Legacies.* Charlottesville, Va., 1993.

Onuf, Peter S., and Nicholas G. Onuf. *Federal Union, Modern World: The Law of Nations in an Age of Revolutions, 1776–1814.* Madison, Wis., 1993.

Pagden, Anthony. *Lords of All the World: Ideologies of Empire in Spain, Britain, and France, c.1500–c.1800.* New Haven, 1995.

Pasley, Jeffrey L. "'A Journeyman, Either in Law or Politics': John Beckley and the Social Origins of Political Campaigning." *JER* 16 (1996): 531–69.

———. *"The Tyranny of Printers": The Rise of Newspaper Politics in the Early American Republic.* Charlottesville, Va., forthcoming.

Pearce, Roy Harvey. *The Savages of America: A Study of the Indian and the Idea of Civilization.* Baltimore, 1953.

Perkins, Bradford. *The Creation of a Republican Empire, 1776–1865.* Vol. 1 of *The Cambridge History of American Foreign Relations.* New York, 1993.

Peterson, Merrill D. "Jefferson and Commercial Policy, 1783–1793." *WMQ* 22 (1965): 584–610.

———. *The Jefferson Image in the American Mind.* New York, 1960.

———. *Thomas Jefferson and the New Nation: A Biography.* New York, 1970.

———, ed. *Thomas Jefferson: A Reference Biography.* New York, 1986.

Philbrick, Francis. *The Laws of the Illinois Territory, 1809–1818.* Illinois State Historical Society, *Collections* 25 (1950): introduction.

Pocock, J. G. A. "States, Republics, and Empires: The American Founding in Early Modern Perspective." In Terence Ball, ed., *Conceptual Change and the Constitution,* 55–77. Lawrence, Kans., 1988.

Powell, H. Jefferson. "The Original Understanding of Original Intent." *Harvard Law Review* 98 (1984–85): 885–948.

Prucha, Francis Paul. *American Indian Treaties: The History of a Political Anomaly.* Berkeley, Calif., 1994.

Rakove, Jack N. *The Beginnings of National Politics: An Interpretive History of the Continental Congress.* New York, 1979.

Reid, John Phillip. *The Authority of Rights.* Vol. 1 of *Constitutional History of the American Revolution.* 4 vols. Madison, Wis., 1986–93.

Richter, Daniel K. "Native Peoples of North America and the Eighteenth-Century British Empire." In Marshall, *The Eighteenth Century,* 347–71.

Robertson, Lindsay. *"Johnson v. M'Intosh:* Land, Law, and the Politics of Federalism, 1773–1842." Ph.D. diss., University of Virginia, 1997.

Scott, James Brown. *The United States of America: A Study in International Organization.* Washington, D.C., 1920.

Seelye, John. *Beautiful Machine: Rivers and the Republican Plan, 1755–1825.* New York, 1991.

Shalhope, Robert E. *John Taylor of Caroline: Pastoral Republican.* Columbia, S.C., 1980.

———. "Thomas Jefferson's Republicanism and Antebellum Southern Thought." *Journal of Southern History* 62 (1976): 529–56.

Sharp, James Roger. *American Politics in the Early Republic: The New Nation in Crisis.* New Haven, 1993.

Sheehan, Bernard W. "The Indian Problem in the Northwest: From Conquest to Philanthropy." In Ronald Hoffman and Peter J. Albert, eds., *Launching the "Extended Republic": The Federalist Era,* 190–222. Charlottesville, Va., 1996.

——. *Seeds of Extinction: Jeffersonian Philanthropy and the American Indian.* Chapel Hill, N.C., 1973.

Sheldon, Garrett Ward. *The Political Philosophy of Thomas Jefferson.* Baltimore, 1991.

Simpson, Lewis P. "The Ferocity of Self: History and Consciousness in Southern Literature." *South Central Review* 1 (1984): 67–84.

——. *Mind and the American Civil War: A Meditation on Lost Causes.* Baton Rouge, La., 1989.

Sisson, Daniel. *The American Revolution of 1800.* New York, 1974.

Sloan, Herbert. "'The Earth Belongs in Usufruct to the Living.'" In Onuf, *Jeffersonian Legacies,* 281–315.

——. *Principle and Interest: Thomas Jefferson and the Problem of Debt.* New York, 1995.

Smith, Henry Nash. *Virgin Land: The American West as Symbol and Myth.* Cambridge, Mass., 1950.

Smith, James Morton. *Freedom's Fetters: The Alien and Sedition Laws and American Civil Liberties.* Ithaca, N.Y., 1956.

Smith, Mark Augustus. "Crisis, Unity, and Partisanship: The Road to the Sedition Act." Ph.D. diss., University of Virginia, 1998.

Smith, Rogers M. *Civic Ideals: Conflicting Visions of Citizenship in American Public Law.* New Haven, 1997.

Stagg, J. C. A. *Mr. Madison's War: Politics, Diplomacy, and Warfare in the Early American Republic, 1783–1830.* Princeton, N.J., 1983.

Stanton, Lucia C. "'Those Who Labor for My Happiness': Thomas Jefferson and His Slaves." In Onuf, *Jeffersonian Legacies,* 147–80.

Stuart, Reginald C. *The Half-Way Pacifist: Thomas Jefferson's View of War.* Toronto, 1978.

Tucker, Robert W., and David C. Hendrickson. *Empire of Liberty: The Statecraft of Thomas Jefferson.* New York, 1990.

——. *The Fall of the First British Empire: Origins of the War of American Independence.* Baltimore, 1982.

Tyler-McGraw, Marie. "Thomas Jefferson and the American Colonization Society." Paper delivered at the International Center of Jefferson Studies, Sept. 1998.

Van Alstyne, Richard W. *The Rising American Empire.* New York, 1960.

Waldstreicher, David. *In the Midst of Perpetual Fetes: The Making of American Nationalism, 1776–1820.* Chapel Hill, N.C., 1997.

Weinberg, Albert K. *Manifest Destiny: A Study in Nationalist Expansionism in American History.* Baltimore, 1935.

White, Richard. *The Middle Ground: Indians, Empires, and Republics in the Great Lakes Region, 1650–1815.* New York, 1991.

Wiebe, Robert H. *The Opening of American Society: From the Adoption of the Constitution to the Eve of Disunion.* New York, 1984.

Wilentz, Sean. "Life, Liberty, and the Pursuit of Thomas Jefferson." *New Republic,* 10 March 1997: 32–42.

Wills, Garry. *Inventing America: Jefferson's Declaration of Independence.* Garden City, N.Y., 1978.

Wilson, Douglas L. "The American Agricola: Jefferson's Agrarianism and the Classical Tradition." *South Atlantic Quarterly* 80 (1981): 339–54.

———. "Jefferson and the Republic of Letters." In Onuf, *Jeffersonian Legacies,* 50–76.

———. "Thomas Jefferson and the Character Issue." *Atlantic Monthly* 270 (Nov. 1992): 57–74.

Wood, Gordon S. "Conspiracy and the Paranoid Style: Causality and Deceit in the Eighteenth Century." *WMQ* 39 (1982): 401–41.

———. *The Creation of the American Republic, 1776–1787.* Chapel Hill, N.C., 1969.

———. *The Radicalism of the American Revolution.* New York, 1992.

———. "The Trials and Tribulations of Thomas Jefferson." In Onuf, *Jeffersonian Legacies,* 395–417.

Yarbrough, Jean M. *American Virtues: Thomas Jefferson on the Character of a Free People.* Lawrence, Kans., 1998.

Zuckerman, Michael. "The Power of Blackness: Thomas Jefferson and the Revolution in St. Domingue." In Zuckerman, *Almost Chosen People: Oblique Biographies in the American Grain,* 175–218. Berkeley, Calif., 1993.

Zuckert, Michael P. *Natural Rights and the New Republicanism.* Princeton, N.J., 1994.

Index

Jeffersonian America

Jan Ellen Lewis and Peter S. Onuf, editors
Sally Hemings and Thomas Jefferson: History, Memory, and Civic Culture

Peter S. Onuf
Jefferson's Empire: The Language of American Nationhood

Printed in the United States
151328LV00017B/1/P

9 780813 920900